HOW TO SETUP
SUCCESSFUL

AN ENTREPRENEUR'S GUIDE TO RUNNING A
PROFITABLE CLUB OPERATION

First Edition

by Robert Smith

UPLAND PUBLISHING

HOW TO SETUP AND OPERATE A SUCCESSFUL NIGHTCLUB

An Entrepreneur's Guide To Running A Profitable Club Operation

By Robert Smith

Upland Publications
308 E. Burlington St. Suite 305 Iowa City, IA 52240

ISBN 0-9710400-2-8

Printed in the United States of America.

Disclaimer: This book is sold with the understanding that the author and publisher are not engaged in rendering legal, accounting or any other professional advice. If legal or other expert assistance is required, the services of a competent professional should be sought. Every attempt has been made to ensure the accuracy and completeness of this book. However, it is not a substitute for vital business and legal advice that must be considered when establishing any business. This book should only be used as a general guide and as a source for creative ideas that can be applied toward setting up and managing a nightclub.

Contents

INTRODUCTION

Operating a nightclub can be a very rewarding and financially lucrative business opportunity for the success-minded entrepreneur. As with any business, nightclubs carry their own unique challenges and obstacles in which operators may have to overcome. Careful and astute planning will help to avoid many problems that may lay ahead.

There are many different categories of entertainment venues that range in size, status and style. These operations include small bars, usually referred to as taverns or pubs, Brewpubs, lounges, dance clubs and adult venues to name a few. These are all examples of different types of venues that specialize in specific forms of entertainment and leisure. The one thing all bars of any type or size have in common is that they all exist to provide a social atmosphere for the patrons that walk through their doors. Therefore, this book encompasses all types of venues and refers to all clubs collectively as nightclubs.

Who Should Read This Book

This book is written for everyone who has ever wondered or has had the desire to know what it would be like to run and operate their own nightclub. How to Setup and Operate a Successful Nightclub goes one step further and stimulates ideas and identifies both the potential problems and benefits of a nightclub operation. The ideas, suggestions and methods presented within this reference can assist aspiring nightclub owners by helping to turn wonders into reality.

This book is also meant for operators who already own or manage a nightclub. By reading and applying the techniques and methods that have been carefully laid out, it is expected that current nightclub operators will gain invaluable insight into the internal, operational workings of their current venues, which can help to improve upon those existing businesses in ways that will aid to increase customer traffic and ultimately profits.

GETTING STARTED

THE BASICS OF
THE BEGINNING

Getting started is perhaps one of the most important phases operators must undertake because the decision must be made to take the leap and actually decide to take on the endeavor of running, managing and owning a nightclub. This is better known as the *idea* phase. The idea phase is just the beginning and more important, the phase that will be returned to again and again to answer questions and solve problems, regardless of how long an operation exists.

After making the decision that this is the business for you, a transition into the research and planning stages must occur. Researching and planning includes gathering all the information possible and developing a formula as to how plans will be implemented. During research and planning, hundreds and even thousands of crucial decisions must be examined and answered. Planning continues on from having the unique ideas to run a nightclub operation to choosing an appropriate name, deciding what kind of club yours will specialize in, employee issues, equipment, inventory matters and much more.

Becoming an entrepreneur can be fraught with unforeseen dangers, challenges and even adventures. On the other hand, taking control of your destiny and your finances is a rewarding experience that can leave you with an immeasurable amount of personal achievement. Making the decision to become your own boss is what separates you from everyone else.

Most nightclub operators don't find themselves in the nightclub trade by accident rather, their decision to enter this field of business stems from a strong desire to succeed and usually from past years of frequenting nightclubs themselves on a personal level. Very early on, most successful nightclub operators, made a decision that they were going to someday *set up* their own nightclub. Does this sound like you? Running a nightclub operation is something that seems to drive and burn inside of a person. It's that kind of drive and commitment that makes nightclubs successful and stand out from one another. Because you are reading this book, it's safe to assume that you are one of the elite. You either have a long-ing to open your own nightclub or a desire to improve upon the one you are currently running.

Running a nightclub is no longer an easy business where one can just sit back and count all the money. In order to make the six or seven figures a year in today's nightclubs, one will need to be very involved in many different aspects of operations and management. Soon you'll learn the techniques of the trade which will give you a head start to becoming a dynamic operator.

> BECOMING AN ENTREPRENEUR CAN BE FRAUGHT WITH UNFORESEEN DANGERS, CHALLENGES AND EVEN ADVENTURES. ON THE OTHER HAND, TAKING CONTROL OF YOUR DESTINY AND YOUR FINANCES IS A REWARDING EXPERIENCE THAT CAN LEAVE YOU WITH AN IMMEASURABLE AMOUNT OF PERSONAL ACHIEVEMENT.

THE FUTURE OF NIGHTCLUBS
The future for the nightclub entertainment industry looks good. Although for many years in the past, the industry as a whole suffered tapered salesand difficulties drawing in healthy crowds because people had more

to do in their everyday lives. The outlook in the new millennium promises a new trend with increasing revenues and more people frequenting nightclubs.

There is an estimated 50 million people in the U.S. alone, between the ages of 20-29, which represent the most active nightclub patrons. These patrons are entering nightclubs on a nightly basis more and more often. In addition, the industry is also seeing older customers between the ages of 25-45 returning to nightclubs more often than ever. These trends ensure that nightclubs will continue to strive and succeed for decades to come.

> COMPETITION ENSURES THAT NIGHTCLUB PATRONS WILL ALWAYS ENJOY THEMSELVES INSIDE OF A NIGHTCLUB BECAUSE CLUBS ARE ALWAYS STRUGGLING TO OUT DO ONE ANOTHER TO INCREASE BUSINESS.

TODAY'S ISSUES

Increased competition amongst nightclubs, social trends, legislative and regulatory mandates are all issues that can strain every nightclub operator. These factors force operators to constantly change the way in which they run their businesses in order to cope with the constantly changing demands and pressures placed upon them. Operators must constantly be thinking of new ideas and concepts to stay on top of situations and the ever-changing needs of their customers.

COMPETITION

Competition is both a useful issue and one that can put you out of business if you're not up to the challenge. In a perfect world, you would own the only nightclub in town and everyone would line up outside your front doors just dying to get in. Unfortunately, chances are yours won't be the only nightclub on the block and so you'll have to convince people to choose yours over other clubs. Once they come, you'll have to entertain them to make sure that they leave with a favorable impression so they'll come back again and again rather than taking their business somewhere else the next time.

Competition ensures that nightclub patrons will always enjoy themselves inside of a nightclub because clubs are always struggling to out do one another to increase business. A nightclub that falls behind in the race will lose the game and maybe even go out of business. Fresh and innovative ideas are so important to keep the industry thriving and to keep the customers interested.

SOCIAL TRENDS

Trends and fads can also have an effect on operations. Nightclubs must always be able to give the customers want they want.

Sometimes want they want today isn't the same thing they wanted last week. So what does that mean to a nightclub operator? That means that in addition to the day to day operations of actually running the club itself, the operator has to keep up with what's going on outside the club. The average operator must have some idea of what kinds of social trends are occurring outside his or her front doors. Sometimes certain trends may slow down business for a while and other times, trends may cause business to boom.

A good example of a negative social trend is when a community stands together and revolts against issues such as drunk driving, underage drinking, public intoxication and a whole plethora of other sometimes controversial issues. Not that your nightclub would promote or allow any type of illegal activity, but your competition might and because of that, your business could be a little slow.

When a community makes a big enough deal about social issues, cities may be compelled to take action. Maybe they may decide to increase law enforcement efforts— causing more police officers to be seen inside clubs on a nightly basis. Police officers can often make bar patrons feel uncomfortable and their presence can often drive them out of a bar even if they haven't done anything wrong. Or, maybe a city begins to pass more laws or regulations which directly affect an operation and make it even harder to do the job. In that example, as an operator you'd have to be able to overcome any negativity's that may be inflicted on the club and try to make the best out of a bad situation. Sometimes you can actually use those things to your advantage through special promotions or PR to show the community that you too care about the same issues.

LEGISLATION
Pressures from laws, government regulations and restrictions can play an important role in the operation of a nightclub. Operating a legal venue means adhering to a number of specific laws and regulations. Fortunately, some of these laws can serve to keep the industry in check and actually improve the environment within any nightclub. But, more often, most laws handicap or tie the hands of a nightclub. Social trends and community problems also have a tremendous influence in establishing new laws and the enforcement of those laws.

In recent years, pressure from legislature to lower the legal blood alcohol level to operate motor vehicles and pressure to enforce laws such as DUI, has made it harder for the nightclub industry. Hefty fines and sanctions imposed on nightclubs for violations such as serving minors or intoxicated persons, don't help much either.

THE CHALLENGES
By now some of the challenges of operating a nightclub should be apparent. These challenges are real but any crafty operator will get around them and make them work to his or her advantage. In addition to challenges such as legislation, competition and trends, there is the challenge of change. What that means is that what worked last year might not work this year and what works this year might not work next year. Why, because people change. People change because our society is constantly and rapidly changing. People sometimes change, whether they realize it or not just to keep up with what's happening around them.

YESTERDAY'S CHALLENGES
Nightclub venues of yesteryear didn't really have to compete for peoples' time. Large televisions that featured either music videos or sports programming were easy entertainers. Large theme-designed clubs, unique specialty drinks and spectacular lighting and sound effects, also used to be more than enough to draw in large crowds for the industry. Most of the challenges of those days used to come from competition from other

area nightclubs. Even then, most venues could do quite well, and boasted big profits from customers with lots of time to throw away.

TODAY'S CHALLENGES

New technology such as the Internet now make it possible for people to relax at home by getting online and going into a chat room. People no longer have to go out to meet new and interesting people. People have less free time than they used to and competing for that time has become increasingly demanding for the industry. Factors like the Internet, movie rentals, coffee houses, home entertainment centers, sports venues and other non traditional types of entertainment all vie for peoples' time.

Many forms of social entertainment and interaction are fast becoming popular or *the thing to do,* so nightclubs must keep up in order to avoid being completely pushed out. Spectacular light shows, themes, TV, videos or specialty drinks are no longer enough by themselves, to draw customers in and keep them happy. For example, in years past, most people had to go to a club in order to buy a hard to get favorite drink of theirs. Nowadays, they can probably go into just about any supermarket or liquor store and buy any drink they want— and pay less for it than they would inside a nightclub.

Also, with the ever-improving capabilities of TV programming like digital cable or satellite programming, some sports bar operations are feeling the heat. It's now very easy for a group of people to stay at home and watch, say the Superbowl on a wide screen TV, in exceptional video and sound quality—complete with a state-of-the-art stereo and surround system. With all of that who needs to leave the house anymore?

This isn't to suggest that it is now impossible to run a successful nightclub, but merely that nowadays it takes a culmination of different aspects of operations— marketing, design and layout, lights and sounds, customer interaction, managerial know how and more to run a highly successful club with today's more sophisticated customers.

Ideas and methods of the past still work today but they must all work together or they probably won't work at all. Today, you won't be able to just rent or buy a large one-room building, throw up some lights, hook up a sound system, serve alcohol then sit back and expect that the place will be overcrowded with customers. It just won't happen anymore.

Today's club requires careful planning and demographic research. It's important that you know who your customers are and what they want. Special amenities such as lights, light shows, high quality sound systems, drink specials, excellent customer service, dance floors, high and low-tech games and special events like, live bands are all still powerful influences that keep patrons coming back for more. These things brought together along with a solid marketing plan is just the beginning in the race to get people out of their homes or away from other activities and get them into your nightclub.

TOMORROW'S CHALLENGES

Like any other successful business operation, nightclubs must try to continually look ahead into the future to prepare for the challenges that await. The only way that operators can stay ahead of their patrons is by constantly rating the success of their operation and improving upon what is or isn't working. The future can sometimes be a guessing game and tomorrow's challenges will start with trying to anticipate your customers' needs and wants and finding a way to deliver upon those demands.

The ultimate challenge of all is to keep the audience entertained, interested and happy. You'll soon learn how to do that through the many important aspects of a club and how patrons are affected by different fundamentals. You must also learn the importance of changing food and drink menus, working with the sound and lights, the design and layout and learn how to make customers more comfortable to persuade their feelings about the nightclub.

SUCCESS VERSUS FAILURE

This chapter is not meant to discourage anyone from operating a night-club. Rather, it is meant to enlighten anyone who yearns to become a nightclub operator by preparing you for this rewarding career by helping you to realize some of the pitfalls within the industry. So, don't worry, millions of people still frequent clubs every year seeking entertainment and nightclubs are still very profitable businesses if they are operated correctly. Success is a relative term. If you ask ten people, what success means to them, you'll probably get ten different answers. To define your own success, you must first realize what it is that you hope to achieve as an operator. Opening a nightclub is a fun experience but in order for a club to survive in today's nightclub climate, it takes a lot of hard work— day in and day out.

Before you go off and get a loan to open up a nightclub, first take some time and think about what goals you want to reach if you do proceed. Sit down and write down some simple goals. Once done, you should have several objectives on paper that you'll want to aim for within your venue. These goals should help to give you some focus and a direction to work toward. Make sure that both the short-term and long-term goals are feasible and attainable. Otherwise, you could set yourself up for failure. Transpose those goals into a business plan and after those goals are met, only then should you consider yourself successful.

> OPENING A NIGHTCLUB IS A FUN EXPERIENCE BUT, IN ORDER FOR A CLUB TO SURVIVE IN TODAY'S NIGHTCLUB CLIMATE, IT TAKES A LOT OF HARD WORK— DAY IN AND DAY OUT.

Everytime a set of goals is reached, sit down and write out new ones that are even higher and then begin working towards them. This process should continue on throughout the duration of a nightclub. Setting and arriving at goals will keep you, employees and the nightclub on track because everything that is done will revolve around achieving those goals.

START-UP TIPS

Getting any nightclub off the ground is usually the hardest part of becoming an operator. But once you've jumped through all of the hoops, there are a number of things you should strive for very early on to increase your likelihood of running a successful operation. The following are some tips for start-up operations which can help you to grow a club in a healthy manner from the very beginning:

- **Avoid Getting into Debt:** Debt is the number one reason a night-club will go out of business, so do your best when making financial decisions to avoid it. For most prospective operators, it will be nearly impossible to get started without a loan from a financial institution. If you do need to borrow money, make it a primary objective to repay the loan as soon as possible. Loans come with interest that have to be repaid which can quickly add up over a period of time. Why pay a bank money when you could be accruing that money as profit. After settling your debts with a financial institution, if any, never return to them again requesting money. If you need cash for renovations, remodeling or expansion, work toward those projects by saving the needed funding from profits. If you arrive at a point where you feel you need cash for projects or activities quickly, but don't readily have the necessary funding, seek out investors, friends or family members to assist rather than asking a bank if at all possible. The bottom line is the less debt you have the better off you'll be in the long run.

- **Keep the Atmosphere Entertaining:** People go to nightclubs to enjoy themselves and to relax. If that doesn't happen, there's little reason anyone will return to any club. You should swiftly try and create an environment that allows guests to be entertained and happy. If it isn't entertaining the very first time they arrive, why should they come back the next week?

- **Use Lighting to Create a Relaxing Environment:** Lights are powerful elements inside nightclubs which help to create and enhance themes. They have the ability to make guests feel uncomfortable or comfortable. Use lights abundantly to create moods but try not to make them the center of attention. They should just be part of the total package.

> DEBT IS THE NUMBER ONE REASON A NIGHTCLUB WILL GO OUT OF BUSINESS, SO DO YOUR BEST WHEN MAKING FINANCIAL DECISIONS TO AVOID IT.

- **Properly Research and Plan Your Venue:** An excellent approach to a start up will revolve around the research and planning phase. Proper research and development can eliminate surprises and save a lot of money in unexpected expenses and problems.

- **Make Good Food:** If you plan to run a nightclub/restaurant operation, the food that is served should be excellent. Food should complement the drinks that are served and vice versa. If the food doesn't taste good, it won't matter how good the drinks are because the lunch or a dinner crowd will be nonexistent.

- **Hire the Right Employees:** The people that are employed to carry out your intentions and to communicate with guests are the life-blood of an operation. Customers will form opinions about a club based on their interactions with employees. Therefore, employees should project a positive image as well as deliver a quality, friendly service to guests every working day of the week.

- **Visit Other Nightclubs:** Seeing firsthand what other nightclubs or the competition is doing can set the stage for your operation. Visiting other nightclubs is one of the best ways to see what entertains bar patrons, especially if you visit a club that is very similar to yours. When you go to a neighboring nightclub, pay close attention to everything that's happening, how the nightclub is making money and how it treats customers. You may see things that you can duplicate within your own nightclub or things that you don't want to do at all. Use those observations to make the nightclub experience that much more enjoyable inside your club.

- **Develop a Solid Workable Business Plan:** A good business plan should cover every aspect of an operation. In order to secure a loan from a bank you'll need to develop a business plan that a loan officer or committee will review, then appeal or approve. The business plan needs to be very concise and explanatory. Even if you have enough money to start your operation and won't require a business loan from a bank or other lending institution, you should still develop a workable that you should abide by. The business plan should include everything from daily operations, food service, beverages to advertising and promotions. A business plan should clearly spell out these things and more in a clear manner. Try to keep it short, less than 12 pages. If it's longer than that it's likely to be too hard to read and probably won't be read by the people it really matters to—you and/or your bank.

RESEARCH AND PLANNING

You need to have a plan. What does that mean? It means that if you truly want to pursue your dream of owning a nightclub, you need to have a plan to get it done. Planning includes gathering all the information possible about a project, figuring out how much capital you'll need, selecting a location; *will you buy a building, lease one or purchase an existing operation?* Will you own the bar alone or will others be involved and share ownership? If so, who will do what?

Gathering the information needed about an endeavor is very important, especially if you and/or your partners intend to obtain financing. At this point, one of the many decisions that must be made is deciding which type of nightclub you intend to operate. Will yours be the small bar on the corner or the multi-level club that is equipped to cater to hundreds of patrons at any time? The size, design and style of the club will be dependent on how much capital you and/or your partners will be able to raise. There is absolutely nothing wrong with starting small and expanding over the years. In fact, many very successful clubs, started out exactly that way by using a smaller venue as a financial springboard to eventually open a larger club.

Figure out how much capital you and/or your partners are able to raise. It is important that you be realistic here. Don't overestimate your financial potential and definitely don't underestimate it either. You'll learn about raising capital, later in *Obtaining the Cash.*

THE IDEA

Now that you have made the decision that you want to open your own nightclub, you must now bring some ideas to the table. Ideas are how you plan to make a nightclub successful. Grab a piece of paper and begin writing down all of the ideas that you would like to implement and do inside a club. These ideas will help later on when it comes time to piece together a business plan. Some of the ideas that you may want to think about addressing should include issues such as: *Naming your club, deciding on what type of club to open, design and layout, putting together the sound and light systems, employee issues and organizing an overall strategy.*

To get you started in the idea stage, Below are a few questions to ask yourself. Keep in mind that there is an infinite number of ideas out there and the number one source for them is your brain power. Don't limit yourself when it comes to ideas— Give each of your ideas equal consideration and strategically choose or eliminate each one carefully:

- What will make my club stand out from the rest and make it different from other clubs like it? What kind of club will it be?

- Where would be the best or ideal place to buy or build a nightclub to ensure maximum visibility and traffic?

- How much advertising will I do on a weekly, monthly or yearly basis?

- What kind of advertising will I do to convince people to give my club a chance?

- How large of a nightclub should I open; What can I afford?

- Will I serve food? If so, what kind? What is my competition serving? How can I serve better food than they are?

- Should I put an emphasis on sound? Design?

- What kind of music will my club play? Which nightclubs in the area are playing the same music?

- Will I have drink specials? Cover charges?

- Will I buy or rent my equipment?

Again, these are just a few of the many questions that must be answered. In order for a club to become successful, hundreds of questions will have to be carefully studied and no question or idea should be overlooked. Each nightclub is an individual entity so many questions and potential problems will often have to be solved and addressed specifically to a club itself. Keep that in mind while brainstorming ideas.

SELECTING A LOCATION
Selecting a suitable location for a nightclub is critical. Where will it be? Take into consideration other nightclubs that are presently in the area that may pose competition. If there are other clubs already established, what will you do differently to compete? Starting out, try to avoid building a site near an already successful club. It could be difficult to compete against an already popular nightclub, especially if you are planning to start a smaller operation. The exception to this however, is if you plan to run a large nightclub and expect to win over your competitions' customers relatively early on. This can be done, but usually requires a significant investment in advertising and marketing, which must be a priority in the beginning phases of an operation.

Utilize Census figures to find out how many clubs or bars are in the area or look in the yellow pages to see who is where and personally visit each one to check out what and how they are doing.

Ideally, you'll want to set up an operation in high traffic areas, preferably in prosperous *commercial zones* within a city. The more customers that pass by a business in a normal day, the higher the chance of that business getting noticed by people who didn't realize it was even there. Simply being in the right place or being exposed to more potential customers can spell more business and ultimately more profits for you.

This is especially true if you hope to establish a food crowd during the day and evening hours. People appreciate convenience and don'tlike hard to find places. Take some time, do your homework and find a location that provides excellent access to customers to maximize exposure.

Unfortunately, some cities attempt to zone nightclubs as far away as they can away from everything else. In these situations, operators may find themselves bordering on the outskirts of town or neighbors with factories or large companies in industrial zones. These zones are usually not traveled heavily by average citizens, which makes it *harder* for a nightclub in this situation to attract a food crowd. If you find yourself in a predicament such as this, don't worry too much, you'll still be able to run a successful club, but chances are you'll need to place less of an emphasis on food sales and more on late evening entertainment.

> THE MORE CUSTOMERS THAT PASS BY A BUSINESS IN A NORMAL DAY, THE HIGHER THE CHANCE OF THAT BUSINESS GETTING NOTICED BY PEOPLE WHO DIDN'T REALIZE IT WAS EVEN THERE.

Other considerations to take into account are the available parking for guests and the size of the property; is it an empty lot or is there already a building there? If there is a building there, is there enough available property to support future expansion if it becomes necessary?

LEASING OR BUYING A BUILDING

Do you plan to buy the property outright or will you lease? There are advantages and disadvantages to both. Advantages of owning a building will be that you won't have to worry about answering to others. That means, as the property owner, you can do whatever you want to it to improve it as you see fit. Also as the years pass, you'll gain equity in the property which will increase its overall value. A disadvantage would be, if for some reason a club is not a huge success within a period of time and it was forced to go out of business, you would be stuck with the property and would still be responsible for repaying any loans you took out to obtain it. The only way to recoup any losses would be to try and sell the property to another potential business entrepreneur which could take a long time to do in some cases.

For that reason, leasing a premise is an advantage. Leasing can become a disadvantage in that you may be limited by contract in what you can and can't do. For instance, as a tenant you could be prohibited from making major necessary structural changes inside the building because a lease could strictly prohibit any such activity. Also, the owner of the building will always have the final say in matters and you could be forced to abide by his or her rules in order to keep the lease and stay in business.

Leasing also causes the costs of starting up considerably less than if you were to purchase property. Depending on the property's location and quality, it could quickly add up to hundreds of thousands of dollars that would be required on top of everything else needed to get an operation off the ground. Entering into a lease, in most cases, only requires a lease agreement, possibly a security deposit and the current month's rent to get started which, in a nightclub's case, can range from several hundred dollars to several thousand dollars, depending on the area and property values.

You'll have to decide which option will best suit your financial situation and how much you are willing to spend in order to get started. Leasing a building will require some remodeling to design the layout (bars, dance floors, kitchen area, etc.) and will then require you to purchase or rent all of the needed equipment and furniture to decorate how it should look. Even though a lease isn't buying a piece of property, adding all the necessary amenities can cost thousands of dollars. The money spent on a lease project is usually still considerably less than buying property or a building outright and can save money from the onset.

Regardless of which route you decide upon, visit several properties and carefully evaluate each one's potential. Each location you evaluate should have adequate space for your needs and should be somewhere between 2700 square feet to 15,000 square feet or more. Anything between 2700 and 3500 Square feet, falls into the *small* venue category. 3500 to 15,000 square feet is considered a *medium sized* or a *large venue*. Anything over 15,000 square feet is considered a *huge* nightclub. When looking for rental properties, it'll be harder to find properties over 3500 square feet that are in decent locations and are cost effective. When seeking to establish a medium to a large sized venue, in most cases you'd be better off purchasing an existing building or buying an empty lot to build on.

Get estimates from construction contractors and then find out about property taxes and rental rates. Make offers on properties you can afford and learn all you can about the utilities at each site. Absorb as much information as possible from each location so that you'll be able to accurately determine a financial projection which you'll need when you write the business plan so that everything can fall into place.

PURCHASING AN EXISTING NIGHTCLUB
Few successful nightclubs are ever placed up for sale. For that reason, you should carefully approach another operator who is selling an existing nightclub. Find out quickly what his or her motives are for selling. If it's because business isn't so good, be leery of buying a failing nightclub unless you think you have what it takes to turn it around.

Thoroughly investigate the business and request to see profit and loss statements for as many past years as the owner(s) can provide. Evaluate everything else on the premise as if you were buying a brand-new property or business. If you do decide to buy an existing nightclub, it doesn't mean that time spent on research and planning, and other critical start-up basics should be eliminated. Take the approach, that even though the club has been around for a while, it's still new to you and you are going to run it your way— The right way, preceded with careful and well thought out objectives.

DECIDING ON THE TYPE OF NIGHTCLUB TO OPEN
The decision as to what type of nightclub to open is a big one. This decision can be an especially important one if you intend to open your club in an area that already has competition from other nightclubs. Which type of bar you establish should rely on what competition is or isn't doing and your own personal preferences.

TYPES OF ESTABLISHMENTS

Brewpubs: Brewpubs are clubs or bars that produce and sell their own beers. Usually in addition to the specialty house beers they make and sell, they also have available common, commercially sold beers, liquors and wines. Those interested in opening their own Brewpub should be familiar with the process of making beer or should employ an expert who would be responsible for manufacturing beer. Brewpubs require sophisticated equipment in order to brew beer which increases start-up costs.

Cigar or Martini Bars: Cigar and Martini Bars suggest just what the names imply. These bars specialize in the sale of quality cigars and a wide variety of delicious martinis. Often these types of bars are one in the same. Martini bars usually also promote and sell cigars and vice versa.

Wine Bars: Another type of bar whose name suggests its specialty. Typically built in elegant settings that suit themselves toward the older segment of the nightclub crowd. Very Cultural.

Latin/Salsa: An increasingly popular type of nightclub in the United States. Salsa clubs boast upbeat Latin dance music.

Sports Bar: Sports bars are very popular and offer patrons the ability to watch a wide variety of live sports programming on television. Sports bars are usually laid out in a sports genre complete with sports memorabilia to increase visual effects.

Rock Club: Rock clubs tailor to hard rock, heavy metal and soft rock. In addition, rock clubs usually feature golden-oldies music from the past.

Country/Western: The name says it all. Country/western clubs are usually a combination of dance clubs and pubs that play only country/western music.

Jazz Club: Jazz clubs are normally smaller establishments that specialize in jazz, piano or blues music. Live jazz bands are a must for these clubs to be successful.

Karaoke: Bars that are strictly karaoke are rare and require excellent managerial skills to be successful. However, successful karaoke bars can be highly profitable.

Dance Club: Dance clubs are the most popular of all bars and nightclubs. Dance clubs are very versatile and allow for a number of different activities and music genres.

Comedy Club: You guessed it. Comedy clubs specialize in amateur and professional live stand-up comedy acts.

Gay/Lesbian: Increasing in numbers throughout the U.S., gay and lesbian clubs provide a social setting for alternative lifestyles.

Pub or Tavern: Pub or tavern is a common reference to a smaller bar. Pubs or taverns usually lack features such as a dance floor and a DJ which would make it a dance club.

Rap/Hip Hop: These bars originated both on the east and west coast of the U.S. and now have surfaced in the Midwest and south. They also feature some professional acts on stage as well as amateur performers.

Rap/Hip Hop: These bars originated both on the east and west coast of the U.S. and now have surfaced in the Midwest and south. They also feature some professional acts on stage as well as amateur performers.

Lounge/Hotel: These are rare for small, independent operators to own. They are found inside hotels, airports or other major places where people frequent as they travel. Typically these establishments are very expensive to own but can be very profitable.

Adult Clubs: These clubs feature nude or topless dancers (men or women, but predominately women), who entertain the clientele with both intimate and exciting dances. The dancers usually draw in a large crowd, willing to spend a lot of money on a nightly basis which makes these venues highly profitable for the operators who own and run them.

REACHING YOUR CUSTOMERS

Finally, a solid plan is needed, which spells out how you intend to attract the target customers to the nightclub. Knowing how to do this will require knowing what the intended customers will want and also knowing the competition.

A good location is important, but it isn't everything. You'll still have to have a good advertising campaign in place to entice, inform, educate and let many customers know where you are and why they should choose your nightclub over another. Think creatively and do whatever it takes to bring customers inside. Once they come, help them to entertain themselves and your almost guaranteed repeat business. Happy customers convey their experiences through word of mouth to others. Word of mouth is the most powerful form of advertising and the word can quickly spread like wildfires if your nightclub is a fun and entertaining place to be.

THE BUSINESS OF DOING BUSINESS

BUSINESS ESSENTIALS

Okay, if you've made it this far, it's safe to assume that you are still interested in going into business for yourself. More importantly, you still want to start and run your own nightclub. But before jumping right into running a bar, first it needs to built or acquired. This is going to require some planning and financing on your part so establish a plan and stick to it if you hope to succeed. You'll need to make many important legal decisions during the formation of the nightclub. Some decisions will be best made by the aid of an attorney. Other operational decisions such as choosing the right accountant and getting adequate insurance coverage will also need to be given some thought in order to give a venue a healthy start.

SELECTING AN ACCOUNTANT

If you don't already have an accountant, don't wait until the last minute to try to find one. Get one now. Although it's not necessary to have an accountant to assist in handling the financial aspects of a club, it's highly recommended because a good accountant can free you from the tedious process of managing financial reports, accounts and other book work such as the payroll. An accountant should also be able to take care of the business income taxes and guide you in the right direction financially. The services an accountant can provide will allow you to concentrate more on the operation of your nightclub and less on record keeping and tax matters.

A good accountant can also serve to be a trusted financial business advisor who can give you invaluable business insight and ideas.

ACCOUNTANT CHECKLIST

Some accountants specialize in specific industries and others in services such as taxes or audits. Choosing the right accountant for your nightclub should be just like shopping around for any service that a business would need. Check with other business owners and get referrals. Interview those referrals and make a list of potential accountants. While you interview those accountants and later thereafter, make sure you've covered the following:

❑ Does the accountant specialize in businesses such as nightclubs?

❑ Does the prospective accountant specialize in income taxes?

❑ Does the accountant come with high recommendations from other business owners and are others familiar with the accountant?

❑ Does the accountant fully understand my nightclub and all the unique problems that comes with it?

❑ Has the accountant clearly explained all the fees and costs, and do I fully understand them? Most importantly— will I be comfortable with this accountant as my business advisor?

Certified Public Accountants get their (CPA) title by passing accounting, auditing, tax and business law examinations. In addition to being required to hold a college degree, Certified Public Accounts must also annually fulfill a continued education requirement. Certified Public Accountants are required to abide by a code of professional ethics and are overseen by a state board of accountancy.

Most business owners choose a CPA, over a non-CPA, to become their accountant because of the expected high level of professional competence. Non-certified accountants may not have the broad level of education as a CPA, but might have the right accounting or tax experience to serve you well, so don't eliminate them based on the lack of a CPA title.

If you decide that you want to employ an accountant to handle the financial matters of your nightclub, don't wait too long to try to find one. The busiest time of the year for accountants is between January and April (tax season). If you try to interview these professionals during this time, you'll probably find out they won't have much time for you.

SELECTING AN ATTORNEY

Having an attorney in the nightclub industry is a must. You absolutely cannot function without one. Without a doubt, there will be times that legal questions will arise that'll need to be answered quickly. You'll need an attorney on the team so that he or she is only a phone call away. Select an attorney who understands you and the nightclub industry in order to offer the appropriate legal business advice. Attorneys should also be able to offer preventive legal services— preventing you from entering into contracts that are not in the best interest of the nightclub.

An attorney can also help to properly structure a nightclub, negotiate and draw up contracts and review the legalities of policies and procedures. In addition to the invaluable business advice an attorney can offer, a nightclub will need an attorney to represent it as a plaintiff or defendant in criminal proceedings or in a civil lawsuit, should any legal problems arise.

FINDING THE RIGHT ATTORNEY

Try to be very cautious about hiring the right attorney for you and your nightclub. Don't worry about legal fees because they are just part of the cost of doing business, just like rent, labor, supplies and inventory.

Manage legal services just like you'll manage everything else in your business. Investigate and pursue hiring an attorney just as you would with hiring an accountant or any other business service needed. You can start with the yellow pages because you're guaranteed to find pages of attorneys. When you contact and speak to attorneys, use the checklist to help you decide on one that will best meet the needs of your nightclub:

❏ **Consult with other business owners.** Most likely, others already in business will be able to give you a reference to the business attorney(s) they are using and any recommendations or problems that they've had regarding a specific attorney.

❏ **Shop around.** Just when you think you've found the perfect attorney for your nightclub, don't stop there. It won't hurt any to talk to other attorneys and compare them all to each another. You just might find one even better than the one you thought you were going to hire.

❏ **Interview all prospective attorneys just as you would employees or an accountant.** You can learn a lot about a person by conducting an interview. Interviewing an attorney is no different. During an interview you may find personality conflicts that could affect your relationship with an attorney down the line. It's best to find that out sooner rather than later.

If a particular attorney is too high strung to allow you to interview him or her, don't waste your time and move onto the next one, you don't need those types of attorneys on your side.

❏ **Don't hire a relative.** Attempt to stay away from hiring anyone who is related to you. In most cases, relatives lead to problems down the road. When your wife's brother isn't performing as expected, firing him becomes a difficult decision to make, because not only is it just business, but it can become personal too.

❏ **Clearly understand all of the fees.** Before making any decisions whatsoever, make sure you clearly understand everything and get it in writing. For example, if the attorney you decide to hire charges you a rate for all telephone calls made to him or her for advice, get it in writing so that there are no billing surprises later on.

❏ **An attorney should have the same style as you.** If you're a fast paced individual and expect things to happen yesterday, then you better hire an attorney who thinks the same way. In this example, you wouldn't want an attorney who likes to take his or her time to get a job done. This can be a serious conflict.

❏ **Be cautious of advertisements.** Don't rely on any advertisements that an attorney promotes, whether found in the yellow pages, newspapers, radio, a television commercial, whatever or wherever. Advertisements are meant for only one thing— to draw in business. These ads are usually hyped up in efforts to produce maximum responses. Attorneys need clients to make money and the more clients they have the more money they can make. It isn't uncommon for them to sometimes over promote themselves to try to appeal to potential clients. If you contact an attorney in response to an advertisement you saw or read about, make sure you thoroughly apply all of the above principles to determine if the attorney is right for your business.

Finally, if you take the time to carefully research hiring an attorney and find the one that has a good understanding of your night-club and its needs, you will eliminate many problems that normally arise between attorneys and clients, which in turn, will serve to make your nightclub even more successful.

BUSINESS OWNERSHIP
The decision as to whether or not you will own the business by yourself, or if others will share ownership is a necessary consideration. You must understand the laws and rules by which business must be conducted. There are three legal structures for conducting business and you must choose and operate under one of them before you can open your doors to the general public.

The three structures are the *sole proprietorship*, the *partnership* and the *corporation*. You and/or your partners must decide which one of these entities your nightclub will operate under in order to best fulfill the needs of the club. To figure out which entity your nightclub will assume, carefully weigh each of the advantages and disadvantages of each legal formation.

SOLE PROPRIETORSHIP
This is the most common type of business entity and is normally described as a business owned and operated by one person. Sole proprietorships are also the easiest to form and usually require only a business license issued by a local county or city clerk's office. Unlike partnerships or corporations, sole proprietorships are not separate entities from the owner and other than obtaining a business license, and/or fictitious name statement— if the business name is different from the owner's name, no other legal formalities are necessary.

Also, unlike the corporation or partnership, sole proprietors have complete and total control over the business. Sole proprietorships, however do not have perpetual existence. If the owner dies, becomes disabled or retires, the business does not have continuity and ceases to exist.

ADVANTAGES:
1. The proprietor keeps all of the profits and doesn't have to share them with anyone else except of course, the expenses of overhead and employee salaries.
2. There are not as many restrictions or formalities with establishing a sole proprietorship and it is less expensive to obtain the necessary licenses than a partnership or corporation.
3. There are no co-owners or partners to consult with.
4. Management is able to respond quickly to business needs in the form of day to day management decisions as governed by various operational policies and good sense.
5. Special taxation.

DISADVANTAGES:
1. The individual proprietor is responsible for the full amount of all business debts which may exceed the proprietor's total investment. This liability extends to all the proprietors' assets, such as house and car. Additional problems of liability, such as physical loss or personal injury, may be lessened by obtaining proper insurance coverage.
2. Usually there is less capital for start-up. Since this form of business is usually started and run by one person, the one person usually is limited by the amount of money in his or her bank accounts for start-up capital.
3. Usually more difficult to obtain long-term financing, unless the proprietor has a proven track record in business. It may be a little harder (not impossible) for the sole proprietor to win banks over and obtain a loan without the proprietor having a substantial investment in the business.
4. A limited experience and viewpoint. This is more often the case with new operators than with other business owners. Being the only one in charge of the business can limit creative thinking and there is often no form of constructive criticism to help analyze or evaluate operations.

THE PARTNERSHIP

With a partnership, business ownership is divided up between two or more persons. There are two types of partnerships to form. The general partnership and the limited partnership. The general partnership is the most common of the two. All partners involved in the general partnership are equally involved in the operation of the business and all share the profits and liabilities of the business.

Limited partnerships provide limited liability for each of the partners. Liability can be no greater than a partner's initial investment in the business. If forming a limited partnership, you should consult with an attorney because the formation of the limited liability partnership is slightly more complicated than forming a sole proprietorship.

Whichever type of partnership you and your partners decide to form there are advantages and disadvantages to both. They are as follows:

ADVANTAGES:
1. Collective thought processes and reasoning to solve problems.
2. Partnerships are not required to pay federal income taxes. Each partner will separately file an informational tax return. *IRS form 1065.*
3. Liability of the business can be spread amongst each partner.
4. Any loans or investments from any of the partners create a business deduction and interest income for all partners.

DISADVANTAGES:
1. Complexities of formation.
2. Any problems that arise between partners can create potential problems for the business.
3. All general partners have an unlimited liability and may be responsible for their partners' commitments should the business fail.

CHOOSING A PARTNER
If you decide to enter into a partnership agreement with one or more persons do so with great care and caution. Typically, partnerships in the nightclub industry are formed by two or more friends who share a common desire to get into the business. Even still, friends or not—be careful. Partners who aren't properly prepared to go into business with each other can end up bitter and possibly even enemies as a result of business conflicts.

Before opening up the front doors to the public, be sure that each partner's role and responsibilities are properly defined. What this means is that each partner has a clear understanding of what he or she must do on a day to day basis in order to equally contribute to the success of the nightclub. Each partner's profit should be commensurable to their investment and the work that each performs.

For example, if one partner initially invested 80% of the start-up capital and the other 20% and both do an equal amount of work, then the payoff should be proportional—80/20, respectively.

Regardless of the relationships that you may have with any potential partner(s), you'll need to sit down with them and go over all of the relevant details in depth and if possible create a workable contract that all partners must agree upon. Any contract that you enter into with your partner(s) should be reviewed by an attorney for any errors and to obviously make sure its properly done and legal. Even if you decide to go into business with your lifelong best friend, you should strongly consider entering into a contract with him or her. Why? Because money is a very powerful instrument capable of destroying just about any relationship. If problems do arise, they most likely will evolve around money. That's why it's important to have a clearly defined contract in place to eliminate any potential disputes that may or may not lie ahead.

CORPORATION
Some nightclub operators have taken advantage of incorporation. There are both benefits and drawbacks to this form of business ownership. Incorporating probably isn't for all clubs, especially the smaller ones. But for the clubs that draw in a larger crowd and turn over substantial profits year after year, incorporating might be the way to go. Generally speaking, most nightclub corporations are a result of very successful operations. The owners of these successful nightclubs have learned how to successfully run and expand their nightclubs and usually have multiple venues in different areas.

Corporations are complex legal structures and the detailed complexities and applicable laws of each vary from state to state. They are more expensive to form than the proprietorship or partnership. If you or your partners are considering a corporation, seeking legal advice is highly recommended.

The greatest benefit in incorporating a nightclub is the liability protection. Any debt that the nightclub incurs is not yours but is the debt of the business. Incorporating also makes it easier to raise money through the sale of stocks. Also, if you plan to seek outside investors, the corporation is a must.

There are typically three types of corporations to form. The Regular Corporation, S-Corporation and the Limited Liability Corporation. Your attorney should be able to assist you in determining which type of corporation you should form as well as other crucial information about the various aspects of incorporating including, appointing officers or a board of directors.

Corporations are taxed by the government. You, as a shareholder, are also required to pay personal taxes on your income. This is better known as double taxation. This is a significant disadvantage. But if you were to incorporate a nightclub it should be easier to obtain loans from banks and easier to establish credit with vendors and suppliers.

Carefully study the advantages and disadvantages of the corporation and if you believe that incorporating your nightclub is for you, then by all means go for it.

ADVANTAGES:
1. Shareholders (you) have personal limited liability.
2. Indefinite life of a nightclub. If you die or if ownership in stocks changes, the corporation will continue on.
3. Ease in obtaining business capital.
4. Medical, disability, life insurance plans, and other employee fringe benefit from special tax treatments.
5. Deductible dividends.
6. Reduced taxes by dividing profits amongst owners and the corporation.

DISADVANTAGES:
1. More expensive to establish than the sole proprietorship or the partnership.
2. Annual corporate fees.
3. An accountant is most likely needed to complete all necessary tax forms and obligations.
4. Higher tax rates for profits more than $75,000.
5. Double taxation.
6. The corporation cannot deduct any business losses.
7. The forming of a corporation usually requires professional help in the form of lawyers to file papers and to hold the first shareholder meeting. High legal fees can also become a significant part of forming a corporation.

8. Founders of a corporation do not necessarily own the business since a corporation is its own entity. Founders are in essence employees and may have to share profits with investors or other shareholders.

THE BUSINESS PLAN

Regardless of whether or not you'll seek bank or SBA financing, or even if you're independently wealthy and decide to start-up a nightclub with pocket change, you should have a business plan to give the nightclub some direction and a sense of purpose on paper. The business plan should be a well-structured document that answers what your objectives are and how you and your nightclub will accomplish those objectives. A business plan is like a living document for banks, investors and other lending sources to review and then consider the feasibility of your ideas.

Even if you are fortunate in that you'll not need to seek financial assistance, you should still have an honest, workable business plan in place for yourself. One study showed that only 42% of business owners had a business plan in place during start-up. 69% of those who did develop a plan reported that the plan led to their success. In short, if you have a plan you are more likely to succeed and meet your goals than if you don't have one.

THE PLAN

There are many ways to write a business plan but no matter how it's written, certain areas of operation must be addressed. First, a plan needs to lay out a business concept, describe what kind of business it is and what it hopes to achieve. Second, the plan should identify the market or who the customers will be. Lastly, a financial, marketing and strategy plan must be addressed in detail. Each of these areas are usually broken down even further into smaller, more specific components. Your plan can be as long or as short as you need it to be but try to avoid being too wordy because it may become confusing. If it's hard to understand then it's not likely to be read and your point will be missed.

Review the *Sample Business Plan* to get an idea of what one should look like and contain. Keep in mind that the sample is a very simple example and yours will need to be structured appropriately.

SAMPLE BUSINESS PLAN FORMAT
THE APOCALYPSE NIGHTCLUB

I. NAME
Apocalypse Nightclub

II. VISION
To be the number one nightclub/restaurant and entertainment venue on the University campus that will gain an outstanding reputation for service and provide a relaxing social setting and atmosphere for the student community.

III. MISSION/PURPOSE
To provide a centrally located nightclub that will primarily cater to student dining and entertainment needs; *The apocalypse* will provide dine-in food service (restaurant) during the day and offer a high-quality, energetic nightlife during the evening and early morning. During the hours of restaurant service, *The Apocalypse Nightclub*, will offer a free food delivery service, limited to the campus area, to better serve customers.

IV. SCOPE
The Apocalypse will be a full service nightclub/restaurant that will be set in a college environment welcoming all alumni and non-alumni alike.

V. PRODUCTS AND SERVICES
The Apocalypse Nightclub plans to obtain the necessary liquor licenses in order to sell a wide variety of alcoholic beverages, both imported and domestic. An array of fine wines and a large cocktail menu will also compliment the food menu.

The Apocalypse will feature an extensive food menu with an emphasis on Italian foods. The Apocalypse will also host one live band (musical entertainment) a week, one amateur stand-up comedy night and one contest each week where the customers can win a variety of prizes. In addition to the contests and special acts, customers will also have access to a dance floor and can enjoy the most current pop/dance music.

VI. ASSUMPTIONS

There are currently two nightclubs on-campus and neither are equipped as a restaurant which limits their hours of operation due to the inability to serve food during the day and early evening. The apocalypse's ability to serve fine foods will draw students inside during the day, which will result in greater profit.

VII. GOALS AND OBJECTIVES

1. Achieve food sales more than $100K within the first year.
2. Generate at least $750K in gross sales within two years.
3. Expand/remodel *The Apocalypse Nightclub's* building capacity to hold approximately 1000 people.
4. Hire a full-time manager to assume all managerial responsibilities and control the nightclub under my direction within four years.
5. Every year for ten years, build one new Apocalypse Nightclub in each of the Big Ten college communities. (The Big Ten is a collegiate sports conference— states/universities included in the conference are Illinois, Indiana, Iowa, Michigan, Michigan State, Minnesota, Northwestern, Ohio State, Penn State, Purdue and Wisconsin).

VIII. COMPETITION ANALYSIS

Presently, there are two nightclubs established, on-campus. The University currently has an enrollment of 30,573 students. Both of the presently established nightclubs have a combined building capacity of 1,100 people. Competition is minimal and *The Apocalypse* alone will accommodate more than 850 people at one time, giving a larger number of customers a nightclub in which to converge where they couldn't before.

IX. STRATEGIES

The nightclub will feature a host of special events that will change from week to week during the evening. Many popular college club events will be implemented during these activities to entertain the customers. Various drink specials and promotional nights will also be used to encourage customer traffic.

X. FIRST YEAR EXPENSES
$310,000 (see attachment detailing costs break down)

XI. CAPITAL INVESTMENTS
$29,000 (see personal financial statement)

XII. SALES GOAL
$750,000 a year.

XIII. MARKETING PLAN
Three weeks prior to grand opening, a large marketing project will be initiated via various media communications; radio, newspapers, word of mouth, circulars and a 30-second television commercial which will be aired twice a day at random times on a local television channel. Ongoing advertising and promotions will occur on a weekly basis. Many of the campaigns will be initiated inside the nightclub. The remaining efforts will be focused through the use of radio to keep customers informed of upcoming activities, as the entertainment and special events will change on a weekly basis.

Hopefully this sample business plan has given you an idea of what a plan of attack should look like. Remember that this plan is very basic and it's likely that yours will be just a little more in depth. For instance, the estimated start-up and operational costs of your nightclub for the first year will need to be itemized in detail, if you plan on obtaining financing from a bank. That means that thorough research will have to be completed detailing everything you'll plan to purchase, rent or have inside and outside of your nightclub. Banks will also require, a personal balance sheet which details your finances, your assets, your debts and how much you're actually investing in your proposed nightclub.

The business plan can often mean the difference between obtaining the necessary financing and being rejected. Business plans are especially important for those seeking financing and therefore, you should take great care in its inception and utilize an attorney or a nightclub consultant to get through this process.

THE BUSINESS PLAN SHOULD BE A WELL-STRUCTURED DOCUMENT THAT ANSWERS WHAT YOUR OBJECTIVES ARE AND HOW YOU AND YOUR NIGHTCLUB WILL ACCOMPLISH THOSE OBJECTIVES. A BUSINESS PLAN IS LIKE A LIVING DOCUMENT FOR BANKS, INVESTORS AND OTHER LENDING SOURCES TO REVIEW AND THEN CONSIDER THE FEASIBILITY OF YOUR IDEAS.

OBTAINING THE CASH

WHERE TO TURN
FOR THE MONEY

Obtaining the financing needed to open your nightclub is without a doubt the largest obstacle because without cash nothing will happen. Financing can come from several different sources, starting of course with yourself and then with your friends and family.

Most businesses are self-financed, meaning the owner(s) put up all the money needed to start the venue. You and/or your partners must have some funding in order to get off the ground. If you plan to approach either a bank or venture capitalists, they will expect you to invest in your nightclub too. Don't bet on receiving a loan to finance your club if you aren't willing to invest some of your own cash. Why would they risk their money if you don't have faith enough in your nightclub to risk any of your own?

SELF-FINANCING
The first thing to do is to take a thorough look at your personal financial resources. You'll probably be surprised to find out that you have more assets than you thought you had. Vehicles, recreation equipment,

equity in real estate, life insurance policies, your personal bank accounts or even your retirement accounts. You could sell some of these assets or use them as collateral for a loan. Also consider any lines of credit that you have established with your credit cards. This can be an expensive way to get started but if it can help you to raise the necessary capital do it.

Consider getting a home-equity loan if you own your home. Home-equity loans can provide a substantial amount of cash. There are many benefits to obtaining a home-equity loan, including low interest rates. But be careful, if you can't repay the loan you could lose your home! 401(k) retirement plans also offer the ability to borrow against the plan. But, there are some down sides to borrowing from a 401(k) and you should consult with your plan to find out if this route to obtaining the cash is for you.

BANKS

Choosing a bank is a task that you should consider with great care. Banks differ mainly in the services that they provide. Some services you'll need immediately and will be invaluable to you. Other services you may find you don't need at all. Find a bank that can provide assistance and advice on money matters that may affect your nightclub. In addition, you'll need a bank that offers a number of business services such as:

Financing
Lines of Credit
Letters of Credit
SBA Loans
Notary Service
Checking Accounts
Savings Accounts
Federal Tax Deposits
Merchant Credit Card Management
Certificates of Deposits
Wire Transfers
Cash Management Services

Borrowing from a bank can be the number one source for most of your financing needs. Bank loans can provide start-up capital and expansion capital for your nightclub. Banks make their decisions to loan you money based on two factors. 90% of the decision is based on your cash flow and current net worth. The other 10% is based on your credit history and the potential for success of your proposed business.

When you prepare to go to your banker and request consideration for a business loan, make sure that you have all of your documents in order that represent your current financial situation. It won't hurt to bring your accountant along either because he or she can probably talk to the bank, in the bank's language, better than you. At a minimum you will need your business plan, personal balance sheet, cash flow projections and a business pro forma.

Once you obtain a bank loan, you'll be personally liable for the entire balance of the loan and will be required to give a personal guarantee. If you are unable to repay it, the bank will have the right to place liens on your personal assets, such as your home.

SBA (SMALL BUSINESS ADMINISTRATION)
Many small businesses and nightclubs alike owe their presence to the U.S. Small Business Administration. The SBA offers an alternative to entrepreneurs who are turned down by private and commercial financial lending institutions. The SBA is an excellent source for start-up capital and qualifying for an SBA loan is a less stringent process because they often require less of the owner's equity and collateral.

Many banks regularly work with the SBA through SBA loan programs. The SBA doesn't directly loan money to applicants, but rather the federal government (SBA) provides a loan guarantee to potential entrepreneurs and promises to pay back the lending bank a percentage of the loan should the borrower default. The SBA can assist you in preparing your loan package and if a bank approves a loan for you, the bank will submit the application to the SBA for final review.

There is no guarantee that you will automatically qualify for an SBA loan. You'll still have to meet minimum requirements. The SBA will expect that you will have the ability to repay the loan from your cash flow. They will also review your credit history, examine your qualifications to run your business and look at any collateral and equity that you have as assets. They will also expect that you personally guarantee a certain percentage of your loan should you default.

There are several SBA loan packages that potential candidates could be approved for. Also, the SBA has many services to assist entrepreneurs to get their businesses up and running. Each state has at least one SBA office. Contact your local office for additional information on specific programs or visit the SBA Web site at www.sbaonline.sba.gov. You can also contact the SBA Answer Desk by phone at (800) 8-ASK-SBA.

FAMILY AND FRIENDS

Family and friends are excellent sources for loans. Although, it's sometimes tough to approach a friend or family member and ask for money, if you have a good relationship with them, the chance of them saying yes is much greater than a no. In others words, you have a much greater chance of obtaining money from your family than you do your bank. That's not to suggest that bank loans are difficult to get, but with your family and friends, you can often bypass a lot of wordy paperwork.

Chances are your family and friends aren't extremely wealthy or you wouldn't have to worry about approaching them to ask for money. Wealthy or not, people closest to you will usually give as much as they can and that's all you should expect. Please do not talk your parents into mortgaging their house. You need to keep in mind that a nightclub is like any other business and all businesses can be very risky. That means that the possibility always exists that you could lose your entire investment. And your parents' house too if they were to mortgage it.

The best way to approach family and friends when it comes to asking them to invest in your idea is to do your research and then be completely honest with them. Don't leave anything out, thinking that it'll change their minds if they hear the negatives. By presenting all aspects of your proposed operation, including the good and the bad, you will come across as if you know what you're talking about, rather than coming across as if this is just a spur of the moment idea that you haven't given much thought to. Friends and family are much more likely to invest whatever they can in an idea that's well thought-out, organized, honest and feasible.

MANY SMALL BUSINESSES AND NIGHTCLUBS ALIKE OWE THEIR PRESENCE TO THE U.S. SMALL BUSINESS ADMINISTRATION. THE SBA OFFERS AN ALTERNATIVE TO ENTREPRENEURS WHO ARE TURNED DOWN BY PRIVATE AND COMMERCIAL FINANCIAL LENDING INSTITUTIONS.

KNOW THE LAW

RUN A LEGAL OPERATION

Nothing is more important to a nightclub than running an operation according to the laws of the land. In almost every type of business that's open to the public, there are a number of laws, regulations, ordinances, permits and licenses that need to be obtained and adhered to in order to open and stay in business. Unfortunately, a typical nightclub/restaurant operation will have to abide by more rules and laws than other conventional businesses, such as retail stores or other service oriented businesses (hair salons, for example). Nightclub/restaurant venues have to obtain special permits to serve alcohol and food in addition to the standard permits and licenses that other businesses must also obtain.

Many areas of the country are very strict about specific laws that pertain to nightclubs and others are more lenient in the enforcement of the laws. Many operators run their nightclubs based on the level of enforcement that they are forced to abide by from their local governments. Respectively, some clubs are very strict and some are too loose when it comes to abiding by the laws and rules. For the clubs set in easy-going areas this could spell disaster. When an operator takes advantage of a situation where little to no effort is ever made to ensure that they are running a legal operation, a club closing catastrophe is usually just one step away.

It's simple, in the world of politics and public perceptions, the proverbial "shit," rolls downhill. For the nightclub operator who gives little regard for the laws and rules, the "shit" may end up right at his front doors. For the sake of an example, let's say an unfortunate operator routinely served intoxicated guests way too many drinks to the point that they could barely walk. It's bound to happen that at least one of them will decide to drive. Each time they do, the likelihood of someone becoming involved in a traffic accident is relatively high. Sooner or later it will probably happen, and an innocent person, who had nothing to do with the nightclub at all, is killed by a drunk driver who was served too many drinks.

It won't matter much what the operator has to say once the story hits the news and the community starts demanding answers. Situations like this one, are bad and usually get worse for the shameful operator and nightclub. Even though the nightclub in the example, didn't directly kill anyone, if and when civil and criminal proceedings take place, a lot of the blame will be pinned on the nightclub. Judgements made in court can cost a lot of money and even put a nightclub out of business.

ABIDING BY THE LAWS AND ORDINANCES

Knowing how important the laws, rules and regulations are, is what's needed to keep you out of legal trouble in the money. You can't control everything that happens outside of the nightclub and it's impossible to prevent catastrophes involving guests from occurring. No matter how hard you work to prevent such things, as serving an intoxicated guest too much to drink, inevitably someone will slip through the cracks, drink way too much and drive away in a car. Although, it's not your responsibility to prevent guests from driving cars if they've had too much to drink, your attack and the measures you take to encourage customers not to do such things can relieve any legal burdens placed on you in the event that an undesirable event does occur involving one of your guests. You should care about sensitive, social issues such as DUI and others. Your caring should extend to your employees who will ultimately carry out your wishes and demands while dealing with customers. The attitude about certain issues and the stances you, employees and the nightclub itself takes can be greatly beneficial to a community as a whole. Abiding by the laws, will not only help to keep you out of legal troubles, if they arise, but will also serve to make your nightclub a better place for your customers, as well as making you and your employees better people. Sometimes, the extra buck or two you can make just isn't worth it. So, regardless of where your operation is set up, make sure that you not only know the laws, but you abide by them too.

Failing to abide by the laws can be costly because they typically affect the liquor license that belongs to a nightclub. Most laws that pertain to nightclub operations deal with the service of alcohol. A nightclub could lose its liquor license for a period of time and sometimes even permanently for violations against the license. Liquor licenses usually aren't cheap and can cost thousands of dollars to obtain one. Without a liquor license, a club obviously can't sell alcohol and usually has to close until the matter is resolved which can cause a substantial amount of lost money for any club.

For nightclub/restaurant venues, losing a health department permit or license can be as equally devastating as losing a liquor license. The inability to serve food for a typical restaurant would very well put them out of business. There's little difference for a nightclub/restaurant that relies on a certain proportion of food sales to be part of the overall gross sales.

The many laws, regulations, codes or ordinances vary greatly across the country but for the most part, many are very similar and yet some are very different. You should thoroughly educate yourself on the laws in your particular state, county or city of operation before opening. Utilizing your attorney should also be helpful as he or she had better be able to instruct you in the do's and don'ts within your area. Some of the typical laws that apply to nightclubs are listed below:

- **Serving Minors**— Most localities or states require that the nightclub have knowledge that they are serving a minor and other states are more stringent and require less knowledge from the nightclub before a violation of this kind of ordinance is broken. Do your best to avoid breaking this law regardless of where you're at. Underage drinkers are easy for the police to pick out if they decide to visit. This could be costly also if a minor gets into trouble with the police hours later after leaving your club. Increased enforcement at the front doors by checking IDs is the solution to controlling the underage drinking situation.

• **Serving Intoxicated Persons**—Many of the examples contained within this book deal with serving intoxicated guests. This is prohibited in nearly all states. You, your bartenders, security and your wait staff need to be able to recognize when a customer has had too much to drink and cut them off. Knowingly serving an intoxicated customer can have many disadvantages for a nightclub including; violent or assaultive situations (inside and out), passed out customers, guests who later commit DUI and possible legal ramifications should an intoxicated guest damage property or injure another person.

• **Permitting Alcohol Outside**— States usually adapt laws such as this one to quell or discourage citizens from roaming the streets with alcoholic beverages. These kinds of laws however, usually do not apply directly to the citizens, they apply to the nightclub. Fines may be in order for nightclubs that allow customers to leave with alcoholic beverages. Again, not all laws regarding nightclubs apply in all states or areas, so keep that in mind.

• **Serving After Hours**— Serving after hours is a very common violation that some operations commit on their liquor licenses. Most states prohibit the sale of alcohol after two o'clock A.M. In some states the cut off-hour is three o'clock and others four o'clock A.M. Yet, for a few, the parties can go on all night until 6:00 or 7:00 A.M.— before a nightclub must stop serving alcohol. The most common closing time is 2:00 A.M. which is regarded as early by many people but to ensure that no alcohol is drank or served past that hour, most clubs make it a habit to stop serving around 1:30 A.M. or one-half hour before closing respectively, in order to abide by this law.

- **Exceeding Occupancy**— An unfortunate situation for any club. Why? If a club exceeds its occupancy rating it's because it's a busy night. It's hard to turn people away, especially when everything else just seems to be running smoothly. In all likelihood, the chance of a fire breaking out, which is why there are usually such laws, is remote. It's easy to try and get away with breaking occupancy laws, but always beware that if the fire department shows up unexpectedly, they take these laws seriously and they normally have the power to revoke fire department permits or close you down until occupancy, fire escapes, extinguishers or alarm problems are fixed and handled to their liking.

- **Noise Violations**— Some, but not all, locales require nightclubs that play music loud enough to be heard from the outside to acquire a noise permit. Most areas don't require a permit and any noise or sound that's emitted outside only becomes a problem if nearby citizens complain about it.

- **Allowing Underage Patrons Inside**— Some cities strictly forbid minors (persons less than 21 years of age) from entering nightclubs. Others don't have any specific laws regarding this issue, which means that anyone over 18 can enter. This is where many clubs run into problems with serving minors. Nightclubs that do allow 18, 19 or 20-year-old patrons inside, run the risk of them obtaining alcohol. On a very busy night with several hundred guests inside, it may be impossible to prevent all minors from illegally drinking while on the premises.

NOTE: If you decide to allow entrance to persons under 21, you need to take measures to identify those who are old enough to drink from those who aren't. Hand stamps or wristbands are the two preferred ways of dealing with this issue.

- **Various Health Violations**— Nightclubs that also double as restaurants during the day and early evening have to be careful and observe all applicable laws related to serving food. Many of the laws revolve around sanitation and proper food handling techniques. Failure to comply with health department standards could result in the loss of a permit or license, not to mention the bad PR that will follow if any health or epidemic problems arise from a negligent operation.

Listed below are common permits and licenses that most operations will need to acquire at a minimum:

(DBA) FICTITIOUS NAME

If you are planning on using your own name as the name of the nightclub then you won't need to complete a fictitious name statement, which is commonly referred to as, *Doing Business As* (DBA). Otherwise, most localities will require that you register your business name with the appropriate governmental department.

Most states, counties or cities have a business name bureau which will allow you to search through all of the business names currently in use. This process will save you a lot of time and money, especially if the name you have chosen for your nightclub is already in use by another business somewhere in your state. Checking existing names can prevent you from being sued by another business or company with the same name and hopefully prevent you from having a gigantic headache, if you had to change it because of that and any promotional materials, commercials or ads that might have already been created before the error was found out.

NAMING YOUR NIGHTCLUB

Choosing a dynamic name for your nightclub is one of the many important tasks involved in your start-up and planning phases. Some believe that choosing an effective name is actually the hardest part of getting started. This can be a difficult process but it doesn't have to be if you are prepared and up to the challenge.

A name doesn't have to be long or complicated either. It could be as simple as "Bill's Tavern and Eatery." This example is short and to the point. It advertises that Bill is the owner and that one can order drinks and food. But that is about all it says. If someone were looking to go out on the town and have a fun night dancing, share a few drinks with friends and maybe even meet a mate, they may think twice about going to Bill's because the name seems rather boring. Yes, the name of a nightclub can create a mental image of the nightclub and because of it, you could either gain or lose customers.

There is nothing wrong with a name like "Bill's Tavern and Eatery" if it denotes a quiet peaceful pub where one can sit and enjoy a cold beer and a good meal. But it you plan on packing in large numbers of patrons, you'll have to do better than that.

You may already have a name picked out that you thought of a long time ago. If so, you are a step ahead of the rest of us. But if not you may need a little help. As you read the following session, keep in mind not to overlook other sources for helping you decide on a name. Family and friends are often great idea banks for coming up with excellent night-club names. If they don't readily have ideas, get them in the process of choosing a name by getting together and brainstorming.

HOW TO CHOOSE A NAME

Get a pen and a piece of paper, a dictionary (a multi-language conver-sion dictionary is preferable) and a thesaurus. Sit down and visualize what your nightclub will be all about. How do you feel about it and how do you want others to feel about it once it's up and running? Write it down. Don't worry about how it flows on the paper or how it's all organized. The purpose here is to just get some ideas down on paper.

Then take your pen and paper and begin writing down some thoughts about your potential customers. Think about your expectations of your patrons. Who will they be, what do you think they'll look like, and what are their expectations? This should give you a start.

Next, take those ideas and look them up in a dictionary or a multi-language conversion dictionary and begin making a list of words— possible names. These names probably aren't going to sound very good at first but the deeper you dig the more you'll come up with. After that, take your list of words, look each one up in the thesaurus and continue to expand upon the lists of words you have created.

You should then have a pretty decent list of names. Study each name as a possibility and also consider combining some of the words to form one name. This process is pretty simple and if you don't come up with anything the first time, keep doing it until you find something you like and believe will best describe your nightclub.

FOR EVERY NIGHTCLUB, A LIQUOR LICENSE IS AN ESSENTIAL PART OF BUSINESS AND WITHOUT ONE YOU CANNOT LEGALLY SELL ALCOHOLIC BEVERAGES.

The name of your nightclub along with everything else should help to draw attention to your venue. A catchy name always helps. Try to find a name that's relatively easy to remember. Try to avoid very long names, names no one can pronounce and try to avoid tongue twisters. Generally the shorter the better. The name you choose should be able to sell your club and leave a good impression on all that entered.

BUSINESS LICENSE

This is the most basic and common type of licenses that one will need to obtain. In most cities throughout the U.S., you will be required to register all businesses with the local city or county clerk's office. Obtaining a business license normally requires a very small fee. Check with your local clerk's office to get the details that are specific to your area.

LIQUOR, WINE AND BEER LICENSES

For every nightclub, a liquor license is an essential part of business and without one you cannot legally sell alcoholic beverages. Liquor, wine and beer licenses usually need to be purchased from your state or local government. Often, these special licenses come with many strings attached that vary from city to city. For example, most locales will require that you submit an application in person and include information such as general business information, proposed business information, personal information or a personal background, the proximity of hospitals, schools, public parks or churches to your nightclub and/or residents within a certain distance of your nightclub.

Normally, if your application is approved, you'll be required to display the permit or license in a common area which is accessible and can be easily viewed by the general public. Also in many areas, you may also have to notify any residents within a certain distance of your nightclub of your intent to sell and distribute alcoholic beverages. Most liquor licenses are issued for a specific time period (normally one year) and must be renewed by the applicant once it expires. States, cities or municipalities can reserve the right not to renew a liquor license based on whatever criteria they may so choose to establish. So, it's important that a nightclub abide by all the rules set forth in the licenses and the local laws of the land that a nightclub happens to reside in order to avoid ever being denied a liquor license.

Many states also make the distinction between beer, wine and hard alcohol and require separate licenses for each type of beverages. In these cases you simply need to apply for each one separately and most likely will be required to place each license in a highly visible place where they can be seen by the general public.

When it's time to apply for the appropriate alcohol permits or licenses, check with your state, county or local government for additional details. You should also utilize your attorney in this area just to make sure that you're complying with all of the necessary rules and required laws.

HEALTH DEPARTMENT PERMIT

Before you can begin business and serve food to any customers, you'll need to obtain a food service permit to do so from your health department. Usually there is no fee for this permit and they are typically issued only after your nightclub is completed, ready to do business and only after the department ensures that you are in compliance with the rules and regulations established for food service operations.

To obtain a food service permit, many important questions about the nightclub will have to be answered such as:
• What type of water supply will be utilized? Public or private?

- What type of sewage system will be used?
- Are the floors grease resistant and easily cleanable in the kitchen and restrooms?
- Are the walls and ceilings of light color, smooth and easily cleanable in the kitchen and restrooms?
- Are employee restroom facilities conveniently located?
- Are public restrooms provided?
- Are restrooms facilities ventilated?
- Are all light fixtures shielded and covered to protect food and utensils in the food processing area? Are heat lamps protected from breakage?
- Is there an inside refuge storage room?
- Is there an outside refuge storage area?
- Are container washing facilities available?

The list goes on and on and covers other topics like insect and rodent control, housekeeping and food service equipment.

Once you get a health department permit to serve food, understand that you'll need to maintain a standard of operation. The intent of the health department is to prevent your customers from becoming sick from inadequately prepared foods, communicable diseases and to prevent your employees from being injured on the job. In most areas, the health department can impose hefty fines for violations and/or revoke a food service license.

FIRE DEPARTMENT PERMIT
Many areas also require that any business open to the general public, be issued a permit from the fire department. The process of obtaining a permit usually requires an inspector who will carefully evaluate a nightclub. In order to receive a permit, topics like portable fire extinguishers and the placement of those extinguishers will be addressed. Also covered are a nightclub's maximum occupancy rating, sprinkler systems, fire escapes, obstructed escape routes and even hazards such as possible electrical problems are examined.

As with all permits, personally see to it that your club is always in compliance. Don't leave it up to employees to make sure that you are because it's very likely they'll miss things they shouldn't. You wouldn't want the fire department to unexpectedly show up on a very busy night and close you down because your club was exceeding the maximum occupancy by 200 or so people.

FEDERAL, STATE AND COUNTY REQUIREMENTS

Many laws and requirements are set forth by different states, counties and the federal government regarding nightclub businesses, in addition to the local licenses and permits that have already been covered. Many state offices are structured or named differently so it's up to you to find the appropriate state office, in your area, that handles the following requirements. If you want to keep this process as simple as possible, this is a good time to get your attorney involved and let him or her handle it.

FEDERAL REQUIREMENTS

Employer I.D. Number/Taxes: Many nightclubs are unlikely to require the need of a federal permit to operate unless they are making alcohol products, such as the case in a Brewpub, or if they prepare meat products. If you fall into those categories or if you have formed a corporation or a partnership, you'll need to apply for a federal employer identification number (EIN). Even if, for whatever reason, you are the only employee. Contact the IRS office closest to your location and request the Employers Tax Guide, a publication that explains federal income tax, social security tax withholding requirements for employees and unemployment taxes.

STATE REQUIREMENTS

State licenses: Different states impose different license requirements and fees for different business and professions. Check with your appropriate state office to find out whether or not your nightclub is subject to a state license requirement.

State taxes - withholding: If you have employees, you must register with your state department that handles this special tax.

Wages, hours and child labor: Again, if you have employees contact your appropriate state office of department regarding minimum wages, overtime pay, employee termination requirements, the hiring of minors and fair employment practices.

COUNTY REQUIREMENTS
Property taxes: Normally you'll be contacted automatically by your county assessor's office. As the owner of record, you'll be sent a property tax bill.

NOISE PERMIT
A few municipalities will require that nightclubs obtain a noise permit if the music played, can possibly be heard outside of the nightclub. In some places, a noise permit is always necessary during the entire existence of a club. For most areas in the country, it's very rare that any nightclub would actually need to have one of these to do business. But just in case, make sure you check to see if you'll need one. Generally, most noise or sound permits will only need to be obtained if the sound or music will intentionally extend outside of a nightclub's premises. For instance, if a nightclub were to set up a loudspeaker outside, connected to the main sound system, in some sort of a promotional effort to draw in customers, that may be a reason to obtain a noise permit in case any complaints are made.

SIGN PERMIT
Some areas also require a permit if you intend to stake a marquee or business sign with your nightclub's name on it into the ground in front of your business. Some places believe that business signs can take away from the beautification of an area and therefore will require that a business has a permit before one can be erected.

THE INTENT OF THE HEALTH DEPARTMENT IS TO PREVENT YOUR CUSTOMERS FROM BECOMING SICK FROM INADEQUATELY PREPARED FOODS, COMMUNICABLE DISEASES AND TO PREVENT YOUR EMPLOYEES FROM BEING INJURED ON THE JOB.

YOUR SALES

WHERE WILL THE PROFITS COME FROM?

In the nightclub business, sales and profits are derived from four general areas: Entrance fees, food sales, drink sales and revenue generated from coin-operated equipment. Not all venues need to utilize all four of these avenues of profit to become successful. Many are just as successful, relying only on a combination of entrance fees and alcohol sales. Some venues are able to make huge profits just from the sale of alcohol alone. All operators will have to determine which profit avenues they'll choose to exploit to draw in sales.

What customers are charged for and how goods and services are priced should be contingent on a number of different factors including what the competition is or isn't doing. If you recognize differences between your club and your competition that could be to your benefit, take advantage of them and find a way to turn the differences into money. For example, special events in the forms of contests or live entertainment can trigger increased customer traffic. This can place an operator in an advantageous position to charge more for drinks and entrance fees and most guests won't be alienated if they feel the events are worth the extra money.

A common factor to consider is the popularity or success of a nightclub. For instance, if there are lines of people dying to get in every night, take advantage of that and charge more for admission. Vice versa, if a club is struggling it probably wouldn't be prudent to charge high entrance fees. In this case, high prices might drive much needed customers away. The list of factors goes on and on and it's up to operators to be able to recognize when and when not to charge customers. It's also an operator's responsibility to figure out what should customers be charged for and how much should they be charged. The answers to those questions vary from nightclub to nightclub because each club in itself is unique. Those are some of the decisions that will make you worthy of being considered a successful nightclub operator if the answers produce profits.

ENTRANCE FEES
One of the brilliant aspects of the nightclub industry is that one can charge people money just to get in and in most cases, they'll pay almost anything. Entrance fees can be a very lucrative source of income for any nightclub. The key to entrance fees is knowing when to take advantage of the profit potential and when not to.

On average, the revenue gained through the practice of charging customers an entrance fee can account anywhere from 10-40% of a nightclub's total nightly profit and sometimes even more depending on the occasion. For many larger clubs, entrance fees are a major part of the club's profits. Other clubs never charge entrance fees and don't feel the need to because they rely on enormous alcohol and food sales. But even those clubs could benefit from door sales and increase profits at any given time they choose to. Smaller establishments, bars or pubs, traditionally do not charge admission fees because they represent a different type of environment and patrons who frequent them don't expect to pay to get in.

HOW MUCH SHOULD YOU CHARGE AT THE DOOR?
Deciding on how much to charge patrons to enter your nightclub is a

tricky question. After pondering this question the answer should come to you only after you analyze your market— who is your prospective clientele? What would they be willing to spend for a night out? Then ask yourself, "would I spend that much to get into this nightclub?" After asking and answering those questions, you then need to analyze your competition.

If you plan on establishing a nightclub in an area where other nightclubs already exist, you'll need to find out what, if any, door prices they are charging. If other nightclubs in the area are charging door entrance fees, you'll want to stay competitive. It's not a good business practice to charge a $10 entrance fee per person, when your competition

> A REASONABLE ENTRANCE OR COVER FEE ON MOST NIGHTS WILL NOT KEEP PATRONS FROM ENTERING A NIGHTCLUB AND AS A MATTER OF FACT, NOWADAYS MOST PEOPLE EXPECT TO PAY A FEW DOLLARS TO GET INSIDE A DECENT CLUB.

across the street is only charging $2 per person. Once established, you may be able to charge higher entrance fees than the competitors, but only after a solid customer base and an outstanding reputation is built. Otherwise, you will find that once people arrive at the front doors, they'll backtrack and head to another bar up the street seeking a cheaper cover charge.

A reasonable entrance or cover fee on most nights will not keep patrons from entering a nightclub and as a matter of fact, nowadays most people expect to pay a few dollars to get inside a decent club. Excessive entrance fees however will put you out of business in a relatively short period of time, because high fees will only serve to drive patrons away. In most cases, an average or reasonable entrance fee should vary anywhere from $1-$5. For the more successful nightclubs however, it isn't uncommon to see entrance fees in the range of $10 per person and even higher.

WHEN TO CHARGE ENTRANCE FEES
Be prepared to be flexible in establishing and setting admission fees.

And as such, you need to be able to recognize when to lower door fees, when to raise them and when not to charge guests an entrance fee at all. Nightclubs that assume the role of restaurant, bar and nightclub must adjust entrance fees to the time of day. For example, during the afternoon when food sales are at their highest, it doesn't make sense to charge people to come in and dine. You wouldn't pay a cover charge to go into any restaurant to eat so don't expect customers to pay either.

Normally, to maximize profits and reduce customer rejection, start charging door fees at a certain time in the evening, when your dance and bar crowd begins to arrive. After, during or before events like a happy hour are also prime times to begin charging cover charges because many customers will arrive to take advantage of reduced alcohol prices or drink specials.

Also, for many nightclubs, the day of the week plays an important role in determining when and how to price entrance fees. In most places throughout the United States, certain weekdays have a tendency to be somewhat less-busier nights than other days of the week. For that reason alone, you should identify those weekdays that draw smaller crowds and adjust your entrance fees accordingly. You'll probably find that charging less cover charges on slower nights or eliminating cover charges altogether will work out best.

Some areas in the country are fortunate in that just about every night draws a fruitful crowd. If this is the case in your area or with your nightclub, then take full advantage of it and charge those cover prices. Obviously some nights, especially weekends, Friday or Saturday nights tend to be the busiest nights of the week no matter where you are. If you consider raising entrance fees from time to time, nights like those would be ideal nights to do it. That only makes sense, doesn't it?

Don't forget about special events, such as live bands or concerts. A well-publicized special event can serve to draw in thousands of paying patrons so don't forget to raise the cost of admission. A good special event will make it easy for patrons to pay almost anything to get in. For example, have you ever been to a quality nightclub that charges upwards of $50 per person or more just to get inside on a New Year's Eve or during the Superbowl? It happens all the time and every year, millions of patrons eagerly pay high cover charges, just to witness an event or to be a part of history. The $50 or more that they paid becomes just a small fee to them to be able to participate in a special or rare occasion. The best part of all is that they will enjoy those particular moments in life inside your nightclub which hopefully will leave very favorable impressions with them and build stronger customer appreciation and recognition.

ALCOHOL SALES
Regardless of the size of the operation, alcohol sales without a doubt are the main staples of profit income for every nightclub in existence. Alcohol sales are also obviously one of the main reasons people will come. How much profit alcohol sales bring in may vary slightly from venue to venue. Many states have passed laws that only allow a nightclub's alcohol sales to be a certain percentage of the club's total profit depending on its hours of operation and whether or not the nightclub sells food or not.

Even still, the volumes of alcohol sales in the nightclub hospitality industry far outweigh the sale of food, entrance fees, coin operated games, or anything else a particular nightclub may be promoting or selling. This only makes sense because most customers will expect to buy and drink alcoholic beverages when they walk into a nightclub, regardless if they plan to eat, dance, play games or participate in a special/promotional event.

Alcohol plays a very important role in our society and all by itself, has the ability to create a social setting and mood within people. There is no such thing as a nightclub that doesn't serve alcohol. If there were, they wouldn't be nightclubs, and probably wouldn't stay in business for very long. However, the exceptions are those non-alcoholic establishments that cater to people under the legal drinking age (21). Those are commonly referred to as teen bars. Teen bars are slowly increasing in numbers, but don't even come close to measuring up to a real nightclub and probably never will.

SETTING ALCOHOL PRICES

Pricing your alcohol sales is one of the easiest things you'll have to do. After you draw people in, and especially after they have paid to get inside a club, they aren't going to squabble to much over alcohol prices unless prices are extremely outrageous. You'll find that most customers will pay nearly anything for a drink.

As with everything else, you'll want to try and stay somewhat competitive with alcohol pricing. The main reason for being competitive is because you'll want the customers to come back again and again. Customers who enter, after paying a $3 cover charge, will stay for a period of time and pay just about anything for their favorite drinks, even if drink prices are expensive. But the next night out, some of them may reconsider a nightclub they feel overcharged them with high or excessive alcohol prices, and take their business elsewhere.

> ALCOHOL PLAYS A VERY IMPORTANT ROLE IN OUR SOCIETY AND ALL BY ITSELF, HAS THE ABILITY TO CREATE A SOCIAL SETTING AND MOOD WITHIN PEOPLE.

Most people won't have a problem paying a few dollars for a large frothy mug of beer or even a little more, for a shot, shooter or mixed drink. Bar patrons have come to expect that they will spend more in a nightclub for beverages verses if they went to their local convenience store and bought their alcohol there. But they also know a really bad deal when they see one too.

Have you ever been to a baseball or football game? Beer prices are out of control aren't they? You felt ripped off and frustrated after buying an overpriced $5 beer, which was served in a little plastic cup, that you gulped in two or three swallows. After one, two or maybe even three beers, you probably formed an opinion that it just wasn't worth the money, didn't you? It's no different inside a nightclub. Patrons can and do spot sour deals, and will leave them alone if they feel they are unreasonable. That could definitely affect a nightclub's customer traffic.

When setting alcohol prices, remember that you have to pay your bills first and turn a profit, therefore you need to charge more for your alcohol services in order to do that. Your array of alcohol products, which should range from draft beers, bottled beers, cocktails, shooters, wine coolers, shots, wines, etc. should all be separately priced differently to reflect their individual values.

An old trick that has been in existence for years is slightly watering-down the draft or tap beers, which increases the volume of draft beers to sell. Operators then sell the draft beer by the mug, cup, glass or pitcher and can make huge profits on the sales. Ideally it's best not to add carbonated water to the draft beer because it can divide your customers and maybe even cause you to lose some of them.

Customers' opinions about watered down tap beers differ. Some people are indifferent, some don't even notice the difference and others are very passionate about it and really feel ripped off. Not watering down tapped beers will give you an edge over your competition by allowing you to deliver and serve quality draft beers. So if you want to sacrifice quantity for quality, don't do it.

You should establish fixed prices for each beverage your club will serve. Shots and cocktails should typically be priced higher because of their higher inventory costs. Shot drinks and the countless number of cocktail drinks carry a perceived expensive value to customers. Customers know and expect that when they order a shot of alcohol or a mixed drink they'll probably have to pay slightly more money than they would for a draft drink. Why customers feel cocktails and straight drinks, should cost more is unknown. Maybe it's because of the stronger tastes or the perceived potency of those kinds of drinks.

Unless you're planning to do a drink special, average shot drink prices typically range anywhere from $2.00 to $5.00. More often than not, if you price shots higher than that, sales may not be too impressive. With cocktails, simply because there are so many of them, you might choose to categorize and price them separately according to what's in them. However, it's not necessary to do this especially if you want to maintain a standard in pricing.

Some nightclub operators do price cocktails separately and identify the cocktails which take more time to prepare and/or require more ingredients such as some margaritas and price them differently than other cocktails. Standardized mixed drink pricing means that all cocktails cost the same which makes it easier for both bartenders and customers alike.

Beer prices should be set up to be sold by the glass, mug or cup. Pitchers of beer should be priced to give the impression of an economical savings. For instance, if you priced a 16 Oz. mug of beer at $1.50, an ideal price for a 48 Oz. or a smaller pitcher of beer would be $4.50 or higher. A 48 Oz. pitcher pours exactly three 16 Oz. drinks and the price works out to be exactly the same ($4.50). Some of your customers might think that $1.50 is a lot of money for one beer, but will think they are getting more for their money or even a bargain by buying by the pitcher.

Pitchers make it easier for the discriminating beer drinker to buy more without realizing they are paying about the same amount of money or more for the same amount of beer. If you play with the numbers a little bit by changing the price of the same pitcher a few cents or more, or maybe by providing slightly smaller pitchers, you'll increase profits on your pitcher sales.

Bottled or canned beer, whether domestic or imported, should be priced higher than draft beers because they will cost more to obtain and stock. Customers who purchase and drink bottled beer, do so because they expect the true and genuine taste from the brand of beer they ordered. Also, a number of beers can only be bought by the bottle or can because they are not manufactured into kegs or drafts. Another thing to consider about bottled and canned beer is to offer a cold or frosted glass or mug for customers to pour their beer into. This service will be appreciated by many patrons, and could set your nightclub apart from your competition.

SIZE MATTERS

The size of the receptacle or drinkware that you serve your alcoholic beverages in should also play a significant role in price determination. You'll need to make a decision very early in the planning phase of your venue and establish your drinkware styles and sizes. First off, glasses and mugs can be purchased in a variety of sizes. The industry's typical glass or mug sizes vary anywhere from 12 Oz. to as large as 34 Oz. The larger the drink, the higher customers will perceive the drink's value so therefore be prepared to price accordingly to take advantage of this situation. But you'll need to be a little careful here, don't overprice your draft beers or you may get complaints. Just because you choose to serve draft beer out of a 34 Oz. mug don't expect soaring sales by charging $5 or more a beer.

A simple example in size pricing is setting a 12 Oz. draft beer at $1.25 and a 24 Oz. drink at $2.00. In this example, even though the amount or volume of beer is doubled, the price doesn't necessarily have to. You'll still profit well in either situation and won't run the risk of alienating your customers with high prices.

FIGURING THE PROFITS
Figuring out how much money you can make is important for planning and speculation. Figure that one keg of beer will cost you somewhere between $20 and $30, depending on your distributor. A typical *bar keg* is about 15 ½ gallons or about 1,984 ounces. From that same keg you will be able to serve approximately 165-12 Oz. drinks. If you were to price each 12 Oz. drink at $1.75, your profit would be around $289.00 per keg. Bottled or canned beer priced between $2.00-$2.75 should bring in about $60.00 per case.

Shot drinks are usually poured and served in one ounce incre-ments. On average, figure on 30-35 drinks per bottle. If you were selling shots of Southern Comfort or whatever, at $3.50 a shot, you would make something in the neighborhood of $120.00 a bottle.

Cocktails, unlike beers and shot drinks, represent compounded costs. With most recipes, the multiple ingredients involved in the preparation process are minimal in costs to you but they are still costs that you'll absorb and will add up over time and therefore, you must quickly recoup your investments and profit margin by charging a fair price.

These amounts don't reflect losses from employee errors, such as spillage or theft, or from your costs to stock alcohol inventory, but you get the picture. You can obviously play with the numbers a bit to get different figures. Try raising or lowering the prices, or raising or lowering the size of your drinkware (ounce sizes) to change the results.

$1.75 VS. $2.00
The psychological effect of $1.75 compared to $2.00 for example, is enormous. Attempt to end all of your drink prices in $.25 cent increments. What this means is that instead of charging exactly $2.00 or $3.00 for a drink, round the prices down to $1.75 and $2.75 respectively. Why? Although it's only a quarter difference,

> THE PSYCHOLOGICAL EFFECT OF $1.75 COMPARED TO $2.00 FOR EXAMPLE, IS ENORMOUS. ATTEMPT TO END ALL OF YOUR DRINK PRICES IN $.25 CENT INCREMENTS.

$1.75 sounds *A LOT* cheaper than $2.00. People have an easier time remembering the dollar in $1.75 and just as easily forgetting the $.75 cents. For you, this can translate into more sales and the $.25 cents you lose per transaction will make up for itself in increased sales.

Conversely, you could just as easily price a drink at $3.25 rather than $3.00. Once again, customers will probably focus on the even dollar amount of $3.00 and the $.25 cents will most likely be forgotten or underestimated. In this example, the extra $.25 cents adds up quickly and can turn into hundreds or even thousands of dollars of gross profits.

FOOD SALES
Coming in second to alcohol sales are food sales, which are also big moneymakers. Food sales are a major part of most successful nightclubs, and especially for nightclubs that are open for business during the afternoon hours. During the day, patrons are more likely to enter a nightclub with a focus on eating. During the early evening hours, food helps draw in a number of patrons before a club makes a transition from restaurant to nightclub. Many patrons that arrive to eat may opt to stay as the party crowd starts to fill up the club.

FOOD PRICING
Your food menu prices should be consistent with the overall scheme

of your nightclub. If you're planning on running a super-upscale nightclub, having $1.00 chili dogs on the menu may seem odd to patrons, and the upscale effect that you're trying to achieve would be lost. On the other hand, if you were running a very small operation, with a limited local clientele, pricing your menu items expensively may not go over well with those customers. Finding the right food menu and pricing the menu is a task that you'll need to determine based on your operation, and your potential customer's needs and wants. With that, keep in mind two things—don't overprice and don't underprice. Don't be afraid to charge a little more money for a good service along with the food, but be reasonable. Intentionally under pricing foods can be a bad idea. Believe it or not, people have grown accustomed to spending a little money to eat in a restaurant or nightclub.

Low prices may actually scare some away and make them believe the food is not good or not worth it. For whatever reason, when it comes to good food, people will actually be more inclined to order and eat a meal with a higher price tag. The only catch is that your food had better be good if you want them to come back and/or recommend your nightclub to others.

THE FOOD MENU

If you plan to serve food in your establishment then menu selection should be important to you. Generally speaking, the style and look of your food service should be consistent with the style of your nightclub. If you were running an upscale, contemporary operation, then your patrons would be disappointed if their server brought them a sorry looking hamburger with ketchup and juices dripping off of a paper plate. Get the picture?

> LOW PRICES MAY ACTUALLY SCARE SOME AWAY AND MAKE THEM BELIEVE THE FOOD IS NOT GOOD OR NOT WORTH IT. FOR WHATEVER REASON, WHEN IT COMES TO GOOD FOOD, PEOPLE WILL ACTUALLY BE MORE INCLINED TO ORDER AND EAT A MEAL WITH A HIGHER PRICE TAG.

Try to cater to and speculate to what your customers will want and develop a menu based on that. Also, try and be just a little bit different than your competition and have a house specialties that no one else is serving. A good house specialty is sometimes more than enough to draw people to your club during the day for lunch or even later on for dinner.

You'll want to be thinking of a certain style of food that to have available on the menu such as Italian, Greek, Mexican and so on. Try not to limit your menu to just one certain style of food either. For example, if the mainstay of your menu is Mexican food, put hamburgers on the menu somewhere. Simple foods such as hamburgers are big sellers for those folks who just aren't sure what they are in the mood to eat. Other simple ideas for menu items include pizza, hot wings or burger baskets. Simple foods are real nightclub winners.

Don't forget about appetizers either. When people's eyes are bigger than their stomachs, appetizers provide a quick and easy sale. Appetizers can vary but a few ideas to think about are chips and salsa, nachos, French fry or onion ring baskets, salads, soups, potato wedges, bread sticks or biscuits. The list goes on and your imagination and your cooks may come up with even more.

BAR SNACKS

Take advantage of bar snacks. It's true that snacks at the bar encourage more drink orders. Peanuts, popcorn or pretzels are all cheap additions you can put on the bar or for that matter at the tables to satisfy the"munchies." These salted snacks are effective at making customers thirsty after eating a couple of handfuls—a drink ordered from the bar will quench those thirsts.

The possibilities of food entrees, preparations and snacks are enormously broad for the purposes of this section to cover. If you're considering a nightclub/restaurant venue and need more help in the area of food service, you would do better to refer to the countless number of books on the subject of restaurant operations. An experienced cook (employee) or even a restaurant consultant may be an option to really get you off to a good start. Just remember that if you need the assistance of a consultant to plan ahead of time so that start-up goes smoothly.

GAMES, VENDING MACHINES AND PAY PHONES

Games, vending equipment and pay phones are all commonplace in today's nightclubs and you shouldn't hesitate to reap the large profits made from them. Coin-operated machines are easy change eaters which require little to no effort on your part to maintain. All you need to do is collect the money and replenish the inventory, such as in the case of vending machines. This is easy money because these machines are impulse objects and customers often react and put money in them simply because of convenience and they are there for them to use. The money spent on these machines by customers isn't a big deal to them and only costs them a few quarters. However, the quarters dumped into them, quickly add up in revenue for the successful operator.

GAME PROFITS

Profits made from games like foosball, pool, darts, pinball, air hockey, video games and high-tech virtual reality games are big moneymakers for the entertainment industry, regardless of the crowd a nightclub seeks to attract. Many games keep people lined up for hours just waiting to drop quarters into them. Those quarters add up quickly and generate easy, effortless profits.

Unlike other aspects of a nightclub, games have the distinct ability to advertise themselves and draw people to them almost like magnets. People don't have a problem plugging quarter after quarter into these machines because spending quarters is easy. Quarters are merely extra change that seems to burn holes in the pockets of many people. It is so much easier for people to spend four quarters than it is to spend a one dollar bill. In addition, many people feel the need to get rid of change because, as everyone knows, loose change is harder to carry around with you.

More important, games add a special touch to a nightclub and allow a unique socialization to occur. How many times have you been to a nightclub, decided to play pool and ended up playing the game with someone you barely knew or didn't know at all? Interactions with total strangers are rare in peoples' everyday lives. This is one of the many reasons why people go to nightclubs, to meet other people.

As long as nightclubs exist there will always be entertainment in games. The types of games people might play may change over the years but they will always be there in some form or another. Profits from coin-operated games are enormous for many operators throughout the country, which have to potential to earn them $75,000 or more in a year just from the change in their customer's pockets. Just as incredible, those figures are unbelievably made from just a handful of games inside those same nightclubs.

VENDING MACHINES
Vending machines such as condom machines strategically placed in restrooms, medicine dispensers (aspirin, ibuprofen, decongestants, headache/pain relievers and others), cigarette machines, candy-machines and even, those machines called intoximeters which tell guests how high their blood alcohol levels are, are all coin-fed machines that play their own roles. Equally, they can draw in large amounts of money with little to no advertisement at all.

PAY PHONES
Pay phones are consistent change earners and nightclubs can always count on them to bring in money. People need pay phones to stay in touch with others and more importantly to call for a ride when they become too intoxicated to drive.

GIVE PATRONS SOMETHING TO DO

ENTERTAIN YOUR CUSTOMERS

After customers arrive, most of them will need to do something while they are there. Every nightclub must be able to entertain its customers through a variety of activities if it hopes to survive in this competitive industry. Giving patrons something to do, deserves a great deal of thought and implementation. The activities patrons can engage in will largely be contingent on the type and style of the club you decide to set up. For example, if you plan on operating a billiards club, then the main activity would obviously be pool.

Regardless of the type of operation you open up, be sure not to limit customers with the activities provided. Try to provide a variety of different things to do. You can do this by not only setting up games, but by also including special events, such as live bands or maybe even a raffle to win free prizes. Or maybe even a year round pool or dart tournament.

Activities and things to do cannot be over-stressed enough. There is no limit as to what you can do to provide quality entertainment for guests. Be imaginative. Weigh the probabilities of different types of entertainment working by being able to draw in customers and keeping them in, versus activities having an opposite effect and sending customers away.

Whether or not social activities will work, will depend largely on you knowing your market, your competition and your customers. Knowing your competition in this area means knowing what they are doing differently to bring in a crowd. It's imperative that you know because chances are, if your competition is operating the same type of operation as you, then you probably have the same customers from time to time.

You may want to visit your competition incognito a time or two to get a feel for what they are doing. Ask yourself some questions while there; How many pool tables do they have? Do the customers seem to appreciate the pool tables? Do they have video games? If so, which ones and do customers enjoy playing them? How is the dance floor laid out? Do the customers seem to be enjoying the music? Does the competition have any special events such as a live band? If so, which night? Are they pulling in a crowd that's there to listen to the band? These are just a few questions to ask while studying and comparing your club against another to learn what types of things you should aim for to entertain your customers.

> A HAPPY HOUR IS ONE OF THE OLDEST PROMOTIONAL EVENTS USED TO DRAW PATRONS IN DURING SPECIFIC TIME PERIODS BY TYPICALLY ALLOWING CUSTOMERS TO BUY CHEAP DRINKS.

HAPPY HOUR

A happy hour is one of the oldest promotional events used to draw patrons in during specific time periods by typically allowing customers to buy cheap drinks. These specials usually work best for smaller nightclubs with a very defined clientele. The location of a nightclub also plays a crucial role in the success of a happy hour event. The most successful venues that sponsor happy hours are conveniently located and easily accessible to patrons as they travel from work, sporting events or other social gatherings.

Happy hours used to be enough to pack a nightclub full of paying customers for several hours but that isn't the case anymore. A happy hour event that is properly advertised will still work but, as an operator you shouldn't expect that a happy hour will carry a nightclub to success and generate the majority of profits. Today, a happy hour is best used as a transitional event. A happy hour should still be able to draw in patrons seeking cheap drinks and good food. Once the happy hour event ends, the nightclub needs to be able to make a transition, keep all or most of the happy hour customers and move onto another form of entertainment or mood within the club.

DRINK SPECIALS

A drink special, much like a happy hour, is not enough standing alone to support a nightclub. Drink specials are just another *perk* for bar patrons to indulge themselves with. Specials offer some style to any club by helping to give it an identity. Bar patrons love drink specials because they usually feel they are getting more for their money. Drink specials can be employed in a variety of ways, from buy one get two specials to nickel, dime or quarter nights— (special nights where patrons pay either a nickel, dime or a quarter for a draw of beer). Other specials could include rare *house drinks* that are individual only to a nightclub and because of that, the drinks can't be bought anywhere else. Customers who desire a nightclub's house drinks obviously have to go to that nightclub in order to buy their unique drinks. Those are just examples of how to use drink specials, of course it's up to you to find out which sorts of drink specials will work best in your club and on which days of the week.

Drink specials can be powerful incentives for guests to frequent a nightclub. But you wonder, "how do drink specials give a nightclub an identity?" Let's say as an operator, you designated every Wednesday as "Quarter Draw Night" (or whatever you wanted to call it). If you have properly advertised and promoted the special and have been successful in doing so, many customers seeking a Wednesday night on the town will associate cheap drinks and Wednesday with your nightclub. That could help to increase traffic and sales within an establishment on Wednesdays. But, don't stop there, develop specials for every single night of the working week to go along with everything else if you really want to capitalize on the influence of drink specials and events.

In the previous example, it's important to remember that you are in the nightclub business for two reasons:

1. To provide service and entertainment for your guests and;
2. To make a profit from doing so.

As stated earlier in this book, each nightclub has its own unique obstacles and strong points. It's up to you, the operator to understand every aspect of your nightclub in order to maximize success. Let's go back to "Quarter Draw Night." An operator can do a number of different things to make this night even more successful. Let's assume that "Quarter Draw Night" is such a huge success that every Wednesday, the club is packed to capacity. The operator shouldn't forget to charge a reasonable door or cover charge to make a nice profit. At the peak of the evening, why not throw in a small contest or other event to really get the guests' attention? And if an operator can get away with, only host a special like "Quarter Draw Night" for only a limited time during the evening. For instance, the drink special might only be in effect from 7-10 pm. After ten o'clock the prices could go back up to $1.75 or so.

A time frame like that forces guests to come during those hours if they want to take advantage of the cheaper drinks. If the guests are having a good time, chances are, they won't leave after ten and the club will stay relatively busy for the remainder of the night. Whatever you decide to do with drink specials, try to mix it up and find out which combinations of events and specials work better than others to keep your guests on their feet and interested.

LIVE ENTERTAINMENT

From comedy acts, musical bands, to live television programming, live entertainment can definitely set a nightclub apart from another. Live acts and live television shows have proven time and time again to be winners with many nightclub guests. Live entertainment gives bar customers something new, fresh and interactive to be entertained by rather than the typical daily operations of some nightclubs. Live entertainment captures attention like no other events.

Live acts have an obvious advantage and allow nightclubs to be very diverse in the forms of entertainment they provide. Guests appreciate live acts from time to time, which helps to increase a nightclub's identity and popularity. Use live acts such as bands or comedy nights sparingly, don't over do it and book these types of shows every night unless your nightclub will primarily be built around the premise of featuring live shows on a nightly basis.

Choosing the right live band or act should correspond with the style of the club. You should be able to sell bands or acts to clients just like everything else. Common sense will tell you that if you were running a Country and Western club, bringing in a live rap band won't go over very well with the

> LIVE ACTS HAVE AN OBVIOUS ADVANTAGE AND ALLOW NIGHTCLUBS TO BE VERY DIVERSE IN THE FORMS OF ENTERTAINMENT THEY PROVIDE. GUESTS APPRECIATE LIVE ACTS FROM TIME TO TIME, WHICH HELPS TO INCREASE A NIGHTCLUB'S IDENTITY AND POPULARITY.

clients and the event will probably be a disaster. Knowing customers and knowing your club will help you to determine which types of acts will be successful and which ones won't. Don't forget to advertise and promote all live shows to get peak customer turnouts.

KARAOKE

A favorite for many nightclub customers are karaoke nights. Unless you're specifically opening a karaoke bar, use karaoke sparingly. It's one of those things that can get old to people if it's overdone. But on the other hand, karaoke has the ability to draw in large crowds if planned and marketed correctly. It's surprising how many people, with or without a few drinks find it easy to take the stage and the microphone— eager to sing out a favorite song of theirs in front of everyone. They get the chance to let others hear their singing voices and get to perform in front of a live audience— Good or bad.

Sometimes, without proper planning, a karaoke event could backfire. If its forced onto customers who may not be aware of it, you could find that no one has the courage or will be in the mood to get up on stage to perform and the activity will be a failure.

Before going off and designating a night of the week for karaoke, test it out after proper marketing to see how it does. If the bar or club is large enough, has multiple rooms, dance or bar areas, try having the karaoke in a smaller area inside to see how it turns out. That way, the entire mood on the main floor isn't jeopardized if it doesn't work. Afterwards, maybe wait a week or two and do it all again. Pay special attention to how many guests show up for the event and to how they respond to it. If it becomes a hit, then by all means designate a night for karaoke. If it doesn't, maybe think about using it on a very limited basis or eliminating it altogether.

Another thing to keep in mind is that karaoke night does not have to be all night long. You'll have to tailor the event and figure out what times and night for that matter, will work out best. Usually, a karaoke night should only last a few hours in the evening and then the night should either be resumed as normal or another special event should be thrown in.

KARAOKE CONTESTS

Consider hosting a karaoke contest where the winner is decided by the crowd and receives a prize. The prizes can be anything, including cash, gift certificates, merchandise, free drinks or whatever you want as long as the contestants feel that the prizes are worth it. If they are worthwhile prizes people will line up to enter the contest. One of the best prizes to give away is cash. If you do decide to give away cash, make sure it's not too much and definitely not a small amount. Remember if it works, you'll have an increase in customer traffic and sales. Profits should be more than enough to cover any cash awards or other prizes given away and there will be plenty left over to put some extra money in the cash register for you.

One trick when it comes to karaoke contests is to spread the contests out over a period of weeks. How it works is that on each designated karaoke night, a winner is selected by the crowd— You'll have to keep track of all the winners. After say, a month or two or even longer, take each of the winners and have them compete against each other in some sort of karaoke "finals" contest. Once again, let the crowd select a winner, and whomever they choose then becomes the overall winner. Only then, once the overall winner is determined, are any prizes awarded.

> TAKE SOME TIME AND INVENT SPECIAL CONTESTS THAT OCCUR ONLY INSIDE YOUR NIGHTCLUB. USE YOUR IMAGINATION AND YOU'LL COME UP WITH ALL KINDS OF EXCITING IDEAS TO INCREASE SALES AND SET YOU APART FROM THE COMPETITION.

This method really works and you'd be amazed over the increased profits that'll accumulate over the period of the contest. Once it's over and a winner is rewarded, you can do it all over again.

Lastly, try to run a karaoke event in a manner that leaves a favorable impression upon patrons. If you put some time and money into running the event, patrons will see that. If you don't care, neither will they. You might also consider hiring and bringing in a professional for karaoke night or if you have a great DJ let him handle it. Either one of the two should strive to make the night very entertaining and somewhat funny.

FREE PRIZES, RAFFLES AND CONTESTS

Bring out the competitive side of customers through contests. People like to compete in all sorts of events. Those who don't compete, like watching others who do. Contests allow patrons to become involved and create another form of interaction within nightclubs.

There are many different types of contests which all vary from one another. From pool or dart tournaments, drinking contests, to on-stage events such as "Wet T-Shirt" contests and other similar events or fun activities. It doesn't really matter what the contests are as long as they are catered toward the individual nightclub's patrons. For instance, a "Wet T-Shirt" contest may work very well in a popular nightclub where college students make up the majority of the clientele. However, the same contest may not go over very well inside an upscale venue with more particular guests.

Take some time and invent special contests that occur only inside your nightclub. Use your imagination and you'll come up with all kinds of exciting ideas to increase sales and set you apart from the competition. Employees and customers are both excellent sources for coming up with contest ideas. Give all of ideas equal consideration. You never know, one of their ideas may be a huge hit.

Another incentive to give customers a reason to come and stay longer are prize giveaways. Once again, this can be done a hundred different ways and anyway you want. People always appreciate winning stuff. Giving away prizes can become expensive, but if you're turning profit over, you'll come out on top in the long run. Again, as with karaoke prizes, the prizes can be anything as long as they are worth keeping.

How about this? What if you gave every guest a card when they entered through the front door? Your door men also gave each guest instructions about the card and told them that each time they purchased a drink, the bartender would stamp the card. Once their cards were full of stamps— say eight stamps (drinks), they could redeem the card for a free T-shirt.

In this example the T-shirt isn't totally free since guests would kinda have to work for it, but on the other hand it is. Your customers were probably going to drink eight drinks anyway. Right? At least this way they get something back in return. A lot of people will appreciate this and will remember your club in the future.

If you do plan to give T-shirts away, make sure they are of some quality. A really good idea when it comes to T-shirts is to have your club or bar name put on them. Maybe even a logo also. When customers wear the shirts out in public they become walking advertisements for you!

Whatever you do, don't get hung up on the T-shirt. T-shirts are just an example. Other popular examples of things to give away are tickets to concerts or sporting events, free drinks, money, posters, sports memorabilia, glassware (beer mugs, etc.) and gift certificates to specialty stores. The list of prizes goes on and on and your imagination is the only limit. With some free gifts, you may want to contact other businesses, such as a specialty store (maybe a tanning salon), and work together so that you both profit.

A great way to boost traffic and give your patrons something to do and look forward to is to have a raffle. With a raffle, you give customers an opportunity to fill out a raffle ticket to become eligible to win a prize. Be careful that you're not actually charging them money for a chance to win because it may be illegal in certain states. The raffle entry should be free to anyone who is interested and takes the time to fill out an entry form. Also require that they must be present during the drawing to win. Your raffle can be as long and as intense as you want it to. Some clubs sponsor a raffle for just one night. The prizes won are usually small. But if it keeps people happy, so be it.

Other clubs sponsor raffles on a larger scale with a much larger grand prize, like a jet ski or a car. Those raffles are usually spread out over a time period of a year. The drawing for the grand prize is usually the last one, 365 days from the start of the raffle. Each week, typically on a Saturday night, smaller drawings are done and several smaller prizes are given away.

The kicker is, you allow customers to enter the raffle as many times as they want to. But they can only enter the raffle once a night. What does that mean? It means, if they want their name in the raffle one hundred times, then they have to return one hundred separate nights. Also remember that they must be present to win. That means, each Saturday, even if they only want to win the smaller prizes, they have to come inside. Once they're there, they are bound to spend some money.

Most people aren't going to specifically plan to enter a raffle a certain number of times, but if they know that every time they went inside of your place they could enter a raffle, it speaks volumes when they decide to go out. Strongly advertise a raffle to let everyone know about it.

So what does all this do for you? It shouldn't be too hard to see that sponsoring a raffle can greatly influence gross sales because of increased customer traffic. If you don't think people are motivated by the idea of winning a car, then guess again. Think about how many people would be there *hoping to win* the night of the grand prize drawing.

Your club would definitely be on the map. There is one word of caution however. If you do decide to do a raffle type event, consult with an attorney first just to make sure you abide by all the rules and any applicable laws regarding lotteries or raffles.

LET THEM PLAY!
Social activities in the forms of games are important to many guests. Although games by themselves aren't the major source of income for a nightclub, they promote social interaction between guests and can cause people to stay longer, drink more, eat and obviously spend more money. Sometimes just sitting at a table with a group of friends isn't enough and can become boring for some customers. They often like to move around and become involved in something. Games allow that to happen. In fact, the lures of games are so strong that the lack of them can cause you to lose customers on slower nights because they have nothing else to do.

> SOCIAL ACTIVITIES IN THE FORMS OF GAMES ARE IMPORTANT TO MANY GUESTS. ALTHOUGH GAMES BY THEMSELVES AREN'T THE MAJOR SOURCE OF INCOME FOR A NIGHT-CLUB, THEY PROMOTE SOCIAL INTER-ACTION BETWEEN GUESTS AND CAN CAUSE PEOPLE TO STAY LONGER, DRINK MORE, EAT AND OBVIOUSLY SPEND MORE MONEY.

BILLIARDS
Away from the aspects of winning prizes or singing karaoke are the more common features one may expect to see or do in most bars. *Playing pool.* Even if you only have one pool table, it's enough. Pool is one of those things that brings people together and helps people to forget about any stresses or problems they have while they engage in a friendly competition against a friend or even a stranger.

If you don't have a table in your club or aren't planning on getting one, you should strongly consider the potential. Pool tables are one of the most basic of many bar or club sights. Why should you be any different? It's a guarantee that if you don't have at least one pool table, you or your staff will be questioned several times a week from customers, wanting to know where it is.

On top of being a common bar staple, if you own the table, they provide a very stable and consistent form of profit and require little to no maintenance. The important things are to make sure the tables stay clean, all of the balls are with the table and that the cues are in relatively good shape. Be prepared to replace the cues as needed because all of the use will wear them out.

Depending on the size of your place, how many customers frequent it and how many tables you own, expect to bring in anywhere from $100-$1500 or even more a week just from the pool tables. If you were to open a pool hall, expect to make way more than that because that's perhaps the main reason those customers are going in anyway.

To get even more from your tables and give customers even more incentive to come try sponsoring some pool tournaments? Think about it.

VIDEO GAMES

Coin-operated games, or video games are also another common feature and sight. Though normally not as popular as pool tables or darts, they provide another means for people to relax, compete (against the machine or another person) and enjoy themselves.

If you choose to do so, you can actually purchase your own arcade games. Arcade games are expensive and video game fads change regularly. What that means is that people are less likely now, to spend money to play pacman than they are to play the latest shoot 'em up game or interactive sports simulator. Although pacman, and games like it in its day, were awesome, don't expect a line of people waiting to play them these days. For that reason, it's not wise to buy arcade games. What's popular today, probably won't be popular tomorrow in the gaming industry. Most games that are placed inside should be owned by a gaming company. That way it won't cost you a bundle to replace any games that aren't being played. Build a good relationship with a game vendor so that any problems that arise or any game changes that may be needed can be quickly addressed.

Strategically placing certain games, such as small video poker or other electronic games on top of a bar counter will pay off. People who sit at the bar will have easy access to something to do.

This kind of placement also promotes social interaction between strangers who happen to be sitting close to each other at the bar. The bottom line is that games are terrific coin-eaters. Both you and your customers will benefit from them so while planning your venue, don't forget to research and add a few games to the floor.

DARTS

Dart games are also very common and becoming increasingly popular amongst nightclub customers. Darts are beginning to succeed pool as a popular nightclub activity. Most people only play darts once inside a club. And, some of them actually own their own set of darts complete with a little case and everything. Put a little dart stand in the corner next to the dart games where people can buy any necessary dart products they may need. Make sure the stand is locked up and that the bartenders, waiters or waitresses have keys. If you don't lock it, don't be surprised when items are stolen.

Dart games are now electronic and most of them have several preprogrammed games within them, which keep scores, tells who's up next and announce winners. Because of that they are relatively easy to play and the only thing users have to do, is throw the darts and the dart boards keep track of everything else which alleviates the need for customers to have to think too much while playing.

Keep all of the darts and the dart boards in good shape and replace the worn darts as needed. People easily get turned off when they can't find a good set of house darts to play with or if the equipment is shoddy.

> DART GAMES ARE ALSO VERY COMMON AND BECOMING INCREASINGLY POPULAR AMONGST NIGHTCLUB CUSTOMERS. DARTS ARE BEGINNING TO SUCCEED POOL AS A POPULAR NIGHTCLUB ACTIVITY.

DART TOURNAMENTS

Dart tournaments are on the rise so give them some regard. Just like pool tournaments, there are now dart leagues and thousands of participating people are members of those leagues. These tournaments are spread throughout many clubs, bars or taverns in just about every city and often bring in many spectators as well as the players on a tournament night. Tournaments can last for weeks or months and are easy ways to draw in customers on those given nights.

LET THEM WATCH!

Television sets are extremely important, especially if you plan to open up a sports bar. Watching TV allows patrons to focus on something rather than having to stare at the wall if they don't want to play pool, darts or whatever else you have inside on slow nights. It's best to have television sets in several areas so that they can be seen by all guests— no matter where they are, except the restrooms of course. But if you want to place them there that's fine too.

Television often does not have to be exclusively live to be a success. Popular TV programming has the ability to draw people in on a weekly basis. Good examples of this are TV shows like *"Who Wants to be a Millionaire?"* Or even the very popular cartoon, *"South Park."*

These shows and those like them in their prime, can send curious patrons inside nightclubs wanting to watch the shows, during quieter times in the week, while relaxing with friends and enjoying good drinks— on large television screens and in high-quality sound. TV shows can also work very well with happy hours and drink specials.

Televisions, especially when talking about purchasing several wide screens to fill a club, can become expensive but are a must for any modern nightclub. You could actually lose many customers if you don't have television because it's a certainty that when the Superbowl is on, you won't be very busy.

Cable or satellite services offer the ability to tune into a wide variety of channels and show customers programming many can't get at home. Contact your local services to find out more about the rates and packages in your area.

Hire a good TV/video man to hook up the television system and have him put in a camera system. An especially popular way to add some pizzazz to any club is to have a camera pointed at the dance floor. When it's really busy, tune the cameras and televisions to the action on the dance floor. This is a little feature but it will add some touch and style to a nightclub. Most people won't mind at all being on TV others to see. The action inside can actually become entertainment for those watching the televisions.

If you expand some day and open other similar venues, have an audio/video man connect your venues through TV. This works well for very busy and popular nightclubs. Guests in different locations can see what's happening on the floors of your other clubs. It all comes down to the style and the image you want to project.

SPORTS PROGRAMMING
What sports bar would be complete without sports programming? Sports are important benefits to the club industry and watching a sports game in a nightclub is a favorite past time for many sports enthusiasts. Even if you don't plan to operate a sports bar per se, use sporting events to your advantage, especially during slower periods of an evening to keep guests entertained. Sports programming has the ability to set a healthy mood and those who like watching sports enjoy having several drinks while doing so.

LET THEM DANCE!
The benefit of having dance floors speaks for itself. Dance floors allow people to carry out their feelings to the music they listen to and allows them to interact with other customers and the nightclub itself. Carefully construct and place dance floors in convenient locations to let customers easily get to and from them. Use a good light and sound system to enhance the experience of dancing inside your nightclub to really make customers feel uninhibited.

MANAGING EMPLOYEES

EFFECTIVE LEADERSHIP
LEADS TO A PRODUCTIVE STAFF

The employees that are hired and brought onto the crew can make or break a nightclub. Employees are without a doubt the most important aspect to any nightclub. Think of all employees as ambassadors. Their personal appearances, demeanor and work ethics directly affect customers' opinions and perceptions towards the club itself.

HIRING EMPLOYEES
One of the first things to do when it comes to hiring employees is to understand and analyze each of the specific job functions you'll need others to perform to achieve a quality and professional service. Carefully interview each and every applicant that's interested in a particular job. The next step is to evaluate and decide which applicants will best suit the needs of the position and for the nightclub as a whole.

APPLICATIONS
Whenever you interview or hire an employee, see that he or she has

first properly filled out an application. You'd be surprised how many employers forgo the application process leaving themselves to remember each potential employee from memory. Not good. When your nightclub becomes a huge success— like you know it will be, you'll have your hands full with a number of different things. Trying to remember a conversation you had with someone a month ago about getting a job as bartender will be difficult to do.

Have all potential employees complete an application. Have applications available all year round even when you don't necessarily need anyone. Once you're ready to hire someone, go back through all of the applications you have gathered and begin the process of interviewing prospective job candidates. There are some questions on the application itself and during the interview that you cannot and shouldn't ask. *Pay close attention!*—Don't ask for information regarding race, gender, height, weight, disabilities, religion or marital status. Generally speaking, don't ask for anything that might violate any state or federal anti-discrimination regulation. If someone feels that they were discriminated against because of a civil rights issue, they may be able to successfully bring about a lawsuit.

What you can ask for are references. Once you get them, make sure to follow up on them to ensure that your applicant is telling the truth about him or herself.

MANAGERS

If you decide that you don't want to actually run your club and only want to assume the role as owner, you'll need someone who can step forward and fill your shoes. A manager will be the solution and will represent both you and the nightclub. This isn't a position you want to give to just anyone. Seek out people who have outgoing personalities, excellent leadership qualities, integrity and whom you can work well with for this position.

Even if you're going to play an active role in running your nightclub, you still might consider hiring a manager or assistant manager to assist. Managers can take a lot of the burdens off your work load by taking on tasks like scheduling employees and more.

THE BARTENDER

Let's now take a look at the most common job of all in a nightclub outside of a manager. It doesn't really matter how large or small a nightclub is because you are guaranteed to see this employee working inside. Can you guess who this employee is? Give up? It's the bartender!

Hiring a bartender or bartenders is very important. Getting started, the first bartenders should be experienced and knowledgeable in the trade of preparing and serving drinks. You'll have enough to worry about and to do. Leave the art of mixing and pouring drinks to someone who knows what they're doing. This first bartender should also be very outgoing and willing to help your establishment achieve maximum success. He or she should be willing to assist other, less-qualified bartenders get up to speed. Avoid those potential bartenders who are out only for themselves. That sort of selfishness in an individual is no good for your nightclub and will only cause problems in the long run.

> HIRING A BARTENDER OR BARTENDERS IS VERY IMPORTANT. GETTING STARTED, THE FIRST BARTENDERS SHOULD BE EXPERIENCED AND KNOWLEDGEABLE IN THE TRADE OF PREPARING AND SERVING DRINKS. YOU'LL HAVE ENOUGH TO WORRY ABOUT AND TO DO. LEAVE THE ART OF MIXING AND POURING DRINKS TO SOMEONE WHO KNOWS WHAT THEY'RE DOING.

A bartender needs to have a special personality that allows him or her to build a friendly rapport with customers. Communications skills are important too. Communicating with customers is something that must happen at all times. The bartender is probably the most frequent employee that customers will encounter during the course of an evening. The impression that the bartender leaves should be a good one.

THE WAIT STAFF

The next employee is the waiter or waitress. Again, depending on the size of your club, this employee is optional. If you plan on running a medium to a large sized nightclub, waiters and waitresses are essential. They serve as a liaison between the bar and the customers and between the kitchen and the customers— if you'll be serving food.

A good waiter or waitress can and will take the edge off of customers' stresses and make any night a little smoother and a relaxing one. Attempt to find and hire waiters and waitresses with excellent people and communication skills. Ideally, you'll want them to be both excellent servers and excellent people persons. But, if you are unable to find that perfect employee, settle for the one that is an excellent people person— even if their serving skills leave a lot to be desired. A waiter or waitress that has the ability to befriend patrons has a powerful effect over them. In these situations, they can often *sell* more or cause increased sales. Any minor mistakes they make will soon be forgotten by satisfied guests. Conversely, people tend to view a waiter or waitress who doesn't seem to talk much or seem to care as lousy, no matter how good their serving abilities are.

One final point about waiters and waitresses is to hire individuals who have above average personal appearances, mannerisms and hygiene. Think about it. A good-looking female waitress, with a charming personality, serving food or drinks always goes a long way with the men. The same is true of a waiter for women customers.

This may seem a little superficial or sexist to some, but this is reality. People enjoy other good looking people. Being in the nightclub industry is a service and entertainment business and if you want to be successful you need to do the things that work in order to satisfy customers.

"BOUNCERS"

The next employees you should seek to put on your payroll are the persons commonly referred to as *bouncers*. Small operations can get away without one, but larger clubs will definitely need someone to keep the peace, order and to see that all patrons are abiding by the policies and rules set forth by you. They also make sure that the nightclub itself is complying with any and all applicable laws and ordinances in your city and state.

A word of advice about your security or bouncers is to avoid making your customers feel as if they have just walked into a WWF wrestling meet when they come through your front doors. Most of your customers aren't going to cause any problems and won't appreciate seeing a bunch of huge, intimidating thugs hovering around the front door eyeing everyone. That's how they'll perceive it. Keep them out of sight as much as possible. Chances are you'll need no more than two bouncers working at the front door checking ID's and ensuring that no undesirables get in. And as always, make sure you hire security personnel that can maintain a professional appearance.

Every potential security team member *must be able to follow your each and every order at all times!* The ability to listen and obey is important. You don't need any loose cannons. Bouncers who are quick with a heavy hand may possibly expose you to a lawsuit. Lawsuits or the threat of them is one of the downfalls to operating a nightclub, but one that you must get used to. It's part of the business.

THE DISC JOCKEY (DJ)
Hiring a DJ is not at all like hiring a waiter. If the waiter doesn't work out and he quits or you fire him, then the club isn't going to suffer any big loses. DJ's will play such a significant role in establishing an identity for a nightclub that their presence or absence will without a doubt make a noticeable difference.

When seeking out a DJ(s), hire the ones that'll fit into the nightclub's theme or genre. In other words, don't hire a DJ who specializes in country line dancing for a heavy metal nightclub, or whatever. It just won't work out and the nightclub's sales will suffer. Up to 75% of all nightclub failures are caused by inadequate DJ's. The main reason that happens is because the entertainment that the DJ attempts to provide in the form of music and his vocals mismatches the structure or theme of the club itself.

Failure can also be attributed to a nightclub owner's lack of hands-on control of the DJ/music aspect of the nightclub. If you place too much faith and trust in the DJ and leave him to do what he wants, then you could be doomed. You'll have to visit the DJ booth often and communicate with him. Listen to what he's actually playing and evaluate his effectiveness regularly. Listen to how he performs and analyze how customers react to his overall performance. Constantly decide if both the music and the DJ are right for the club.

In order to achieve success in this area, you'll have to constantly rate your DJ's on those criteria and interactions. Don't be afraid to fire a DJ who consistently isn't performing well. The DJ has nothing to lose if he isn't doing well in your club. You on the other hand have a lot to lose.

Another reason for failure is that the DJ(s) doesn't know what he's doing. Before you hire a DJ make sure he knows how to perform basic tasks and has the potential ability to command a crowd. It doesn't hurt either to listen and see how he performs before subjecting customers to him. It's not necessary that potential DJ(s) already be professional or deeply experienced. But, whatever you do, don't just trust and turn over your expensive light and sound system to some kid who claims to be good.

PAYING YOUR DJ

Don't be stingy when it comes to paying the DJ. In the nightclub industry, paying a DJ is usually different than paying the rest of the employees. This is so because the DJ is a pivotal employee for any major venue. He provides a backbone for a club and the music he'll play will bring people in to spend money, dance and have a good time.

Most professional DJs have their own collection of music (CDs and records). In order for him to keep current with the latest

> WHEN SEEKING OUT A DJ(S), HIRE THE ONES THAT'LL FIT INTO THE NIGHTCLUB'S THEME OR GENRE. IN OTHER WORDS, DON'T HIRE A DJ WHO SPECIALIZES IN COUNTRY LINE DANCING FOR A HEAVY METAL NIGHTCLUB, OR WHATEVER. IT JUST WON'T WORK OUT AND THE NIGHTCLUB'S SALES WILL SUFFER.

music, he'll spend his own money to buy the newest songs to play in a club. That in itself, should prompt you to pay him well.

The alternative is for you to buy all of the music and purchase the latest releases as they come out. Doing this will cost you time and more money but may compel you to pay the DJ a little less.

FOOD SERVICE/COOKS

Obviously important employees for the nightclub/restaurant venues. Only after you have made the decision as to the type of foods/entrees your venue will serve to customers, should you seek out qualified personnel. In a start-up operation that serves food, you want to be able to rest assured that the food service is left to competent cooks. Getting a nightclub/restaurant off the ground isn't the time to advertise, "help wanted— No experience necessary."

Interview applicants very carefully for these positions and be prepared to pay them a little more in wages than other positions you'll need filled. The exception to this however will be for the dishwasher positions. If you are planning on doing a lot of food sales during the day and early evening, you'll need dishwashers, who can start out at minimum wages. Otherwise, if you're not expecting huge food sales, your cooks can do double duty and act as the dishwashers between orders.

For even smaller operations, it isn't uncommon for the bartender to also assume the role of cook for small orders such as burger baskets. The decision to hire cooks or dishwashers will rest on the size of your operation and your ultimate plans for selling food.

EMPLOYEE POLICIES

After you decide that you'll go into business for yourself and open your own nightclub that will utilize employees, you must develop a comprehensive employee policy manual. This manual is mandatory and protects both you and your employees. At a minimum your policy manual should cover:

- Compensation/wages/tips
- Pay periods
- Overtime
- Vacation, absent without leave, sick leave
- Holidays
- Work hours/schedules
- Performance and salary reviews
- Time off
- Benefits

- Training
- Promotion
- Grievances
- Termination

Those are both common and very specific topics which you should address when establishing policies. Other topics you should also include in your policies are listed below:

- Job descriptions
- Smoking
- Sexual Harassment
- Disciplinary action
- Retirement
- Dress/uniform policy
- Substance abuse

Try to get your policies right the first time you put the manual together and have it reviewed by an attorney. If you don't, you're sure to have mistakes and changing those policies with mistakes can be a pain down the road. Also, don't attempt to write policy manuals from scratch. Writing one from scratch only increases the likelihood of making many mistakes. It is strongly suggested that you obtain one of the many employee policy manuals that are available as samples from the library in order to avoid having to write one from scratch.

DEALING WITH YOUR EMPLOYEES
Dealing with employees can be both a rewarding and a dreadful experience. In a perfect world, none of your employees would ever have a problem that you would have to take issue with.

Actually in a perfect world, your employees would work extra hard, long hours and would do it for free. But, unfortunately as you well know, it's not a perfect world and no one, including you is perfect.

Managing your employees is challenging work which will put your leadership skills the test. Countless books have been written and dedicated solely on the subject of managing employees. If you feel that your people or leadership skills need a little work before you begin the process of hiring and managing employees, you may want to pick up one of those books to give you more insight on the issue.

The following are a few common methods for dealing with employee situations. As you read on, keep in mind that this list is not by any means the only or best way to deal with any and all situations that might arise:

1. If possible, you should always commend and praise employees in public and criticize them in a private setting, alone with them.
2. Be accessible. All of your employees should be able to speak with you when they need to and have the peace of mind to know that you will listen.
3. Show your appreciation to your employees by talking. Everyone likes feeling that they are needed.
4. Make sure that you have written very specific and concise job descriptions so that everyone knows what their responsibilities are and how they are to perform their tasks. Doing this will eliminate confusions, misunderstandings and will promote better job performance.
5. Give employees objectives. Either personal objectives or objectives for the overall growth of the nightclub. One way to motivate all employees and promote teamwork is to create an objective that you wish your nightclub to achieve. You will see real results as each employee works towards the objective rather than each employee simply fulfilling the minimum requirements of his or her job descriptions.
6. Personally request input and suggestions from your employees. Also host group meetings on a weekly or monthly basis to promote unity and give an opportunity for all employees to get together and brainstorm, complain or plan for any upcoming nightclub objectives.
7. Don't let your employees feel that they are in a dead-end job. If they do, performances will suffer and they probably won't be around for long. When, and if possible allow them the opportunity for

advancement, no matter how small or large the promotion may be.
8. Thoroughly train your employees and present monthly or bi-monthly training sessions.
9. Don't always insist that things are always done your way. Sometimes your employees may have a better way of doing something.
10. Lastly, pay your employees for what they are worth and for the jobs that they do. Remember, in the long run, you'll get what you pay for.

SCHEDULING EMPLOYEES

Scheduling employees for your nightclub is yet another task that can become grueling if you let it get away from you. Once your nightclub is up and running you'll get a feel for the number of employees you'll need on each given night. You'll find that on some nights you need more and other nights you'll need less. It's important that you be able to find out exactly how many employees each night needs to correctly schedule your staff to reduce the payroll and maximize employee effectiveness. Schedule too many on a slower night and you'll end up with employees standing around doing nothing costing you a bundle in payroll expenses. Not enough employees on a busy night and the nightclub may suffer because of the lack of customer service.

Don't be afraid to send employees home on a slow night and don't be afraid to call them in at home to help out during an unexpected busy night that leaves you short-handed.

If it works out best for your operation, you may consider appointing an employee from each of the nightclub's specialized jobs. Have that designated employee, most likely one who is experienced and has excellent communication skills with other employees, be responsible for scheduling employees of the same like job. For example, you could create positions such as head bartender. The head bartender could be responsible for tracking every bartenders' schedule. You would then of course, give the schedule final approval each week or if you hire and utilize managers or assistant managers, leave the approving to them.

EMPLOYEE TRAINING

Properly trained staff will dramatically improve the relationship between a nightclub and the customers. Trained staff work more efficiently and with a sense of purpose. Training eliminates confusion and promotes confidence. In turn, the wait staff can actually increase your overall profits and increase their tips. The more money they are able to get in wages and tips, the happier they'll be.

The worst thing that can happen is to have a bunch of employees standing around, not sure of themselves or staring at the walls when they are needed. Training is the best way to solve this problem. Training doesn't have to be expensive and there are a variety of ways to do it. You could do it yourself with regular staff meetings, give the responsibility to a senior bartender, waiter or cook, let a manager take care of it or you could hire an outside agency to handle it.

The wait staff is probably the one position where training is the most important. Regular on-going training is a must. You'll probably have more turnovers with the wait staff than with any other position. Generally, a promotion in the wait field means getting a better station that has a greater potential for earning bigger tips.

> THE WAIT STAFF IS PROBABLY THE ONE POSITION WHERE TRAINING IS THE MOST IMPORTANT. REGULAR ON-GOING TRAINING IS A MUST. YOU'LL PROBABLY HAVE MORE TURNOVERS WITH THE WAIT STAFF THAN WITH ANY OTHER POSITION.

Another promotion could depend on job performance or experience. Those promotions could result in being appointed a head waiter or waitress. Because advancement in this field is so limited, it is sometimes perceived as a dead-end job. That means you could have to train new waiters or waitresses on a fairly regular basis than for any other position. However, with proper management and training, employee turnover can be reduced.

Treat all employees like professionals rather than hired help. After all, they will have the most contact with customers and the interaction between them can often determine if a customer will come back again. As professionals, they deserve the best opportunity to excel at their jobs.

Proper training allows them a clear understanding of the roles that they play, what you expect from them and what customers expect from them.

With that in mind, you must realize that training is an ongoing procedure that must occur no matter how long your nightclub is in business. Each week you should make mental or written notes of things that can be done better or things that shouldn't be done at all. Translate problems, concerns, suggestions, comments or even praise into annual training sessions.

Typical waitress training should include, at the very least, the following:

- Seating customers and menu presentation (During food service hours).
- Proper food and drink serving etiquette.
- Removal of dirty dishes and empty glasses to keep the tables free.
- Checking for customer satisfaction.
- Preparing totals and presenting checks to customers (During food service hours).
- Collecting and making change for drink orders.
- Courteous service, greeting guests and profitable conversations.
- Host or hostess responsibilities (During food service hours).
- Efficiency.
- Personal appearance/Dress codes and uniforms.
- Spotting fake IDs.

For all nightclub/restaurant venues, training for the line or prep cooks is very necessary. Here are some of the training issues that should be addressed for food service employees in the kitchen:

- Sanitation.
- Food presentation and preparation techniques.
- Updates in the food menu.
- OSHA standards.
- Clean-up.
- Safety issues and hazards.
- Inventory control.
- Communication skills with the wait staff.

Bartenders will also require regular training. Bartenders are the leaders on the bar floor and their knowledge of the job they must perform is crucial. Bartenders often learn their trades through experience or on-the-job-training from other bartenders. Even still, annual bartending meetings/training sessions should be established, which covers:

• Cocktail recipes.
• Attire and personal appearances.
• Loss prevention.
• Inventory control.
• Customer satisfaction.
• Customer relations.
• Preparing drink orders.
• Sanitation.
• Spotting Fake IDs.
• Laws and regulations.
• Safety issues and hazards.
• Stocking the bar.
• Communication skills with the wait staff.

The last important group of employees that'll need ongoing training is the security staff. Read more about security issues in *THE SECURITY TEAM.*

Security members will need to be well-versed in the following areas of expertise:

• When to use force.
• Spotting fake IDs.
• Laws and regulations.
• Crowd control.
• Customer relations.
• Dealing with intoxicated persons.
• Employee theft.
• Attire and personal appearances.

EMPLOYEE INCENTIVES EQUALS BETTER SERVICE

It's no secret that motivating employees with financial rewards makes them happier, harder workers. This means that customers receive better service and the nightclub gets a better review. Incentives increase employee moral and can even make working fun. This in turn, decreases employee turnover (especially amongst the wait staff) and promotes a congruent work ethic within all employees.

Incentives can be implemented in a number of ways. Employee contests are perhaps the most popular way to do it. Contests offer fun to the job as employees work harder to try to win. The rules of the contests can vary and should be tailored to be consistent with your operation. Generally, an employee contest is one that is set for a specific time period, usually thirty-days. During that time, the sales that employees bring in are carefully tracked. Use a chalk board with participating employee names and sales standings somewhere in an employee only area so that they can all see where they're at each day. After the specified time period elapses, the employee with the most sales wins a predetermined amount of money (*bonus*). After the winner is rewarded, start the contest all over again.

Contests such as this one, do work but there are a few problems with them. First, it's very likely that you'll have employees that are consistently better than others. These employees will beat the dud employees in a sales contest every time. That means that your less capable employees will never win a contest and at some point will realize it and never even try.

Secondly, sales contests are usually suited towards the wait staff. The employees in the kitchen rarely have direct contact with customers and the likelihood of them taking an order or closing a sale is improbable. So what do they get out of a contest? Increased food orders and more work.

In a sales contest, bartenders may profit because they should be receiving a percentage of the tips that the wait staff receives whenever they prepare drink orders. Increased orders brought on by the wait staff means more tips for them. But, increased orders means less time to deal with other patrons at the bar. This could cause a breakdown and the remedy is manning the bar with more bartenders, which means more payroll expenses for you.

Your security staff, who probably won't deal much with sales at all, except at the front door collecting cover charges, won't benefit much from a contest either. It's not very likely that security personnel are going to receive many tips while working the door. To add to it, *more often than not,* entrance into a club will be free and cover will be charged only during certain hours of operation.

So what do you do in order to get everyone into the game? Simple, you host a variety of incentives at all times. Offer all employees an overall club objective incentive, such as a sales mark. Inform them during a meeting, that if the club reaches a certain gross sales profit, that everyone will receive a bonus. This kind of incentive is usually established on a 12-month basis. For example, you could set a sales mark of $650,000 in gross annual sales. If this mark is met or exceeded, all employees that worked during the 12-month period will receive a $400 bonus.

This kind of an incentive gives your employees something to work towards each day. Customer relations will improve and hopefully overall sales will increase. Everyone likes a bonus, especially when it is given in appreciation for hard work. Objectives also help employees work together, unlike a sales contest where some may be so influenced by winning the top prize, they'll step on other employees' feet while trying to win— Animosities and ruined friendships may become the result in some instances.

Also, reward the little things. Reward security personnel, the wait staff and the bartenders for such things as spotting fake IDs. Establish a policy that states anyone who reveals or confiscates a fake ID, will receive $10 per ID. This works two-fold. First, it increases employee awareness when checking IDs and second, more minors are identified and kept out of your club which keeps you operating a legal nightclub. Keep an eye on your kitchen staff also by monitoring the quality of the food dishes they prepare. Give them rewards and praises for quality.

Motivating and offering incentives to employees is an important managerial task. Sometimes, the small things you do to show your appreciation, is what really counts. You don't always necessarily have to give cash incentives to show them that you need them. Certificates of appreciation, plaques and other awards such as an employee of the month award, can all strengthen your employees' bond with your business, which in the long run will benefit everyone including the customer.

UNIFORMS

Believe it or not, deciding which types of uniforms employees will wear, is a crucial managerial decision. Uniforms are very powerful outfits that have the ability to set a tone for any nightclub and identify the wait staff from customers. Anyone who has ever been to a nightclub, where the wait staff doesn't wear uniforms knows how hard it is to find a waiter or waitress when you need one. It's also embarrassing after asking another customer for a drink because you assumed he or she worked there.

Uniforms often influence how customers perceive an operation and causes many customers to dress based on how employees are dressed. If the staff doesn't wear a uniform and dresses casually (Blue jeans and T-shirts), most customers will wear the same. If the staff is neatly dressed in say, upscale-looking clothing, chances are high that customers will conform with similar clothing.

This isn't to suggest that you should dress your employees up in tuxedos, but merely that the employees' apparel has a tremendous effect on what most customers will show up in.

There is a challenge to finding uniforms that work. Actually, for the bartending and security staff this usually isn't too hard to do. Most bartenders are traditionally dressed in a tux shirt and bow tie. Black slacks and sometimes even jeans finish off the uniform. Customers have come to expect seeing bartenders dressed this way. Many bars however have gotten away from that traditional look and their bartenders wear T-shirts embroidered with the club's name or logo.

Security staff outfits vary, but most people are conditioned to seeing these guys wearing jeans and a shirt that says something like "security." Although this is common, it doesn't necessarily have to be the case if you don't want it to be. You can dress security personnel up into matched outfits if an image you want to project dictates it— for example.

THE WAITRESS

The wait staff however, is where uniform selection becomes more complicated. Choosing a uniform that works for both the staff and the customer is almost impossible to do. Mainly, whatever uniform the wait staff is required to wear will almost always cause some controversy between them and you. You'll inevitably receive all kinds of complaints

First of all, the majority of your wait staff will probably be females— especially during the evening hours of operation. This is not meant in any sexiest way shape or form but, the simple fact is most clubs experience higher traffic of men customers looking to have a good time than women customers. *Waitresses* are an obvious choice given that situation. It's just business and waitresses can outsell waiters in a nightclub environment any day of the week.

With that out of the way, the most common uniform complaints you'll get from waitresses are that they are uncomfortable, they don't fit right, they don't look good, they just don't like them or they are causing them to lose money (tips).

To work around these problems you must take control of the situation. You won't be able to find any one uniform that'll satisfy all of waitresses but with a few simple ideas you may just find that you'll cut down on complaints.

The key to selecting the right uniforms is to use them to set the tone and establish an image for your club. The uniform should also be comfortable for your waitresses to wear. Comfort, all by itself will eliminate most complaints. If waitresses are comfortable, they'll feel more relaxed, confident and won't come across to the customers that they are unhappy.

The other criterion for uniform selection is durability. Uniforms that are made to withstand regular wear and tear will last longer and look better. Go with a fabric such as polyester, that won't fade easily after several washes. Uniforms that are not durable are subject to tears or ripping much easier, which does not look good at all. A poor looking uniform during a waitress' shift will surely make her uncomfortable and upset. Durable uniforms also cut down on the costs of replacement which will save you money in the future.

Uniforms are an affordable way to give a nightclub a minor face lift. Because uniforms can influence impressions, set tones and establish an overall mood, changing them from time to time makes customers feel almost as if they have walked into a brand-new club. They are just that powerful. As an operator or manager, whenever you feel that the club needs something new or fresh to get customers energized, think about changing the waitresses' uniforms.

If you plan to change out the waitresses' uniforms on a regular basis, every six months or so, get the waitresses themselves involved in the process. Take comments, suggestions and complaints into consideration. Allowing the waitresses to have input on the uniforms they will wear will reduce complaints from them and make them a little happier knowing they had something to say about their outfits.

To tie durability and comfort together, you'll need to stress personal appearances to the waitresses. Appearances and neatness are important. A poorly dressed waitress leaves a bad impression and customers will take notice. Physical appearances and excellent hygiene will play a role just as important as neatness. It's simple, customers want to be served by others who look good.

ALLOWING THE WAITRESSES TO HAVE INPUT ON THE UNIFORMS THEY WILL WEAR WILL REDUCE COMPLAINTS FROM THEM AND MAKE THEM A LITTLE HAPPIER KNOWING THEY HAD SOMETHING TO SAY ABOUT THEIR OUTFITS.

THE DESIGN

THE RIGHT DESIGN CAN
MAKE A DIFFERENCE

The design and layout of how a nightclub is set up is very important. You should carefully consider a number of different aspects when deciding how to lay out the main floor. Your decisions could mean the difference between a customer returning another night or never coming back again, or at least for a while. The business of providing a service of entertainment is plagued, for better or worse, by the opinions of your customers— whether real or perceived. Those opinions are passed on by word of mouth to others. Opinions that get passed on are powerful and can cause an operation to go out of business if they are negative. But on the other hand, if they are positive opinions, you could see an increase in traffic which translates to more profit for you.

Here you want to really impress your customers. When they walk in for the first time you want them to admire the looks and make them feel comfortable. Can you remember the last time you were in a bar and couldn't find the restroom for a half an hour and then when you did, there was a long waiting line? Or how about when you were sitting at a table trying to relax and enjoy a cold beer, and you were constantly being brushed up against by that guy on the dance floor trying to get his groove on? You didn't stay at that bar very long and the next time you were getting ready to go out for a night on the town and thought about where to go, you probably remembered not being comfortable and probably passed on going to that same bar.

CREATIVITY

Designing and laying out a flavorful nightclub will call for a little creativity on your part. The goal should be to strive for uniqueness and create a total environment with themes/concepts and through the placement of decoration, equipment and furniture.

Even if you have to design and layout your nightclub on a limited budget, you can still create an environment to be proud of using the things you can afford, such as lights and light fixtures, to enhance the interior scheme. It all comes down to imagination and a little innovation to get it right.

10 Tips to Create a Successful Environment:

1. Use the design to flatter your concept.
2. Spend as much money on the design and decorations as you do on equipment and other aspects of your venue.
3. Use lighting to enhance the design and layout.
4. Create a design and layout that customers will be able to relate to.
5. Create spaces so that customers feel comfortable.
6. Control and create traffic areas.
7. Use decorations to stimulate a visual appeal.
8. Think like your customers and employees and envision what they'll see and feel.
9. Give the layout of the dance floor some extra attention to create a luring effect.
10. Consider hiring a professional interior design service that has experience working with nightclub venues.

THE DESIGN

The architectural design of any nightclub should be a primary concern. Unfortunately, many operators don't realize the importance of design and layout as it relates to their business. The design of a nightclub is what gives a club it's personality and creates appeal which can influence the clientele. A nightclub should have a concept, and the design should be built around and support that concept.

The design should also reflect upon the location that nightclub is operated in and customers must be able to relate to it. For example, one theme or design and decor may work well in one part of the world but in another location, in a completely different environment, the same design and decor may not work well at all. Colors play a big part in this phenomenon. Colors and tones can influence moods and enhance the atmosphere that is created. Think carefully about your color selections and make colors work with the design.

When making the important decisions regarding the style and design of your club address the following basic questions, which will make the process a little easer:

- **Who are your customers?:** This is the most important question you'll have to answer. Not only as it relates to the design but to many other aspects of the nightclub as well. There are a variety of nightclub patrons that fall into groups of different tastes, styles, wants and needs. You'll need to define which group of patrons you wish to draw in before you make any definite decisions about the design of the nightclub.

- **What will customers expect?:** Again, because there are many different groups of patrons, expectations will differ. If you know your clientele, you'll have a firm grasp on what they will expect when they walk into your business.

> THE DESIGN OF A NIGHTCLUB IS WHAT GIVES A CLUB IT'S PERSONALITY AND CREATES APPEAL, WHICH CAN INFLUENCE THE CLIENTELE.

- **What kind of image do you want project?**: Image is everything! The design helps to project a desired concept by creating an image. Images and concepts are often the same things. The design and layout inside a nightclub, won't create an image but they'll play a role in enhancing one.

- **Where will your nightclub be located?**: The size and location should cause you to give some consideration when determining a design. The design should agree with the area it's established in.

- **How will your design identify with your location?**: The areas or locations that people go to are normally consistent with their lifestyles. In other words, if you design an upscale, glamourous nightclub in a poorly maintained or run down area of town, you probably won't draw in the clientele you wish to cater to.

THEMES AND CONCEPTS

A design should revolve around a theme or a concept. These are the impressions that a nightclub propels. A theme or concept can be anything and everything but should be acceptable to the target clientele in order to work. An example of a theme/concept would be that of a nightclub that places an emphasis on pirates. Maybe the employees are in uniforms/costumes that resemble pirates. The menus are even construed in a way that drinks and foods suggest something about pirates, ships or the high seas in their descriptions. The design would be laid out to stimulate and enhance images of pirates, ships, swords, eye patches and so forth. All of this creates a certain feeling for the customers and is a powerful method of influence.

The most common theme or concept venues are sports bars. Sports bars obviously promote sports and rely heavily upon sports enthusiasts to frequent these bars. Every attempt should be made with all concepts to design the nightclub accordingly. It would be difficult to try and run a sports bar, for example, that doesn't look, feel or conjure up images of sports— regardless of anything else or of what employees might be doing to try and create that mood or those images. It just won't work which is why the design is so important.

CREATE SPACES

It's no longer possible to open a large nightclub with wide-open spaces. Open spaces are very uncomfortable and don't provide guests the opportunity of privacy and intimacy. This is a big issue for modern nightclubs because people must be able to have conversations with each other and not feel that everyone else is listening. Spaces also allow guests to avoid high traffic areas so that they are not constantly being bombarded by others.

Spaces can be created a number of ways. Simple placement of furniture can establish traffic routes which can alleviate the traffic from other areas which can cause small spaces to be originated. Multiple room or multiple floor venues can also create the feelings of spaces. Rooms and floors can divide the crowd which causes doorways and stairways to become high traffic areas, which can relieve other areas from being congested with traveling customers. This allows customers to relax away from those areas and can increase personal spaces.

> SIMPLE PLACEMENT OF FURNITURE CAN ESTABLISH TRAFFIC ROUTES WHICH CAN ALLEVIATE THE TRAFFIC FROM OTHER AREAS WHICH CAN CAUSE SMALL SPACES TO BE ORIGINATED.

BIGGER ISN'T NECESSARILY BETTER

How large a club you establish is up to you but just remember that size isn't everything. Just because you open a nightclub that can handle 3000 guests at a time doesn't necessarily mean that you'll pack the house every night with that many guests. If it's too big and not enough guests come in on a regular basis, the emptiness will give the appearance of it being a slow nightclub even if 600-800 guests are typically there. The visual appearance of it being slow or empty can influence guests and sometimes make them think it may be busier elsewhere.

The bigger a venue is, the more work there is to do and more employees are required to maintain it and serve customers. Mega venues are also much harder to make comfortable through design and layout and require a lot of money to get it right. Nightclub guests need smaller spaces to relax and socialize in, which means that much time will be needed to properly design hundreds of little spaces throughout a mega club.

This isn't to suggest that it's not possible to operate a large club, just that it demands much more attention to detail, money, time and planning to make it worthwhile. If one can pull it off and maintain the club and fill it to capacity every weekend, the profits can be enormous. That in itself is a tremendous task, which is why most operators opt for a small or medium sized venue. Medium sized venues can still pack in thousands of people and are a little more realistic to have to deal with. Even a small operation, can have a longer life span than a mega club, simply because smaller clubs are much easier to make customers feel at home and relaxed, on top of being easier to run and manage. Most operators will have a much greater chance of success with a small or medium sized venue.

Typical sizes for nightclubs fall into three measures; small, medium and large. The general rule of thumb is 100 square feet per 10 people. But, don't make the mistake of thinking that just because you have 5000 square feet to work with that you'll be able to accommodate 500 people. Keep in mind that layout features such as the bar or a dance floor will take up considerable space, which will decrease your overall, usable space in which people can actually occupy.

These are the usual dimensions for the three *nightclub sizes:*

- **Small:** Usually considered a nightclub that can handle less than 250 people and is anywhere between 2600 and 4000 square feet.

- **Medium:** Accommodates between 500 and 2500 guests at a time. Square feet for medium sized nightclubs range from 5500 and 15000 square feet.

- **Large:** These are massive and rare nightclubs that are built to handle more than 2500 guests and are 15,000 upwards to 40,000 square feet in size.

COSTS CONSIDERATIONS

Obviously the more space you deal with the more money it will cost to purchase it or rent in lease agreements. Buying property will shoot start-up costs to $50,000 to well over $100,000, depending on the condition and location of the property. Leasing on the other hand is no different from paying rent for an apartment. The rent payments are an expense and no equity is built up. Leasing commercial property could cost as little as $1100 a month to as much as $10,000 a month depending on the venue size and property location.

You'll have to carefully consider which option you choose to go with. Most operators get off the ground by entering into a lease simply because leases minimize costs even if required to post a large security deposit and make necessary renovations beforehand. Try to bargain a lease so that the owner pays for any repairs that are needed prior to signing the lease. If you have to make repairs on your own, you'll be more or less fixing up the property for the owner and will still have no vested interest in the property. Depending on what your long-term goals are, also consider asking for an option to buy the property after a certain period of years, especially if you will put a lot of money into the building itself. If the owner agrees, make sure he takes the property off the market so that no one other than you has the opportunity to buy it.

Whichever option you choose, make sure that you fully understand all the costs that are involved and write the costs into your business plan. Your plan should also add in the costs of designing and laying out the particular property and any fees, such as repairs or renovations, that'll be needed after you acquire the property and begin set up and begin operations.

DECORATIONS

The way your customers feel can be dominated by decorative creativeness. Decorative pieces, such as pictures, paintings, railings, furniture, collages, aquariums, memorabilia, lights and other creative assortments serve to enhance design and theme features even further. Decorations make statements and are visual references for the clientele which helps to provide an identity for a nightclub. Decorations are a part of a nightclub and give it energy by setting an atmosphere.

WHEN PEOPLE GO TO NIGHTCLUBS, THEY EXPECT TO ENJOY THEMSELVES AND HAVE EXPERIENCES THEY WOULDN'T ORDINARILY HAVE. IN ORDER TO MAKE THEIR STAYS INTERESTING OR UNIQUE, EXPOSE THEM TO CREATIVE DECORATIONS TO CATCH THEIR EYES AND TO HELP INSTILL A POSITIVE MOOD WITHIN THEM.

When people go to nightclubs, they expect to enjoy themselves and have experiences they wouldn't ordinarily have. In order to make their stays interesting or unique, expose them to creative decorations to catch their eyes and to help instill a positive mood within them.

You can also control where people will pool by properly placing decorations. By enhancing areas with decorations, people will tend to congregate around those areas (without realizing it), which can help to clear them from pathways, doorways, seating areas and other areas you don't want large crowds to gather.

EQUIPMENT CONSIDERATIONS

All designs will have to incorporate the equipment. Placement for equipment such as the sound system's speakers or televisions must not be taken lightly. Equipment location will affect decisions made about the final design, layout and decorations. If done correctly, the equipment will flow smoothly with the ultimate product. The goal is to make the equipment part of the design and not to appear as if it's out of place.

The unique problem with speakers is the sound emissions from them. Therefore, where the speakers end up is a critical decision. Music should be focused toward the dance floor to provide a maximum level of excitement for the dance crowd. But, the music should still be loud enough to fill the rest of the nightclub so that other customers can enjoy it without it being so loud they can't hear themselves think or have to yell to carry on a conversation with someone else standing right next to them.

For multiple room or floor venues the problem gets even more tricky if some rooms or floors have different themes and play different music. Speaker placement and sound projection should be contained within the area or room that the music is played from so that noise doesn't spill into the next room or floor.

Other equipment considerations include heat, air conditioning, air purification and ventilation systems. These are all comfort issues and being comfortable is what nightclubs are all about. The larger a venue is, the harder it may be to control the atmosphere. Access to fresh air is important to most guests even if they don't realize it. People won't like being too cold or too hot and won't appreciate breathing in a lot of cigarette smoke. That means that the placement of these systems will have to be considered into the design to control the environment all throughout the club.

Lastly, consider also the placement of equipment such as lights and special effects. On the dance floor, these are very entertaining pieces of equipment which help to make the customers' experiences that much better. But, what about the guests who aren't on the dance floor? They still appreciate lights and light shows to entertain them. Incorporate special lighting effects in various places, not just on the dance floor, to expose everyone to dazzling lights. Don't over do it because too many lights can become annoying. The goal should be to use light effects to enhance areas to bring out the nightclub feeling in everyone.

KEEP A CLEAN HOUSE

Keeping a nightclub clean and presentable to the guests is very much a day to day operation. Professional establishments cannot strive without a clean operation. Cleanliness or the lack of it says a lot about a nightclub to customers. Customers inside of a dirty club will feel uncomfortable and probably won't stay long. However, customers inside of a clean nightclub will stay longer and eventually spend more money and return at a later date.

Establish several cleaning procedures that employees are responsible for on a routine basis. The cleaning habits of the employees must be overseen and adhered to or else the routines won't be done properly or when they're supposed to.

Good cleaning regiments also promote a hygienic nightclub. We live in a world full of all types of viruses, diseases and bacteria and people are hosts to most of them. When people come together, like in a nightclub setting, bacteria can run wild throughout a place.

Knowing that, it's important to properly sanitize to prevent biological contaminants from running rampant throughout a nightclub and make the nightclub a healthy place for the general public.

Cleaning is a never-ending task that must be performed without hesitation. Always stress the importance of cleaning to employees and encourage them to do it often. Even when it's not busy at all there will always be something that should be wiped down, swept, trashed or washed. When an employee is standing around doing nothing, send them out to find something to clean and if they look, they'll come across something that needs some attention.

Follow these cleaning suggestions at a minimum to keep your nightclub at a first-class establishment status. The following are general suggestions so modify them to meet the cleaning objectives within your operation.

THE KITCHEN

All of the kitchen or food service employees need to take great care when handling food, for obvious reasons. Food is extremely susceptible to disease organisms. Improper sanitation and poor food handling techniques could actually cause an epidemic. As an operator, you couldn't buy worse PR if you had to. Proper training and supervision of your kitchen employees will give them a clear understanding of the importance of sanitation in their work spaces.

• **Stainless Steel Equipment and Surfaces** — At all times the kitchen staff should keep these areas free from contaminants because these are the main areas of food prep. Wipe down all surfaces using sanitation products and keep them clean with a routine cleansing throughout a shift.

- **Refrigerators** — Keep both the exterior and interior of the refrigerator free from debris. Do not allow corrosion to build up on any surface inside or outside of the refrigerator. Follow a weekly schedule that involves removing all items from the refrigerator so that it can be thoroughly cleaned. If you don't, it's possible that mold may build up in area that you can't see and that could raise some health issues with the foods that are stored there and ultimately served.

- **Cooking, Eating Utensils and Tableware Equipment** — A good automatic dishwasher is usually enough to keep plates, bowls, pots, pans, forks, knifes, spoons and so on, sanitized and ready for service. Prior to placing items inside of a dishwasher, they should undergo a rinsing process that removes most of the debris from them. Doing this relieves stress on the dishwasher and increases the likelihood of the utensils being completely cleaned after the dishwashing cycle. Monitor the dishwasher and make sure that it is washing at the correct temperatures and that the proper sanitizing solutions are being used in all washes.

- **Floors** —The floors in the kitchen are both a sanitation issue and one of safety. Restaurant kitchen floors easily accumulate grease. Over-accumulation of grease without adequate clean-up procedures could result in an employee slipping and falling. If this occurs, the nightclub could be held civilly liable for any injuries the employee suffered. Kitchen floors should be thoroughly cleaned at the end of each night. Mopping and hosing the floors are both effective ways to do it. After cleaning the floors, don't forget to have an employee set out the *"wet floor"* sign to notify others that the floor is wet and that they should use caution.

- **Griddles, Fryers, Ovens and Broilers** —The main purpose for cleaning these very important pieces of kitchen equipment is to preserve their quality. Very dirty griddles, fryers, ovens and broilers can affect cooking times and the quality of the foods they cook.

There are many models and brands to choose from but each will come with a manufacturer's suggested cleaning routine. Establish a schedule that states how often these cookers will be thoroughly cleaned to remove the excesses of food and particle build-ups that'll plaque them.

> ASIDE FROM BEING THE MOST VISIBLE LOCATION, THE BAR EXPERIENCES HEAVIER FOOT TRAFFIC THAN OTHER AREAS.

THE BAR

Aside from being the most visible location, the bar experiences heavier foot traffic than other areas. The bar needs to be kept clean and presentable at all times. Also, because the bar is where drinks are prepared for human consumption, some simple sanitation measures need to be taken to ensure that bartenders are serving not only quality drinks, but ones that won't transmit diseases and make customers ill.

* **Drawers, Cabinets and Containers** — Clean these areas routinely. These are areas that normally contain foods/garnishments or liquor inventory. Keep them free from contaminants like dust and other non-productive obstructions. Properly clean all garnish containers as you would any other cooking utensil or tableware item.

* **Draft and Dispensing Systems** — Cleaning both of the these systems is important. They deliver the beer, soda, soda water or just plain old water into the glasses that customers will drink from. Clean dispensing equipment by wiping and soaking the dispensing heads with soda water. Also carefully wipe and clean the couplers and racks with soda water. Decide on a thorough cleaning schedule which involves bringing in a professional to clean the soda and beer lines. Do not do this yourself. With the draft system, also hire a professional to thoroughly clean the draft lines and draft equipment. Routine cleaning that bartenders can do on the draft system is to wipe down the faucets and pour hot water down the drains on a daily basis.

- **Refrigerators and Ice bins** — Routinely wipe the outer surfaces of both pieces of equipment. With ice bins, remove the ice with the ice scoop only to clean the interior. Remove the shelves and drawers inside the refrigerator daily. Wipe down the inside walls as well as the rest of the refrigerator. Thoroughly clean the shelves and the drawers with an appropriate cleanser. Your emphasis on cleaning refrigerators and ice bins should be placed on the prevention or the removal of corrosion.

- **Drinkware** — All beverages should be served in properly sanitized glasses or mugs without exception. Develop a system for cleaning drinkware quickly so that they can be used over and over in a night. No matter how busy it gets, see to it that your bartending and bar back staff isn't inadequately cleaning the drinkware with quick rinses. At times it may be tempting for the bartenders or bar backs to cheat in order to get drinkware ready as quickly as possible to be used. Several drinkware cleaning systems or equipment exists to the job. Make sure that whichever cleaning system you utilize, the drinkware is being washed and rinsed at the proper temperatures with the appropriate amounts of sanitation solutions.

- **Counter tops, Bar Surfaces and Stainless Steel** — Cleaning surfaces is a non-stop activity performed by bartenders during their entire shifts. Keeping counter tops, the bar and other hard surfaces clear of unsightly and dirty debris is almost enough all by itself to keep bartenders busy all day long. Emptying dirty ashtrays, removing empty glasses, napkins and other trash that people leave behind has to be done. A customer may not appreciate sitting at a bar cluttered with trash and might not stay long. Arm bartenders with bar towels and they'll get plenty used as the bartenders work to keep the bar and other surfaces shiny and presentable.

- **Garnishes and Cutting Surfaces** — If you went to the supermarket and picked up some strawberries, you would thoroughly rinse them before you ate them wouldn't you? It's no different inside of a nightclub when it comes to serving fruits and vegetables in cocktails. Keep the cutting boards and knives clean. Properly store fruits and vegetable that aren't being used inside of the refrigerator to preserve them and keep them from any bacteria that might be floating around.

THE FLOOR

Leave the responsibility to cleaning the "floor area" or "common area" to the wait staff. The floor is more or less their environment and as such they spend more time on it with the guests. During the performances of their jobs, they should be taking notice of areas and equipment that will require cleaning to keep customers cozy.

- **Carpet and Hard Floors** — Floors take a heavy beating from customers and need to be well maintained to project a clean image. Vacuuming carpeted floors should be a routine that's performed at the end of every night. Carpet can often be the breeding grounds for all kinds of airborne diseases and because of that proper cleaning is a preventative measure. Vacuuming also helps to preserve the physical appearance of carpet by removing dirt, cigarette ashes, small trash particles and everything else that might find its way onto the floor. Hard floors will require sweeping and probably a routine of waxing and buffing in order to keep up a good appearance.

- **Windows** — Use a good window cleaner and remove smudges and other undesirable markings from all of the windows. This should be done at least once a day, at the beginning or the end of a business day.

- **Tables and Chairs** — Wipe off all tables and the chairs too, if needed, after they've been used even if they don't look too dirty. Empty out used ashtrays even if they aren't full, arrange the salt or pepper shakers and any advertising the way they're supposed to look on the tables. Clean tables are a must, especially for a food crowd in a nightclub/restaurant establishment. You yourself would be dissatisfied if you went to a restaurant and had to sit a table that wasn't clean and saw remnants of food and trash from the last person who sat there.

- **Restrooms** — This is a dreaded and sometimes disgusting job that no one likes to do. The restrooms are areas in which customers obviously relieve themselves, wash up and sometimes even vomit in. Nightclub/restaurant venues may choose to go with separate cleaning schedules for the restrooms. One during the day or restaurant hours where the restrooms are checked and cleaned on an hourly basis. The second schedule is during the evening where the restroom is cleaned after the close of business. During a busy evening, getting into and cleaning the restrooms will probably be an impossible task. Prior to every evening, the restrooms should be stocked with enough paper towels to serve customers through the night. Proper restroom cleaning involves cleaning the floors, sinks, faucets, mirrors, walls, stools, urinals, paper towel dispensing equipment and the exteriors and interiors of toilet stalls.

- **Light Equipment** — Lights and lighting fixtures normally will only require routine dusting. The wait staff should be careful not to touch any bulbs with their bare hands because human oils can greatly decrease the lifespan of the light bulbs. The key to cleaning the lights is to remove the dirt and dust that will accumulate on them. Dirt and dust just like human oils, can shorten the lives of light bulbs.

If profits and payroll allow it, consider hiring an after-hours janitor or a cleaning service to thoroughly clean the entire nightclub or night-club/restaurant after closing. Janitors and cleaning services are only paid to do one job, clean. They aren't distracted as easily as the bartending and wait staff may be when the ends of their shifts arrive. Janitors and cleaning services are usually focused on the task that you specifically pay them for and do a very good job at it.

If you don't hire a professional cleaning staff and decide to leave the burden to your regular employees, make sure that they are properly trained in what they have to clean, when they have to clean and why they have to clean. Cleaning should be stressed at all times and employees should feel that it is a major part of their jobs.

Supervision should follow up with training. Cleaning schedules should be strictly adhered to and you should make sure that employees are doing it right and when they're supposed to. The end of the shift is often the point in which employees who work late are ready to go home. They'll often work fast and try to cut corners in order to leave as soon as possible. Your policy should indicate that no employee is allowed to end his or her shift until their areas of cleaning responsibilities are inspected and approved. Doing that can eliminate the cutting of corners because the employees will know that they have to do a good job in order to leave.

> THE END OF THE SHIFT IS OFTEN THE POINT IN WHICH EMPLOYEES WHO WORK LATE ARE READY TO GO HOME. THEY'LL OFTEN WORK FAST AND TRY TO CUT CORNERS IN ORDER TO LEAVE AS SOON AS POSSIBLE. YOUR POLICY SHOULD INDICATE THAT NO EMPLOYEE IS ALLOWED TO END HIS OR HER SHIFT UNTIL THEIR AREAS OF CLEANING RESPONSIBILITIES ARE INSPECTED AND APPROVED.

THE LAYOUT

PROPER FLOOR PLANNING CREATES
AN EFFICIENT NIGHTCLUB

Properly laying out the floor includes deciding on issues such as where to place the bars, coat rooms and so on to keep everything running smoothly and efficiently. A good layout will control and create pathways, make it easier for customers to access the bars, dance floors, seating areas and will make the jobs of the wait staff much easier. The bottom line is that a good layout plan will create an efficient flow of traffic as customers and employees travel and create spaces where people can engage in conversations, keep bottlenecks to a minimum and provide space for special activities.

The layout will also determine a total occupancy rating or capacity, because arrangement of rooms and areas can increase or decrease the total capacity. A poor layout will without a doubt reduce the areas in which customers can occupy. The goal should be to create as much space as possible to accommodate as many guests as possible in a comfortable manner. A poor layout plan can cause the following to occur:

- Bottlenecks.

- Inability of the room to move around freely.

- Overcrowding in major pathways, such as the front door.

- Long lines to the restrooms, which flow into a main area.

- Poor alcohol sales on a very busy night.

- Poor employee efficiency; waitresses have a hard time getting to and from the bars and customers.

- Complete chaos; Large crowds are unable to move at all.

THE BAR

The main bar should be strategically placed so that it is one of the first sights people see once they walk through the doors. The main bar amazingly eases any tensions that customers may bring with them and provides them with a direction to travel to. Make sure you have plenty of bar tenders to cope with them and get them served quickly to close the sale. When they first get there, they better not have to wait an extended period of time or they just may leave. The bar should be easy to access from several different directions of travel so that customers don't bottleneck in long lines to get to there.

The size and look of the main bar gives a certain style to a nightclub. There are many ways to design a bar, but all designs should allow for both customer and employee efficiency. The bar area takes up a lot of space and is a common area where people congregate, so make sure that not only is it easily accessible, but that its laid out in a way to cope with many people so that overcrowding doesn't spill into others area.

ADDITIONAL BARS

If you are building or buying a building with plenty of space or has multiple floors or rooms, building two or more bars is a good idea.

Additional bars carefully placed allow easy access for customers, because no matter where they are, there's always a bar nearby. If you plan to open a large nightclub and only have one main bar, expect to lose out on many alcohol sales because few customers will wait in a long line or tread through a large crowd, if there is one, to get a drink. You'll find that customers will either wait for a waitress, leave or go without. Either action could cost money.

Additional bars do not have to be as large or as elaborate as the main bar but of course it doesn't hurt if you can afford it. Your secondary bars simply serve as satellite bars to decrease the distance your patrons must travel to give you more money. They lessen the burden placed on the main bar and to the waitresses and waiters—who'll hopefully be very busy anyway. The less-load the main bar carries, the more they can cater to those just arriving in the bar and serve them quicker. The waitresses

> ADDITIONAL BARS CAREFULLY PLACED ALLOW EASY ACCESS FOR CUSTOMERS, BECAUSE NO MATTER WHERE THEY ARE, THERE'S ALWAYS A BAR NEARBY.

and waiters will benefit from the decrease in demand and will actually become more efficient and will have more time for interaction with each and every customer they serve.

The customers' relationship with waitresses and waiters is very important and can actually help to establish an ambiance for a club. Who wants to go to a nightclub where the staff doesn't have any time to socialize because they are constantly on the go? This business of owning a nightclub is all about socializing and interaction.

BEER ISLANDS/TUBS

This is an excellent way to maximize alcohol sales. By placing small beer islands, or tubs filled ice and bottled beer in key locations, many customers passing by will impulsively approach and order drinks from the employees manning the stations.

Prime locations for beer tubs are next to highly traveled pathways, such as the front door, entrances to rooms, stairways and near the dance floors.

DJ BOOTH

The DJ booth is a very popular place for guests to hang out. Because of that, consideration must be given to the booth's position to prevent too many people crowding the area. Locate booths in areas opposite main rooms, which are not likely to be overcrowded and spill into other crucial areas, such as intimate spaces. The DJ should also be set up to have an unimpeded view of the main area so that he can view what's happening.

DANCE FLOORS

The majority of bars, especially very small ones, do not have a dance floor and that's all right. Small bars can do just fine without one. The patrons who visit those small bars usually find a corner or an isle to dispense their energy and move to the music.

If your establishment will have a dance floor, make sure that it'll be large enough to accommodate many guests at a time. The floor should be deep inside the club, but if possible, should be able to be seen from the front door. People entering should see others dancing and having a good time. That view will serve to reinforce their reason for being there and encourage them even more to enter and head for the bar.

Inside some clubs, the dance floor is the first thing you see when you walk into the inside. As a matter of fact, you have to walk through the dance floors just to get into the place. Some customers don't have a problem with this but some do. If all one sees when they walk into a bar is a bunch of dancing bodies, he or she may get the impression that the place is too packed and may move onto the next hot spot. Yet, others may see the action and say to themselves, "this place is hopping!" Why not place the dance floor in a visible place, away from the front doors, where people entering the club can see the entire main area? If the place is hopping, people in the mood to dance are coming in anyway. The other customers, who may not be in a dancing mood just then, won't have to worry about pushing their way through the dance crowd and then locating the main bar.

Locating a dance floor within your nightclub should be a balancing act between placing it close enough to allow easy access for all and keeping it far enough away from the main floor so that dancing doesn't flood into those guests who aren't dancing. Be reasonable, don't over-build a dance floor and eliminate much needed space. And, make sure not to under build it either—There's nothing worse than people packed back to back on the dance floor and others seeing that they can't get on the floor because it's too small—You might lose some business as a result. Raising or sinking the dance floor can also help to separate it from the rest of the main floor and prevent dancers from spilling onto the main floor and vice versa.

FURNITURE
Tables, chairs and furniture say a lot about a club. Believe it or not the condition, style and look of your tables and chairs reflect greatly upon a club. Nightclubs that have shoddy chairs, half of them broken, say to patrons that the nightclub is run down and not well maintained. If it comes to your attention that a chair, table or any piece of equipment is broken, you should immediately fix or replace it. If you don't, over time the amount of broken furniture or equipment will only accumulate and you'll be faced with a much greater problem of fixing or replacing everything at once— if you decide to address the problem at all. If you choose to do nothing, you'll force patrons to put up with the chairs that when sat in, feel as if they could break apart at any moment or make them sit at those tables that rock back and forth. Both are annoying to customers. Remember you are attempting to provide a casual and relaxing atmosphere, and broken furniture is counter productive.

Another common problem is not enough chairs or tables to handle the clientele. When designing the layout of your nightclub, you should know how many people on a good night the club can handle. Figure that if the place is jammed packed with happy customers, you will want seating for at least 70% of them at any time. Turnover with customers leaving and arriving should allow the other 30% to eventually be seated if they so choose.

Basically, if you plan on bringing in 200 guests at a time, then 140 of those guests should be able to find a seat and the other 60 will be left standing, dancing or enjoying the other features of your establishment.

Hopefully outbound traffic will be less than the incoming traffic. We'll discuss how to keep customers inside longer, once they arrive later on.

There are many different types and styles of bar chairs and tables. These can become very expensive as the quality of each increases. If you can afford to buy good quality tables and chairs then by all means do it. If you are opening a nightclub on a shoestring budget, and figure you can only afford to buy a dozen or so plastic chairs and tables, kind of like patio furniture, then do that also but definitely plan for the future and eventually phase those out as your revenues increase. Also attempt to make the tables and chairs fit into the scheme of your nightclub. If planning on a small operation with limited, loyal guests, where everyone knows everyone else, then this isn't so important. But if you are opening an upscale nightclub, then you better have upscale furniture to go with it or it won't work. This is also common sense.

Placement of furniture should be given consideration because furniture can cause certain areas to be filled with customers, pathways to be created and can help to separate seating areas from other areas. Mindfully place furniture so that too much space isn't taken away from where they end up when people start using and congregating around them.

BEER GARDENS ARE VERY POPULAR AREAS, WHEN THE WEATHER IS GOOD, THAT ALLOW CUSTOMERS TO ENJOY THEMSELVES OUTSIDE OF A NIGHTCLUB WITHIN A CONTAINED AREA.

BEER GARDENS

Beer gardens are very popular areas when the weather is good, that allow customers to enjoy themselves outside of a nightclub within a contained area. Typically, furniture and decorations are the only things inside of beer gardens and so they are primarily seating areas, which means that there is little foot traffic. That makes these areas that much more relaxing for guests. Beer gardens can be built in front, in back or beside a nightclub. Either of those locations will serve customers well.

THE STAGE

Stages provide a platform for a nightclub to be diverse in the forms of activities it provides. Special events, contests and live acts can all take place on stage. The stage can take up a lot of space so plan accordingly. Be sure to place it so that the action can be easily seen by all customers in the same room or else they may become a little let down if they can't view what's going on because of where they're at.

Many clubs make use of the dance floor and have it double as the stage, during special events. This is okay but again, it should be located in an area that is easy to see from just about anywhere in the room. For dance floors that are level with the floor or sunken below it, it is usually difficult for all customers to see unless they are in front. Raised dance floors work better because the action is elevated which allows it to be seen easier.

RESTROOMS

The need for restrooms should be easy to understand. Much detail won't be bothered with here because the relationship between your customers and the restroom is most important. Why? Obviously with all that alcohol you'll be serving, folks will need a quick place to relieve themselves every half hour or so. The size and number of restrooms should be carefully laid out in the planning phase. How many restrooms will you have? The answer to that question should be dependent upon the size of your nightclub and how many levels it has. Can you imagine being on the top floor inside a multi-level nightclub that only has two restrooms on the first floor, one for men and the other for women? Imagine having to walk all the way downstairs, through a crowd, and then having to wait in a line. Anyone who's been there knows it's no fun and it's especially annoying when you really have to go.

Sometimes, especially if your leasing a building, you won't have much choice where the restrooms are or how many there are. In these cases, do the best to lay out the floor area so that the restrooms are easy to locate and that foot traffic is diverted away from them to prevent crowding.

This is common sense, but you'd be surprised, how many businesses fail to do this—*Put signs on your restrooms!* MEN for men and WOMEN for women. And, try to avoid unisex restroom facilities if possible because they only brew trouble.

NIGHTCLUB/RESTAURANT LAYOUT

The kitchen is a very important part for nightclub/restaurant operations. Kitchens should be far away from view but yet easily accessible for your waitresses and waiters. There's no reason to put the kitchen in the middle of your nightclub and layout the club around it. That would be a tremendous waste of space. A good kitchen location is one where no one is exactly sure where it is, but know there's one somewhere.

Always keep in mind that socializing is the primary reason that anyone will come to your place. So, unlike many restaurants, food preparation is something that should be kept out of view from your patrons. Customers will know whether or not you serve food, and if they're hungry, they're going to ask for a menu. It's recommended that the kitchen is laid out so that once an order is prepared by cooks, waiters or waitresses must actually walk into the kitchen and get that order rather than a completed order being placed onto a counter top in a little window between the main bar area and the kitchen.

During food service hours, seating areas is a concern and should be set up to allow as many seated guests as possible. Don't worry about trying to seat everyone. If you have to, make a waiting line. Customers won't mind waiting a few minutes for good food and drinks. The wait will be part of their experience.

ALWAYS KEEP IN MIND THAT SOCIALIZING IS THE PRIMARY REASON THAT ANYONE WILL COME TO YOUR PLACE. SO, UNLIKE MANY RESTAURANTS, FOOD PREPARATION IS SOMETHING THAT SHOULD BE KEPT OUT OF VIEW FROM YOUR PATRONS. CUSTOMERS WILL KNOW WHETHER OR NOT YOU SERVE FOOD, AND IF THEY'RE HUNGRY, THEY'RE GOING TO ASK FOR A MENU.

CREATE AMBIANCE WITH LIGHTS

LIGHTS SET THE MOOD

The main lights inside a nightclub or bar should be used sparingly. Lights, like many other things, play an important role in establishing an overall mood. Too bright and patrons may have a difficult time relaxing. Too dark and, they can't see the person across the table from them. Find a middle ground and make them feel comfortable. The idea with lighting is to not only make customers feel comfortable, but to make them feel so comfortable, that they lose track of time.

Coincidentally, the number of or lack of windows and clocks that customers can use to reference time also enhances the sensation of lost time. Windows and clocks are issues that should be addresses during the design phase of your club. Windows are kind of like a double-edged sword. They allow people on the outside to look in and see what's going on. Many decisions as to enter or leave, are made from what people see from the outside looking in. If the place is hopping, it usually results in an easy decision for customers to enter and if it's not, they may leave. This works the same way from the inside, especially for operations that are set up near competition within eyesight of each other.

SET THE MOOD WITH PROPER LIGHTING

It's amazing how many people go out to a nightclub or bar with the intention of only having one drink or even two before calling it quits and going home. Once these people arrive, time passes and the next thing they know they've been there for hours and ordering their eight or ninth drink. The reason this happens is a combination of several things. One being good drinks, another being customer satisfaction and the other is the ability of your guests to lose themselves and forget about all of their worries and stresses. Lights play a tremendous role in this entire process.

Lighting effects can add an impeccable touch to any room or theme concept. The moods that lights can create serve to encourage customers to stay longer and ultimately spend more, which amounts to more profits for you. Lights are a very subtle way of treating customers right. Customers probably aren't going to realize it and say to themselves, "I really like the lighting here," but the simple truth is that proper lighting will make everyone feel more at home.

Lights are so powerful that they control the environment and help to give each nightclub an identity. Sometimes the design of how lights are arranged on a ceiling is enough to set one club apart from another. Many clubs are able to use lights to create or accent themes and the way that some particular lights reflect or bend to create effects, can influence peoples' moods.

Although lights can do a lot of things, all by themselves they may not be enough to magically draw in customers, but they certainly have a way of telling people how they should feel or act. If you don't believe it, how do you explain closing time? Probably every nightclub in existence, brightens the lighting during closing time. The sudden

> LIGHTING EFFECTS CAN ADD AN IMPECCABLE TOUCH TO ANY ROOM OR THEME CONCEPT. THE MOODS THAT LIGHTS CAN CREATE SERVE TO ENCOURAGE CUSTOMERS TO STAY LONGER AND ULTIMATELY SPEND MORE, WHICH AMOUNTS TO MORE PROFITS FOR YOU.

increase from dark to bright during a closing, informs people that it's closing time and thanks for their business. The brighter light can quickly change even the most relaxed of moods by making the environment uncomfortable to be in, thus, sending a message that it's time to go.

USE LIGHT DIMMERS

Every light inside your nightclub should be connected and controlled by a dimmer switch. Dimmers afford you with more versatility by allowing you to take control of the lighting situation at any given time. During the early part of an evening and during prime hours of food sales, you'll probably need lighting that's just a little bit brighter. When the social crowd moves in later on in an evening, you will definitely want to decrease the lighting to give the impression that your club is warm and inviting to all that enter.

Dimmers let you adjust the lights to every situation. Often, the proper light settings will be determined by your feel for the room or the attitudes that your customers bring in on a given night. When it comes to attitudes, people in a community often reflect similar, overall moods. These moods are often set in motion by influences outside of a nightclub. Example, if your nightclub where set up and run in Minnesota and shortly after the Minnesota Vikings won the Superbowl, your nightclub experienced a rush of highly enthusiastic, excited patrons and sales began flying through the roof! These patrons would be in the mood to party hard and would want to go on all night long. In this example, you would go with the flow, so to speak, and work off the moods that are already flourishing. Since you know that low lighting has a tendency to relax people, why dim them and spoil an upbeat mood?

With dimmers, you can always find that perfect setting. The flip side to dimmers, are the conventional on/off switches which have two obvious setting— on or off, leaving operators with absolutely no real control over the lighting. To simply state the role of dimmer switches, use them to lower or brighten the lights until you find a setting which works best to subconsciously create or sustain moods within the club.

UV LIGHTING

UV, or ultraviolet lighting has been around for many years and the effects that UV light creates will never go away. UV lighting has many applications. Because UV has a unique effect in complete darkness, it can be used to highlight areas of a club, with just about any UV paint color, including invisible UV paint. Invisible UV paint can create two different rooms if an entire room is coated. One is when the lights are on and the other is when the lights are off. Invisible UV paint causes a highlighted or painted room to appear totally different in darkness.

One of the most common nightclub uses for UV lights are to accent people. Black UV light in complete darkness, has a one and only illuminating effect. Black light has an interesting fluorescent pigment that creates cool visual images.

USE LIGHT SYSTEMS TO CREATE SPECIAL EFFECTS

It's no secret that fantastic lights and special effects transform any club into a first class venue. There are a variety of effects that any operator can implement to enhance a nightclub's atmosphere. These effects often need to work together in unison to deliver a powerful impact. Lights and sounds all by themselves probably aren't going to magically sell more drinks, but they definitely serve to influence customer opinion and a good setup will cause repeat visits more often which in the long run is what you'll want.

Although most effects are focused on the dance floor, special effects are just as important away from it. For a dance crowd, special effects make it fun to be there. For the non-dancing crowd, visual effects can still make the experience much more interesting. No where is this more true than with stunning laser light shows. The spectacular brilliant shows that lasers create, for instance, are the bread and butter for many nightclub lighting effects as the entire club crowd is wide-eyed when the shows start and finish.

It's likely that if you plan to impress a crowd with light effects, you'll need various light and special effect setups to get the job done. Some lights help in their own ways to produce effects to influences peoples' emotions such as a special effects projector, which can show moving and color-changing psychedelic patterns on a wall or floor. Effects like a fogger which can fill the dance floor or entire club with harmless fog and reduce visibility also enhance special lighting experiences.

Consider hiring someone who is knowledgeable about a nightclub lighting system if you are going to open a brand-new club. Lights and special effects are too important and expensive to get wrong. A good lighting contractor should be able to properly install your light and special effects systems and configure them to work like they're supposed to. Proper installation, can also eliminate future problems such as electrical shorts or light/effect failures.

A nightclub consultant can also assist in determining the best places to install each light and light effects to maximize their performances. A consultant in this regard may be a little pricey but you'll get your money's worth and get the best out of your effects system.

DANCE FLOOR EFFECTS
Dance floor lights work together with the music to create a fun environment. Design a dance floor that not only has a superb, clean sound, but one that also has a life of its own with dazzling lights. Lights make any dance floor come alive and help to keep people dancing for longer periods of time. Lights on the dance floor make it fun to dance. They also have the ability to entice people onto the dance floor. Sometimes people need a little encouragement before they can open up and have a good time.

Think about it, a dance floor without a good light set up is just any old floor where people may or may not congregate. There will be little distinction made between a lightless dance floor and any other area within a nightclub. You can play all the greatest hits in the world, but without a good light setup to go with it, many customers will consider the dance floor a boring place to be.

There are dozens of special effect light manufacturers and hundreds of unique products between them. These manufacturers are constantly producing lights and effects to make the nightclub experience more enjoyable for guests. Contact as many manufacturers as you can and get brochures of their products. Compare the components and purchase what you need to deliver the effects and features that will work best for your club. A consultant should also be able to assist in this area to help you decide what is needed.

For now, familiarize yourself with the following common equipment. Keep in mind that there are many variations and products available but below are some of the basics you'll need to know about to get started.

EFFECT LIGHTS AND SCANNERS
These effects are designed to cover large areas. Effect lights and scanners can transform any venue into a metropolitan nightclub. Multiple beams of light and patterns are created by these types of components in dazzling light shows on and off the dance floor. There are many variations and designs which all do different things. Some effect lights spin, twist or rotate and send multiple beams of colored light in all directions. Some components are fixed and don't move at all but can be just as effective.

Many effect lights are usually no more than a colored image wheel inside of a component that rotates and projects an image onto the floor or wall. These effects usually come with extra image wheels that allow the user to change colors and images whenever desired. Scanners are very similar to both effect lights and laser lights and offer a lot more versatility and create brilliant, preprogrammed light shows.

Most components of these types can be programmed and synchronized to the sound of the music which gives them a cool visual effect. Some are even sound activated, meaning they do nothing until music is played. It is very common to sequence multiple lights together to cover huge areas. When this is done, the visual effects are awesome and the illusions of walls of lights are created. Effect lighting or scanners typically cost between $60-$600 each.

> EFFECT LIGHTS AND SCANNERS CAN TRANSFORM ANY VENUE INTO A METROPOLITAN NIGHTCLUB. MULTIPLE BEAMS OF LIGHT AND PATTERNS ARE CREATED BY THESE TYPES OF COMPONENTS IN DAZZLING LIGHT SHOWS ON AND OFF THE DANCE FLOOR.

SPECIAL EFFECT PROJECTORS

Projectors are often used to place multicolored, psychedelic patterns on the floor or walls. The patterns can rotate and change colors. The speed of the rotation and color changes can also be adjusted from fast to slow.

LIGHT COMPONENTS

GOBOS

These are similar to effect lights. Gobos projectors are great for projecting images or logos wherever you want them. On any wall, the floor or the ceiling. Gobos are excellent promotional platforms to send messages to customers. Project your nightclub's name, logo or even information about drink specials. They also support a wide variety of architectural applications to display large, detailed images such as themes for holidays: Christmas, Halloween, New Year's, etc. Gobos definitely capture the attention of customers and are worth serious consideration.

BEACONS

Simple yet effective. Police beacons are basically the same type of spinning lights that are seen on top of police cars. They spin around and around and project light in 360 degrees. Beacons come in three eye-catching colors; red, blue and amber. To liven up police beacons, use an air horn or a whailing or yelping siren with the beacons. Let the DJ use them to keep the guests on their feet. Beacon prices range from $5 to $70.

PINSPOTS

Miniature spotlights that can be used in a variety of ways to direct intense beams of light wherever they are needed. Every nightclub needs pinspots. Multiple pinspots can be used to create columns of very focused beams, almost like a laser. Individually, they can be used to focus on or highlight a promotional display or an area within a nightclub, like a doorway. If you use a mirror ball, you'll need one pinspot to shine on it so that the ball's reflective qualities take effect.

   Pinspots can also be fitted with various colored light filters (lenses) so that any color needed can be projected. Pinspots can be left on all night or used in conjunction with a controller to create a curtain of lights that are synchronized to the beat of the music.

HELICOPTERS
Helicopters are light structures which incorporate several pinspots into one large spinning lamp. The pinspot lamps on the helicopter can be adjusted individually to shine in different directions as colorful arrays of light swirl in circular motions.

STROBE LIGHTS
Strobes are among the most popular and common of all dance floor light effects. Strobe lights generate tremendously bright light that can flash on and off anywhere from 1-30 times a second depending on the brand or model. Many strobe lights also allow the user to adjust the intervals between the flashes to give greater control over the desired effects. The effects that strobes create are unmistakable as they give the impression that motion is slowed down. Strobe lights range in price anywhere from $12 to $400 a piece.

MIRROR BALLS
Mirror balls are nightclub classics and have been around for decades. They usually do little more than spin 360 degrees and reflect light outwards onto the dance floor in a revolving, mechanical manner. They are common ceiling sights that hover over the center of dance floors. Mirror balls come in several sizes and typically cost less than $100.

LASER LIGHTS
Customers will appreciate a dazzling array of multidirectional laser lights both on and off the dance floor. A good laser light system may be expensive, but will pay for itself time and time again. Laser lights are just another piece of equipment that will leave an imprint on the minds of your customers which always helps to make your nightclub stand out from the competition.

There are many different types of laser light devices and products and which each, you can do several different things. To get you started, here is a little information about three common nightclub laser systems:

Argon lasers are blue green in color and are very basic for general purpose beams of light to spruce up the dance floor. *Yag lasers* are nice setups that can be used to create complex drawings, beams, animation, text, liquid ceiling effects and more. Imagine how the promotions of putting your club name on a wall or delivering a massive light show in laser light would affect business.

The last type of laser light to discuss are the *White Light Lasers*. These lasers are the most beautiful and powerful of all. Unfortunately, the downfall to White Light Lasers is that they are inefficient and require a lot of power and water flow to keep cool but the mesmerizing special effects these lasers have are worth it.

Laser lights are notorious for setting dance moods and getting people to open up on the dance floor. Laser lights are known to give any club a distinct prestige. You may even consider designating a laser light show during a certain time of a given

> LASER LIGHTS ARE NOTORIOUS FOR SETTING DANCE MOODS AND GETTING PEOPLE TO OPEN UP ON THE DANCE FLOOR. LASER LIGHTS ARE KNOWN TO GIVE ANY CLUB A DISTINCT PRESTIGE.

evening. Customers appreciate a powerful laser light show and a good one quickly becomes the focal point in any venue.

Much like scanners or other effect lights, laser lights can be programmed or users can play the preset programs that come with most lasers on the market to deliver incredible light shows. They can also be synchronized to the beat of the music, sequenced with multiple laser components to enhance the visual effects even further or manually controlled by the DJ.

Laser lights used to be only for the elite nightclubs because the cost of owning a laser was incredibly high. Fortunately, recent technological breakthroughs have lowered the cost of owning a laser light system and make it affordable for almost any nightclub to get at least one to produce those disco effects every nightclub deserves. Simple laser systems now cost as low as $50. A fairly decent system will cost from $200-$600 and if you want the best, expect to pay $1000 on up.

EFFECT CONTROLLERS

Finally, effect controllers are a must-have for any nightclub that intends to dazzle customers with lights. Controllers allow all effects, lasers, pinspots, helicopters, scanners, strobes, gobos and more to be manipulated from the DJ booth. Without some way of controlling the light action, the lights would just do their own thing all night long. Effect controllers also allow the DJ to engage other effects such as fog machines or pyrotechnics. Those kind of effects can compliment light systems very well.

Many different models of DMX controllers are on the market and now controllers are better than ever. Most controllers are both lightweight and rugged to sustain heavy use. In addition, most are user-friendly and very easy to program. Today's effect controllers are extremely functional and allow for the programming of several projectors at a time and a good one will have preset light motion patterns. They also have increased memories to allow you to store a number of different light shows. The only thing the DJ needs to do is push a button and the selected show begins. Joysticks, keys and sliders can allow any light to be adjusted as needed from the booth, by turning, panning or tilting.

Basic controllers with limited capabilities range from $50-$300. If you want to pull out all the stops and really take control of an intelligent light system, an above average controller will cost $1000 and more.

OTHER SPECIAL EFFECTS

As briefly talked about before, other effects such bubbles, foam, mist, fog, pyrotechnics, confetti, streamer cannons and launchers all add a certain degree of fun and excitement to the floor. These effects are generally simple in nature and can quickly fill the floor with the desired effect. These effects work well with sound and lights and usually reduce visibility. The result becomes the center of attention for a dance crowd.

Recently, foam has become very popular in a number of nightclubs with younger patrons, especially college bars. The foam, as does mist, bubbles and fog, fills an entire area with thick water-based bubbles, the kind of bubbles similar to an overflowing washing machines. The foam becomes a giant area that people almost have to swim through. The foam itself becomes a source of entertainment as people immerse themselves and their friends in it.

Some special effect systems can be linked directly into an effects controller and others come with remote controls to allow the DJ to dispense the effect when it's needed on the floor.

BUILDING CUSTOMER RELATIONSHIPS

COMMUNICATION BUILDS LOYALTY

Establishing strong customer relationships is not only your job, but is the job of the entire staff and is something that must be done every day. Customers will appreciate the attention that you and your staff can give them. By making them feel more easy they'll know that their business is wanted. Most relationships between a club and customers will be established through the use of effective conversations. Talking to customers builds a stronger bond than any drink special or event could ever do.

GREET GUESTS
Take the time to say "hello." It only takes a moment. This is the chance to make a good impression. Greeting people is a personal experience and when possible, you and your staff should try to take the time to learn a customer's name. You might not remember it later on, but then again you might.

Greeting people and calling them by their names is the best way to show gratitude because people love being remembered. With regular customers, remembering their names is a little bit easier than remembering someone who has only visited once or twice in the past. Even if you don't know a customer's name, you can still make him or her feel welcomed with a warm reception. It doesn't have to be a long draw out process either. Simple salutations like, "How are you this evening?" Or "It's really good to see you," work amazingly well.

> TAKE THE TIME TO SAY "HELLO." IT ONLY TAKES A MOMENT. THIS IS THE CHANCE TO MAKE A GOOD IMPRESSION. GREETING PEOPLE IS A PERSONAL EXPERIENCE AND WHEN POSSIBLE, YOU AND YOUR STAFF SHOULD TRY TO TAKE THE TIME TO LEARN A CUSTOMER'S NAME. YOU MIGHT NOT REMEMBER IT LATER ON, BUT THEN AGAIN YOU MIGHT.

For bartenders and the wait staff, greeting customers is very important and can even increase sales. A bartender, waiter or waitress that greets a customer by name, remembers their favorite drink and has it ready before the customer even has to ask for it creates a strong bond between that particular customer and the nightclub.

When greeting customers, whether you know them or not, make sure that all of your greetings are personal, friendly and sincere. If you fall into the habit of greeting people in a robotic way, then that's the way it will come across and the purpose and importance of greeting guests will be lost.

ENGAGE IN CONVERSATIONS

No matter how busy you are, take a few seconds to have a conversation with a guest. This may become a tiring process but your hospitality will pay off big. A friendly atmosphere always prevails.

Instead of going through the motions whenever a guest orders a drink at the bar, why not briefly strike up a conversation. It doesn't have to be a long conversation. Your goal is to acknowledge the guest and let him or her feel like it's more than just business. You should care how their night is going so ask them about it. At the end of the conversation, proceed to serve that customer if you haven't already prepared the order during the conversation.

This kind of healthy interaction promotes more business by encouraging customers to stay longer and spend more. Many times if a customer has built up a rapport with a bartender or wait person that may influence their decision to stay and order another drink.

Always try to compliment guests during conversations and use words that convey gratefulness. When complimenting, try to avoid getting too personal unless you already know the customer because you might offend him or her. Avoid commenting about things that are none of your business. An example of this would be a man whom you've seen with two different women on the same night inside the nightclub. It's none of your business unless the man chooses to talk about it to you. Showing your appreciation to your customers for their business is easy. Using words like "thank you," or "please come back again soon," show customers that you care and respect them.

Take the time to go out and find customers just to speak with them. Stop by tables or groups of people and find out how they are doing. Let what's currently going on dictate the topic of the conversation that you'll engage in. You can also let the customers themselves choose the topic and go with it. For instance, if a group of male customers are there celebrating a bachelor party get involved with it and even offer the groom a complimentary free drink on the house. You can even take a situation like a bachelor party even further and let other guests know about the occasion through casual conversation.

Not only does talking to guests help to enhance relationships with them, but it also helps to uncover problems, suggestions and things that customers would like to do or see when they are patronizing your bar. You'll never find any of this out if you don't ask or talk to the guests. Many guests might tell you that they wish you had more special contests or live TV events, or whatever they need or want. You might learn that people are upset over drink specials or maybe even over a particular employee that they feel is rude or uncaring. Maybe, they are upset because there aren't enough dart boards or there is always at least an hour wait to play. They might want to see more wait staff because on busy nights they see that your current staff is undermanned and takes a longer time to be served.

Eventually, conversing with your customers will become very easy for both you and your staff. You won't even have to think about it because it will become a natural thing to do. You'll find that many customers will know you by name and seek you out to speak with you on occasion. You'll soon acquire a rather large mental data base of names and faces and will remember a great deal about each of customer.

PROMOTE INTERACTION BETWEEN GUESTS

Among the worst perceptions or reputations that a nightclub can have is that it is boring. One reason this may happen is because people might tend to keep to themselves, especially early in the evening. This can create a very quiet, *boring* atmosphere. Most people go out to nightclubs in order to meet people and socialize, but sometimes you may need to help your guests break the ice when they seem to be frozen.

Encouraging people to talk to each other by bringing them together can be done a number of different ways. Perhaps the best way is to take note of different guests' interest and conversational topics. Instead of engaging in a conversation with just one person at time, try standing between two people who don't know each other and engage in a conversation with both of them at the same time. Get the conversations flowing, then tactfully get both of them talking about the same thing. Essentially you would be including each of them in a mutual conversation with you. Once it's fluent, excuse yourself or quietly slip away from the two. Avoid appearing to force the two on each other, or the interaction will probably fail. Rather, let them do most of the work. Hopefully the interaction between the two will carry on for sometime. You never know, you might help to start new friendships or relationships.

> MOST PEOPLE GO OUT TO NIGHTCLUBS IN ORDER TO MEET PEOPLE AND SOCIALIZE, BUT SOMETIMES YOU MAY NEED TO HELP YOUR GUESTS BREAK THE ICE WHEN THEY SEEM TO BE FROZEN.

This method can also be used to bring two different parties of people together, although it's a little bit harder because parties usually socialize amongst themselves.

After helping two people or parties interact with each other, move onto the next guests who may need a little help breaking the ice. Your goal here is to get everyone in the entire nightclub talking and mingling, thus setting a positive and very social atmosphere.

MAKE CUSTOMERS COMFORTABLE

This is an everyday task that should be accomplished with pride. Customer satisfaction should be something that's at the top of your list of things-to-do every single day. Making customers feel comfortable and at home will seem like more of an art than a chore. It often comes down to the little things, like proper seating arrangements during a lunch crowd, or fine tuning the lighting and playing the appropriate music to set a certain mood.

Customers who feel comfortable stay for longer periods of time, spend more money and usually come back to do it all over again. Sometimes all it takes is switching the television to the right channel on a slow night to make them happy. Other situations may require more thought to figure out how to make them comfortable, such as making a design change. Putting in new carpet, moving furniture or remodeling a room are all examples of structural changes that can influence moods and make guests even more comfortable.

The point is that meeting the needs of your customers by providing an atmosphere that they can kick back and relax in is often easier said than done. The expectations that customers place on the nightclub industry are constantly changing and you'll need to do whatever it takes to please in order to maintain a favorable impression with your guests. Keeping customers comfortable is very much a managerial responsibility and your decisions can mean the difference between more sales and no sales.

Get the employees involved too. As a whole, they will have more contact with customers than you will. Teach them to be aware of the moods customers are in and let them take initiative and come up with solutions to solve problems when customers are uncomfortable. Sometimes you may be preoccupied with other business and may not notice such things like the temperature. Too hot or too cold is a very common complaint and employees had better realize that this sort of situation can be detrimental to business. They should know to bring problems like this to your attention so that immediate action can be taken.

HANDLING PROBLEMS

Problems will show themselves in many different ways in a nightclub. Problems and the way they are dealt with directly reflects upon guests and whether or not they are happy. Customers will usually notice problems all the time but unfortunately, it's very rare that they will actually bring it to your attention. They may not want to get involved or may feel it's none of their business. It's much easier for them just to not come back again if they have a bad experience and you'll never know why.

Talking to guests and employees will often uncover many problems. They could be as minor as a customer not liking a meal to a customer having to wait a longer period of time to be waited on. Problems could be a customer's negative interaction with one of your employees or maybe a customer is unhappy because they gave a waitress a ten-dollar bill and didn't get the right change back. Whatever the problems are, most of them won't be found out until you ask. Employees are usually great sources of information for things you haven't noticed, so keep the lines of communication open at all times.

Randomly establishing dialogue with customers and employees gives them an opportunity for them to tell you what's on their minds. This will give you a greater feel for what's going on and give you the chance to fix it before it gets worse. Conversation also promotes a healthy relationship with customers and gives them a chance to tell you all about how their nights are going. Don't be afraid to ask them what they like, don't like or what they would like to see more or less of. You'll get all kinds of different responses from customers, like someone being upset that they can't pick up a date in your club. To that person, that is a problem. It'll probably be a personal problem and one that you might not be able to help out with anytime soon.

Problems will emerge amongst employees too. Be involved with employees' habits and work ethics. This way you'll gain a greater understanding of them and why problems with them occur. The best way to handle problems with employees is to be flexible whenever possible. You should always be willing to compromise for the greater good of the nightclub. If compromising and flexibility fails, you'll need to handle it by examining another course of action.

Randomly establishing dialogue with customers and employees gives them an opportunity for them to tell you what's on their minds. This will give you a greater feel for what's going on and give you the chance to fix it before it gets worse.

INSURANCE

PROTECT YOURSELF
FROM LIABILITY

In most locales, insurance is not mandatory to operate a business. However, it's a very good idea to get some. Simply because of the nature of the nightclub industry, all clubs in existence need to have adequate insurance coverage. This is common sense. Insurance can alleviate many financial burdens that could be placed upon a nightclub as a result of unintentional or intentional wrongdoings, negligence or property damage such as disasters in the form of a fire or other catastrophe. Other money costing incidents can also be covered such as robbery, burglary or theft. Nightclub insurance coverage should also expand to include liquor liability insurance, which every nightclub operator had better have, in case a damaging situation regarding the sale of alcoholic beverages arises.

The types of insurance coverages vary but at a minimum a nightclub should obtain at least general liability, liquor liability, workers' compensation and property insurance. These coverages should be sufficient to deal with most incidents that materialize in the event of any civil claims made against you and to protect your nightclub from losses beyond your control.

GENERAL LIABILITY

You'll need general liability simply because mistakes will happen. This is a lawsuit-crazed society and nightclubs need insurers who can represent them to pay for damages, legal fees and settlements just in case an episode occurs that could otherwise bankrupt a club. Adequate liability insurance can be there to pay for the mistakes that do happen, giving you coverage for negligent practices and injuries that result from an activity or incident.

A good liability policy should cover at least the following:

- **Property damage or loss:** Covers unintentional loss of property such as glass breakage and other accidents. Should also cover loss prevention such as employee theft.

- **Personal injury:** Covers a wide variety of injurious events that a nightclub could be found liable for (A slip or fall, for example). Personal injury also includes any slander or defamation of character.

- **Bodily injury that results in physical injury or death:** A common example of this type of coverage would include assaults or excessive uses of force by your employees.

- **Advertising injury:** Protects a nightclub from negligent marketing and promotions that infringes upon another's rights.

LIQUOR LIABILITY

Many states require any business that sells alcoholic beverages to have liquor liability. Others don't but just because they don't, a nightclub should obtain liquor liability anyway to protect itself. Nightclubs and alcohol are touchy social subjects and many multi-million dollar settlements have been handed down to victims and family members caught up in bad incidents resulting from intoxicated people who were previously at a nightclub and had too much to drink.

A nightclub cannot be held liable for anything that an intoxicated guest does as a result of being served alcohol. This type of insurance coverage, however, protects a nightclub from liability if you or one of your employees makes a mistake and breaks the law. For instance, if a nightclub were to *knowingly* and *intentionally* sell alcohol to an underage drinker or an already intoxicated guest, the nightclub could be held liable for any damages or injuries that they cause later on. That's where liquor liability comes in to pay out any claims and legal settlements should they arise.

Since most people inclined to sue want huge sums of money, they often perceive all businesses as deep pockets. Because of that, don't be surprised if you and your insurance company have to fight many allegations involving the service of alcohol in court. Since your insurance company stands to lose money, most lawsuits will be successfully defeated. Without liquor liability, you would have to defend each suit on your own, probably with the aid of your personal lawyer, which could quickly add up in legal fees.

PROPERTY INSURANCE

Property insurance is equally important to a nightclub. Property insurance protects against the unimaginable such as a fire, or damaged caused by natural disasters like a tornado, hurricane or even an earthquake. These destructions could permanently cripple some clubs without the right coverage. With property insurance, the insurer steps in and pays the costs to repair the damages or replace what the club has lost. Property insurance also includes losses from major thefts, robbery, burglary or vandalism.

WHAT'S COVERED?

This will depend upon your policy with your insurance company. Some policies only cover the basic equipment such as furniture, the building's structure and equipment. Other policies expand to cover money, securities, stolen or lost cash and lost revenue as a result of temporary closing to make necessary repairs or replacements. Make sure you study the many different aspects of your club and purchase adequate insurance to cover your needs.

WORKERS' COMPENSATION

Workers' compensation is the law and you'll have no choice in the matter if you have employees. If you fail to abide by the law and don't provide workers' compensation coverage to all of your employees, you could face hefty fines and even prison time. This coverage protects you and your employees during injuries and sickness by providing disability and medical coverage.

The Costs: You as an employer are responsible for all of the costs of workers' compensation (100%). Your employees will not have to pay anything into this insurance premium. How much you'll actually pay will vary between insurance companies and therefore you should obtain several quotes before you make any definite decisions. Generally, workers' compensation rates are calculated by the potential risks of on the job injuries to employees and the number of past claims made by a business in past years.

CHOOSE THE RIGHT INSURANCE COMPANY

Selecting an insurance company to represent your nightclub doesn't have to be a difficult process. First of all you should carefully evaluate all potential companies on the basis of money. Choose a company that has a stable history and significant cash reserves. Because, in the worst case scenario, if you were sued for two-million dollars, you don't want an insurance company that defaults on your claim because they can't pay that kind of judgement. In the event something like that happened, you'd still be liable for the full amount and for many clubs, a two-million dollar settlement could be enough to put them out of business.

Try to avoid high-risk insurance companies. These are usually the ones that are fairly new and offer very low premiums. At a glance, the quotes they give you will probably seem like you'll save a lot of money in the long run. You might, but if and when you need to make a large claim, high-risk insurance companies may run you in circles before the claim is ever paid out, if they can afford to pay it at all. A good insurance company is worth the extra money that you'll pay in higher premiums and you'll be able to rest easier.

Insurance coverages, terms, premiums, rates and policies all vary and so you should obtain several quotes from different companies and make comparisons. You'll most likely see differences in the quotes they give. Get quotes on the highest coverages each company offers and once you've decided upon a particular company, it's best to be insured for the highest amounts possible. Some operators may have an inclination to try and save money. Trying to saving money when it comes to insurance could come back to haunt you if you aren't adequately covered when you need to make a large claim.

If you still need some help choosing an insurance company, seek out a broker. Insurance brokers make a living by finding the right insurance packages for businesses. If you hire a broker, make sure that he or she understands the complexities of your operation and the unique problems and risks that you'll face. Like every profession, there are good brokers and bad ones. A good one can introduce you to a good insurance company that fully understands your needs and offer you very competitive premiums. The services of a good broker may be a wise investment because he or she can save you a headache and a little money down the road.

SELECTING AN INSURANCE COMPANY TO REPRESENT YOUR NIGHTCLUB DOESN'T HAVE TO BE A DIFFICULT PROCESS. FIRST OF ALL YOU SHOULD CAREFULLY EVALUATE ALL POTENTIAL COMPANIES ON THE BASIS OF MONEY. CHOOSE A COMPANY THAT HAS A STABLE HISTORY AND SIGNIFICANT CASH RESERVES. BECAUSE, IN THE WORST CASE SCENARIO, IF YOU WERE SUED FOR TWO-MILLION DOLLARS, YOU DON'T WANT AN INSURANCE COMPANY THAT DEFAULTS ON YOUR CLAIM BECAUSE THEY CAN'T PAY THAT KIND OF JUDGEMENT.

THE SECURITY TEAM

THE NIGHTCLUB POLICE

Among a security team's duties are to handle disputes, check IDs, collect door entrance fees, minimize theft from the nightclub and to maintain a visible presence. Presence alone will usually serve as a deterrence. Without the security team, a nightclub has no way to combat problems that can place it in jeopardy.

Not only is it necessary to prevent illegal activity from occurring inside but, guests need to be protected from unwanted or undesirable behavior from other guests. The trick to an effective team of bouncers is to be everywhere at all times but to stay out of the spotlight as much as possible. This may seem like a difficult task to achieve but as the team gains experience, it comes easier with time.

Unfortunately, when people and alcohol are mixed together, there will be bar customers who decide to cause problems. Bouncers will need to respond quickly to handle the problems and head those people off before an incident gets out of hand. Most of the time, inappropriate conduct from some guests will be minor in nature and easily diffused. Small incidents are easy to handle and usually, simply asking the problem patron(s) to leave or calm down will be enough to handle it.

But, sometimes they may not conform and will create a larger problem which will call for another course of action.

ESTABLISH A PLAN OF ACTION

All security staff members should be properly trained and well versed in how to handle many different types of problem scenarios. A plan of action should be written or adopted and even included within employee policy handbooks. Having a written policy will protect you, the security staff and even patrons. A well-written policy that is understood and adhered to, reduces ambiguity in certain situations and defines what bouncers should or should not do in a given situation.

The first line of defense in any plan should always be conversation. Talking to people and treating them with a little respect goes a long way and is the most effective way to handle almost every incident. Just about everyone appreciates being treated with a little dignity, even if their perceptions of an incident are distorted because of their levels of intoxication. Sometimes it's just better to listen. Customers may want to express their dislike for other customers stemming from a negative encounter. You don't have to agree with them personally but letting customers get problems off of their chests and tell you all about it, may be all that is needed to defuse a customer's temper or attitude.

Use these suggestions to talk or listen to an upset customer after a dispute:

- **Never talk down to any troubled customer.** Negative statements just add fuel to the fire.

- **Be aware of your nonverbal communication or body language.** As you are aware, often our mouths can say one thing, but our body can say something else at the same time. What your body says never lies. Words that come out of your mouth sometimes don't convey what you're really thinking. Customers that you deal with, even if they are intoxicated, will pick up on body language. Negative body language is no way to build a rapport with someone. Try to exhibit a body posture of openness rather than of a threatening posture.

- **Avoid touching customers you don't know after they have been involved in a dispute unless you absolutely have to in self-defense or as a safety issue.** Touching someone that is upset may come across as offensive and could lead to further problems.

- **Try to or at least act like you understand their problems.**

- **Kill them with kindness!** It's hard for anyone to stay upset for very long when someone is treating them with respect.

- **Control your own emotions.** Your emotions will dictate how you act. If you're mad, it will be easy for the problem customer to stay upset.

- **Avoid yelling.** Sometimes this will be hard to do when there is music in the background. If you yell, so will the customer and it's very hard for a customer to calm down and think rationally when you or an employee is yelling at them. They'll yell back and you won't get too far with them. It's almost guaranteed that if you talk calmly and in a low voice that the customer will match your demeanor and also talk calmly and in a similar low voice.

With those suggestions in mind, it's extremely important that the security team consist of mature, well-tempered individuals with positive attitudes who understand and communicate well with others. A bouncer that doesn't possess those traits can often escalate a situation and turn it into an even bigger problem just because of the way he acted or spoke during an altercation. *Bouncers are there to prevent problems, not to become part of the problem!*

> IF YOU YELL, SO WILL THE CUSTOMER AND IT'S VERY HARD FOR A CUSTOMER TO CALM DOWN AND THINK RATIONALLY WHEN YOU OR AN EMPLOYEE IS YELLING AT THEM. THEY'LL YELL BACK AND YOU WON'T GET TOO FAR WITH THEM.

Talking will fail sometimes and other courses of action will be necessary. Sometimes, the security staff won't even have a chance to try talking to anyone because a fight has already broken out. Under those circumstances, they'll need to react quickly and attempt to separate all parties involved.

Because the potential exists for violence inside nightclubs, not only should bouncers be equipped with positive attitudes and excellent communication skills, bouncers should be able to defend themselves during fight situations. If they can't, there's a good chance, they or someone else may become injured because of their inefficiency and they may as well be employed as part of the wait staff.

Any fight that breaks out inside a nightclub, should be ended as quickly as possible by separating those involved. It's not a bouncer's job to administer an attitude adjustment to the one who started it by giving him some extra kicks, punches or other painful fight tactics while breaking it up! As soon as possible, all parties involved should be subdued with the *least amount of force as necessary*, then escorted outside of the club. This should be done as low key as possible so as not to alarm other guests.

Once outside of the nightclub, bouncers should end physical contact as soon as possible, with any individuals that were removed, unless safety dictates continued physical measures.

Take notice that the "least amount of force as necessary" is highlighted above. Take careful note of that because it's very important. Security personnel have to respond appropriately to the threat presented to them in every scenario. Too much force could result in civil litigation as well as patrons being unnecessarily injured. If bouncers don't use enough force during a violent confrontation, an innocent customer or employee could become injured.

Knowing what force to use and when to use it can sometimes be tricky. The use of a force continuum may just keep you and your bouncers out of trouble if followed. A force continuum, like most things in life, isn't perfect but it at least gives bouncers a good rule of thumb to work by. In civil proceedings actions will be judged by a legal term called "reasonable." This means what a reasonable, everyday person would do in the same situation.

For instance, it may be considered reasonable for a bouncer to tackle a 250-pound, intoxicated male customer involved in a fist fight to break it up. However, it may not be reasonable for the same bouncer to tackle the same 250-pound male involved in a heated argument with another guest. Although in the second example, any argument inside of a nightclub could quickly turn violent, physically tackling someone over a mere argument is probably unjustified if the people involved in it don't escalate past that point.

Bouncers need also recognize physical differences when intervening in altercations. It's probably safe to assume that your bouncers will be somewhat healthy in weight and muscle. It may not be considered reasonable if a 300-pound plus bouncer jumped on or tackled a 100-pound, intoxicated female, to break up a fight, even thought her actions prompted some sort of a response from the bouncer. In this example, there probably is a better way to handle the situation without jumping on or tackling the female, because the bouncer's actions could easily cause an injury to the much smaller, female opponent. Be aware that the physical appearances of doing such may also be perceived as negative or abusive by many customers and they'll remember it for a long time.

FORCE CONTINUUM

The force continuum is designed as a foundation in which security can utilize during the decision making process to determine when to use force. Further, it provides a basis as to what force would be considered reasonable should it be necessary. Each direction or level defines what type of force is acceptable given the situation.

Level #1. Verbal Communication/Presence. *This is the first line of defense*— Most situations will be effectively handled by talking to the problem individual. A good bouncer can talk sense into most people and get most people to do what he wants. Sometimes, the bouncer won't even have to talk to a problem person because simply being there is enough to deter any problems, someone was thinking of starting, from actually happening. It's impossible to measure the number of conflicts that have been prevented simply by a nightclub showing its force by having bouncers working. Many would be fights never get started just because of presence. If presence and communication fails and an individual is still uncooperative, then you're either at levels #2, #3, #4 or #5. The judgement will have to be made as the situation progresses.

Level #2. Passive Resistance. *This is a common problem for most nightclubs*— A passive resistant patron is one that you want ejected, but he or she is not necessarily a threat to you or other customers. They simply refuse to leave and verbal communication has failed. Usual examples of these types of customers are the ones that are too intoxicated and have been cut off. Passive resistant patrons are best handled by contacting the local police and letting them take care of the problem. If the police won't come, then you'll need to do it yourself. Simple hands on controls such as taking the person by the arm and escorting him or her out is the least amount of force necessary in these situations. If you have to do it, the goal should be to prevent the situation from escalating above level #2.

Level #3. Active Resistance. *This normally happens after a customer refuses to leave and hands on control is necessary to get him or her out*— Typically, this occurs very quickly. Active resistant customers usually start out as passive resistant ones and when a bouncer tries to remove them they begin to resist or pull away from the bouncers. At level #3, they aren't actually assaultive towards anyone, rather their actions are centered around fleeing. Active resistant customers can very easily progress to level #4 or #5 while trying to break free. Active resistant patrons require slightly more aggressive force to remove them because if they escalate to level #4, bouncers will want to already have the upper hand before that happens.

NOTE: There is a very fine line between level #2 and #3. If you were escorting a passive resistant patron out of the bar, and they were to pull their arm away from you, then they've escalated to level #3.

Level #4. Assaultive. *This is when a customer is actively trying to hurt a bouncer or another customer—* This can be a dangerous situation that must be quelled as soon as possible. The worst thing that can happen here is if the problem escalates to level #5. To prevent a serious assault on yourself or others, defensive weapons, strikes, or kicks may be utilized during this step to quickly and reasonably end the assault. Level #4 is very common in a fist fight involving customers. Realize that once bouncers get to the fight, people involved in the fight usually drop to level #3, #2 or #1, so try to avoid sustaining level #4 or allowing it to escalate to level #5.

Level #5. Deadly Force. *This term is often used by law enforcement to describe life threatening situations—* Fortunately, deadly force situations are rare in the nightclub industry but they can and do happen. If faced with a deadly force situation, as a reasonable person, you may do *whatever* it takes to prevent the death or serious injury to anyone inside the club.

In a nightclub scene when hostile customers are full of heated emotion, most of which is fueled by too much alcohol, it's very common for people to escalate and de-escalate through a variety of levels all on their own. Keep this in mind at all times! A person at level #5 could very quickly change his demeanor, de-escalate to level #1 and become cooperative.

The hardest thing bouncers will have to do, will be to also de-escalate if a customer does. For example if a customer were to brandish a

> IN A NIGHTCLUB SCENE WHEN HOSTILE CUSTOMERS ARE FULL OF HEATED EMOTION, MOST OF WHICH IS FUELED BY TOO MUCH ALCOHOL, IT'S VERY COMMON FOR PEOPLE TO ESCALATE AND DE-ESCALATE THROUGH A VARIETY OF LEVELS ALL ON THEIR OWN.

knife and threatening to use it, a reasonable person would feel as if they were at level #5. A reasonable bouncer, for example mind you, might try to defend himself and strike the customer with a bar stool. Just before striking however, the customer drops the knife and de-escalates to level

#1 and decides he's going to cooperate. Should the bouncer still hit the customer with the stool? He had better not!

Quickly adapting to escalation or de-escalation is something that bouncers gain through a combination of experience and adequate training. Each situation is unique and most of the time, plain old common sense will get them through it. Common sense will determine how they will respond or react in any given incident. Common sense will also allow them to assess each situation on the merits of the events which unfold. A bouncer armed with a high degree of common sense will react appropriately and in a reasonable fashion to every circumstance.

There are also many variables in the "reasonable person" term. Sex, age and weight are all variables which change what a "reasonable person" would do in the same situation. Example: Let's say a "healthy" male bouncer caught an 80-pound female minor who managed to sneak into a nightclub illegally. After he asked her to leave, she refused to do so and in the process turned around and starting assaulting him for whatever reason. He probably wouldn't be justified (reasonable) if he decided to zap her a time or two with a stungun, even though her actions pushed the encounter into an assaultive situation.

In that example, simply because the bouncer is a male, older and much larger than the female assailant, it would be unreasonable to expect that the bouncer was in fear of bodily harm or in fear of his life.

The force continuum hopefully will be enough for you to understand what security teams can do in certain security issues but it's not a definitive answer. Without a doubt, consult with your attorney to clarify any questions you have regarding the use of any type of force in any situation. Also draw up your own force continuum in the employee handbook and policy manual, so that all employees have a clear understanding of when and when not any type of force is warranted.

It's not a bad idea to have written into policy that indicates that the police are to be immediately contacted and advised of a situation whenever hands-on control of a patron was required. In most situations, the police will appropriately deal with people that have been ejected from your nightclub. If the police do respond, one of the security personnel involved should debrief the officers and report the incident on behalf of your nightclub. This action can help to reduce any civil litigation against you and your security team.

Whenever any member of the security team is required to take action against a patron(s), no matter how minor the action may be, he should complete an incident report describing the circumstances surrounding the event. All other employees who witnessed the event should be required to fill out a report also. Often guests who witnessed an altercation will be more than happy to tell you what they saw. Many of them won't mind getting involved and filling out a statement for you. If the police are present, get the names of the problem patrons from them and any police report numbers. Avoid having your security people question and demand identification from the people they throw out of the club. They don't have to show bouncers anything and chances are, insisting identification may only lead to continued problems.

The incident reports and all of the witnesses' statements should be kept together in a file and properly stored indefinitely in case one of the patrons who got thrown out makes false allegations and tries to sue.

WHAT TO LOOK FOR

Knowing what kind of behavior to look for can serve as a proactive measure to prevent problems from occurring before they even get a chance to start. All employees, not just the security staff, should get involved in knowing what type of behavior to look for. Training every-one to be on the look out for brewing trouble will make a club much safer. Identifying potential problems is beneficial to the guests' good time, the security team and to the nightclub itself.

Take a look at this common scenario; a young lady sitting at the bar by herself is approached by an intoxicated male who tries desperately to win her attention. The lady is annoyed by the man and tries to tell him several times politely that she would rather be left alone. She is unsuccessful in conveying her feelings and the man persists. The man continues to press hard and makes several inappropriate comments. After a short period of time, she becomes very uncomfortable and the situation between her and the intoxicated man becomes very tense. What happens next is anyone's guess, but it's bound to be a bad experience.

Situations like this can be avoided by an alert employee spotting this problem and intervening. In the above example, if the bartender recognized the unfavorable encounter, he or she could get involved and could subtly speak to both the woman and the aggressive man. The bartender could ask the woman if there was anything that he or she can do for her. As for the man, remember to treat him with a little respect and maybe suggest to him in a polite way that the lady would rather be left alone. Chances are, the forwardness will be enough to handle the problem, and he'll go away. If he doesn't go away or leave the woman alone, then the bartender should report the man to security.

Security personnel should then attempt to quietly talk to the man and suggest he change his behavior because he is making another guest feel uncomfortable. If he does not want to comply then he should be asked to leave. If he does comply, then security should keep a close eye on him—after he leaves the woman alone—wherever he goes inside the bar, because his behavior may resurface with a different guest. He might even start talking to a woman who's obviously already with someone and her husband or boyfriend may become offended and further problems could manifest themselves.

Problems like this, although minor, happen in the nightclub trade frequently and recognizing them quickly is the key to preventing them from getting out of hand. Intoxicated people are perhaps the most common problem that nightclub operators face on a day to day basis and dealing with them is something that you can get good at with time. Most intoxicated people are innocent and are just having a good time. However, there are others who become annoying, nasty or violent, and so you and employees need to be able to spot the troubled drunks from the rest of the guests in order to deal with or monitor them accordingly.

Other problems to look for are people with aggressive or bad attitudes enhanced by being drunk. These people are like magnets to being involved in a fight. Overcrowding is another indicator that should prompt all employees to be on the look out for brewing problems. Most people are very particular about their personal space and are easily offended. Add alcohol to the equation and when someone with a bad attitude gets brushed up against in what they perceive to be the wrong way, a fight breaks out.

Arguments also need to be identified. When patrons appear to be having an argument, no matter how minor it may seem, it's time to get the security team involved. Most arguments about nothing important at all can turn into a fist fight if it starts with the wrong types of people. Whenever an argument is witnessed, it should be quickly broken up by security, and if the patrons who were arguing are allowed to stay inside, they should be closely monitored for further problems.

Rude, aggressive or intoxicated guests, underage drinkers, suspicious people and poor inside environmental conditions for example— too hot or too cold, are all things that need to be monitored. Any of these situations can quickly get out of hand and cause a disturbance inside an establishment. All of employees and especially the security team shouldn't be afraid to talk to guests and get a feel for what's going on. Many times, a guest will see behaviors or problems that employees have missed or haven't seen yet and customers may bring it to their attention. Most problems can be dissolved just by having your security close and conversing with people. Their presence is powerful.

> RUDE, AGGRESSIVE OR INTOXICATED GUESTS, UNDERAGE DRINKERS, SUSPICIOUS PEOPLE AND POOR INSIDE ENVIRONMENTAL CONDITIONS FOR EXAMPLE— TOO HOT OR TOO COLD, ARE ALL THINGS THAT NEED TO BE MONITORED. ANY OF THESE SITUATIONS CAN QUICKLY GET OUT OF HAND AND CAUSE A DISTURBANCE INSIDE AN ESTABLISH-

SECURITY EQUIPMENT

To give the security team some extra leverage, consideration might be given to arming them with additional equipment to handle assaultive problems more efficiently and to reduce the possibilities of staff members or other guests from getting hurt during altercations. There are benefits and drawbacks to using equipment such as *handcuffs*, *stun guns*, *pepper spray* or *mace*. Depending on where you establish your nightclub, there may or may not be laws regarding the use of these types of devices. Contact your attorney for advice prior to using any type of restraint or defensive equipment. Employing these instruments can also carry a civil liability which you need to be aware of. Improper use of security devices could hurt someone if they are not applied correctly and the nightclub could be held responsible.

Pepper spray or mace, is an effective way in dealing with a violent patron. These chemical weapons can bring most people to their knees and end negative behavior quickly. However, chemical weapons have a propensity to affect everyone standing in the area during the time it was used. Innocent guests can become contaminated and suffer the effects of the chemical, such as irritated eyes, nose, throat and even have difficulty breathing.

Handcuffs offer the ability to restrain a violent person. But handcuffs placed on a person improperly can do more harm than good. Tight handcuffs are notorious for leaving marks on peoples' wrists and can even be placed on so tight that they actually cut off circulation to one's hands.

The stungun is a high-powered instrument used to send electricity through a violent person's body in order to subdue them. The downside to these devices are legal actions, which may have to be determined in civil court, if the person it was used against tries to sue. A judge may have to then decide if the use of such a weapon was justified.

The use of these weapons inside a nightclub should be determined on any specific problems within the nightclub. Let's face it, some nightclubs are located in some very shady areas and have a tough crowd where fights break out on a nightly basis. Other nightclubs, located in more prestigious areas can go for long periods of time without a serious altercation ever manifesting. If you consult with your attorney and it's determined that the use of security devices in your area is legal, it may not hurt to have extra equipment on hand in case of a unique circumstance, no matter what type establishment you operate or what kind of neighborhood it's located in.

Having pepper spray, handcuffs or a stungun on hand, doesn't necessarily mean that bouncers have to use them routinely. In fact, if you appoint a security team manager, he should have the ultimate decision whether to employ any defensive weapons and should be the only team member with access to those weapons. Policy should dictate when they can be used and the security team manager should know under what situations he can employ defensive weapons under the policy. Finally, remember to have all team members and witnesses complete an incident report or witness statements if any defensive device is used.

The use of video surveillance inside of a nightclub, though not a direct means of stopping violent behavior, can provide a recorded account of any incident. And if defensive weapons are absolutely needed to handle someone who is out of control, it's all recorded for future use if he attempts to bring about a lawsuit. Actions speak louder than words. Enough said.

DON'T LET PROBLEMS IN
The best way to avoid potential problems is to not invite trouble in. Why allow an overly intoxicated person inside? The chances are high that an overly intoxicated person will only cause problems of some sort once inside. People who arrive at the front door with an attitude problem should be turned away also. You don't really need their business that bad.

Security team members working at the front door should greet each guest that arrives. The moment or two that it takes for door staff to make conversation with someone will give them an opportunity to briefly assess a person's state of mind or demeanor. Many questionable or undesirable guests may be identified during this kind of interaction.

Door security should have a clear understanding of the kind of problems the nightclub seeks to avoid. *Corruption* at the front door can cause you a serious headache. Door staff that isn't properly checking ID's or allowing underage drinkers, known trouble makers or any other bad element inside can set forth criminal or even civil proceedings against you.

A common problem that nightclubs can face is greedy security people working at the door who charge people, who shouldn't be allowed inside in the first place, additional money on top of the cover charge, if there is one. They pocket the difference and look the other way. Be sure to have your employee policy cover such activity and quickly terminate any security member who violates it.

Nightclub security teams generally consist of male bouncers throughout the world. Men working security have a tendency to be more lenient toward female bar patrons. In other words, female minors are more likely to get inside of a nightclub than a male minor simply because male bouncers don't scrutinize female patrons the way that they should. This kind of practice should also not be tolerated.

Probably the absolute worst security issue that any nightclub can face is that of drugs or narcotics dealings. Do not let your nightclub get a reputation that drugs are being sold inside! This is one of the fastest ways that a nightclub will go out of business. Typically what happens is that business increases for a period of time with customers. Not all of them, but some come because they know that they'll be able to purchase some sort of social drug inside of the unwilling nightclub. It won't take long before *police* arrests are being made outside of those kinds of nightclubs.

People in trouble with the law are usually eager to cooperate with the police if they think they can get out of trouble. Soon after, the police will start looking hard at the nightclub in question and then the nightclub will get a bad reputation. The bad reputation is created not only by the police, who will swarm the area on a nightly basis, but by the community itself. That will without a doubt effect business in the long run because law-abiding people will avoid the club. A nightclub is sunk once it loses its customers.

> PROBABLY THE ABSOLUTE WORST SECURITY ISSUE THAT ANY NIGHTCLUB CAN FACE IS THAT OF DRUGS OR NARCOTICS DEALINGS. DO NOT LET YOUR NIGHTCLUB GET A REPUTATION THAT DRUGS ARE BEING SOLD INSIDE!

To control illegal drug transactions, security staff should be aware of the ramifications of such activity. If they are making their rounds and communicating with guests, then it shouldn't be difficult for them to learn of drug activity and deal with it appropriately. In most instances, the proper response would be to immediately contact your local police department and let them handle it. There's a good chance they may already know the drug perpetrators and will want to get them off the streets.

Door staff should also be looking for *any* suspicious behavior. It's not a good business practice to deny suspicious looking people into the bar. Just because someone looks suspicious doesn't necessarily mean they are. If a questionable person does get inside, the entire staff should be informed. Chances are nothing will come of the person, but if the staff isn't prepared for any predicament, that's when something unwanted happens.

Instead of refusing admittance to all suspicious people, most likely the door staff will limit their criteria to those who are known drug dealers or people who have caused problems in the past. People who have been seen distributing drugs before, or those who are suspected of selling drugs inside the nightclub should not be allowed in. Also, depending on your relationship with your local police, they can be a source of information regarding people whose business you do not need.

It's important to remember that it's your business and you reserve the right to refuse admittance to whomever you want for any reason.

SPOTTING FAKE IDS

WHAT EVERY NIGHTCLUB
EMPLOYEE SHOULD KNOW

Because of the lure and excitement of entering a nightclub, the industry will always have people who are under age 21, who will try to get into a nightclub and drink alcohol illegally. Depending on the area in which you set up and run a nightclub, you might decide to allow minors inside. For example, many clubs allow persons aged 19 and up inside their venues. If you do decide to let young guests inside, prepare to have problems with them drinking behind your back. The best advice is to try to enforce a system which identifies the guests who are over 21 years of age, from the guests who aren't. This usually is a tremendous task because underage patrons are very crafty and are continually coming up with new ideas to beat a nightclub's system. Even if you won't allow people under 21 in, they will persistently attempt to get in and drink anyway, so be prepared.

The most common way for minors to circumvent a nightclub's system to get in and drink is by presenting fake IDs. Fake ID's are everywhere and many of them are very hard to tell apart from the real thing. Even if security personnel are doing their jobs, it's almost impossible for them to weed out every single fake ID that's presented to them. Study *helpful hints to look for* and use the suggestions illustrated so that the door security team can identify the majority of fake ID's that cross their paths.

Helpful Hints to Look For:

1. If someone looks too young, they probably are. Door staff should always trust their gut feelings.

2. Scrutinize younger people that pull out a single ID from a pocket. Most people carry their IDs in a wallet or purse.

3. Be observant. Often when minors remove their fake IDs from their wallets of purses, a good observer will see other IDs while the minors make sure they're pulling out the right one.

4. Look hard at the pictures on the IDs. A good portion of the fakes will belong to a friend of the person trying to use it. Comparing the picture and the minor will weed out a lot of them.

5. Many minors will have an ID that belongs to another person and will memorize certain things about the ID that they think they may have to answer in order to get past door security. It's common for minors to memorize the full name, social security number and birth date on a fake ID. To gain the upper hand don't ask those questions, but rather ask what the address is on the ID, or ask about the height, weight or eye color on the ID or anything else you may find peculiar about a particular ID.

6. Ask tricky questions. Most minors expect to be asked "what's your date of birth?" They will quickly recite exactly what's printed on the card–like, "zero-three, two-five, seventy-nine"(03-25-79). Instead, how about asking "what day of the month were you born on?" Or, "which year were you born in?" Those are easy questions that

everyone should know about themselves and can easily answer very quickly. Someone who has memorized an ID will have to briefly think about it and may even get it wrong. Try it— it really works. Also, instead of asking for the full social security number, ask for the last four numbers only; This is another question most people can quickly answer. People who have memorized another's social security number will take a little more time to answer that question.

7. Check the eye color on the fake. If the fake is the ID of another person, there's a strong chance that the eye colors on the fake and the person presenting it aren't the same. Ask them the color of their eyes. If they have to think about it too long as they try to remember what it says on the fake, then there is a good chance you're dealing with a minor. Make sure that you also visually compare the minor's eye color to what it says on the ID.

8. Purposely misread the fake ID. If the minor's sole mission is to get in and illegally drink, they aren't going to dispute security if he read the date of birth aloud and indicated the minor was actually older than what it said on the ID. The minor will think everything is working to his or her advantage. If they agree that you thought they were 22 rather than 21, that's another indicator of possible deceitfulness. This works for other information on the ID as well.

9. With altered or fictitious IDs there are a number of things to examine. Look for anything that looks unusual about an ID in question. If it looks like it's been tampered with, it probably has.

10. Look closely at the year of birth. One of the easiest ways to alter an ID is to scratch out or paint over the year and carefully write in a new year that shows a year that would make the minor of legal drinking age.

11. Check the state seal. Most states have seals that are difficult to reproduce. If you see flaws in a state seal then once again there's a chance that the ID has been tampered with or has been illegally reproduced.

12. Compare. A lot of IDs are produced on personal computers. Check the type face and general appearance of the ID and compare it with your ID if it's in the same state. You are almost guaranteed to find subtle mistakes if you look hard enough.

13. Look at the back of the card. The main purpose of any fake ID is to fool bar security after they look at the front of the card. Most security personnel don't flip the card over and look at it too. If you turn it over, you're bound to find errors, such as sprints or poor reproduction.

14. Keep track of out of state IDs. The number of fake IDs that are manufactured often fluctuate. When you start seeing ID after ID that were issued through Michigan, or any other state, it's possible that someone is making and selling IDs to minors and using a designated state of issuance. The reason this happens is because it is very difficult to exactly replicate an ID in any state and once someone does it or comes close to it, they start selling fakes right away. They probably don't want to take on the task of trying to recreate the IDs of all fifty states. Another reason illegal IDs from other states are made is because the makers often hope that a nightclub security member will be unfamiliar with out of state IDs. They hope that once an out of state fake is placed in the hands of a bouncer, he won't recognize it or have a clue as to how it should look and will mistakenly assume that it's real. Once you put two and two together and realize that there is a relationship between fake IDs and a particular state and minors trying to get in, lights should go off in your head every time you find yourself in that situation.

15. Ask for a second form of ID. Almost all of us travel with more than one form of identification. Additional IDs can be ATM cards, credit cards or even a library card. Be leery of people who appear to be underage who tell you they don't have any other forms of identification.

16. Obtain a reference book from your local library or your Department of Transportation that lists pictures and descriptions of all of the Driver's Licenses and ID cards issued in every state. This should serve as a quick reference whenever in doubt. Most state IDs have seals and authentic markings that are very hard to recreate. Whenever a questionable ID makes its way into your hands, refer to the reference and compare it. Many fakes can be identified this way.

17. Lastly, watch body language. Minors generally aren't going to tell you with their mouths that they are too young to drink but a lot of times their non verbal communication will. Keep an eye out for behavior that's out of the ordinary or that seems deceitful. Nervousness, shyness, lack of eye contact, overconfidence, waiting before approaching or seeming to be in a hurry are all indicators that someone is trying to pull a fast one on you.

Remember, there is no foolproof way to get all of the fake IDs that are presented. Some may slip by, especially on a busy night. But, if you use these tips you are more likely to get most of them, and the more you get, the less often minors will attempt to try to get in because you will build a reputation among minors that your night-club is hard to get into to.

BARTENDING OPERATIONS

10 TIPS TO KEEP YOU IN THE MONEY

You know that bartenders play an important role inside nightclubs and their jobs are never-ending tasks dedicated to serving and interacting with customers directly as well as fulfilling drink orders for the wait staff. Without the bartending staff, nightclubs as people know them today just wouldn't be the same. The profession unfortunately is not without its own set of day to day operational problems and challenges.

To improve the efficiency of your bartenders there is a number of useful tips that you can teach them. These tips can make the job easier, relieve stress on the bartenders, make the entire club run smoother, reduce inventory and profit loss and will allow them to serve customers in a manner that causes longer visits and boosts sales.

Tip #1–Sell it: Bartenders, whether they know it or not, should become salespeople. They aren't just manning the bar ready to fulfill drink requests. Many times will a customer approach the bar with no idea of what or she wants to order. An inexperienced bartender would leave this customer to him or herself until they have made up their minds. To a skillful bartender, this is the opportunity to not only help out a customer, but is the chance to close a sale and more than likely, profit by being tipped well from the customer. It's not at all difficult for a bartender to make suggestions and price comparisons for customers when they are having difficulties deciding on a drink. Sell what you have, sell them what's popular and what's good. If a bartender has spent a few minutes with a person, he should get a feel for what the customer might actually enjoy.

With a little attention and some tact, a good bartender can sell any drink on the menu. Customers will appreciate the help, the bartender will appreciate a tip and the nightclub will have profited from one more sale.

TIP #2–Let Customers Know They Are Next: You'd be surprised at how many bartenders on a busy night don't communicate with the customers who just arrive at the bar. Understandably, when it's busy it's busy, but when a bartender sees someone just reaching the bar standing there with a ten-dollar bill in hand, it's safe to assume that he or she is there to buy a drink. Many bartenders completely ignore these customers until they have time to serve them. Sometimes it may take them awhile to get to these guests, leaving them to stand there for some time, not sure if the bartender is even aware that they are there and need a drink. It's not uncommon for some customers to leave the bar altogether in these situations, causing the club a lost sale and maybe even a lost customer forever.

It doesn't take but a second or two for even the busiest bartender in the world to make eye contact with and briefly speak to a guest who just arrived at the bar wanting to order drinks. A simple "I'll be with you as soon as I can sir," goes a very long way. This acknowledgment, will let a customer know that the bartender is aware of their presence and that they need service. Usually these customers will realize that the bartender is busy and will patiently wait, knowing that soon they will be next in line.

TIP #3–Place Drink Napkins in Front of New Customers: This tip works well with tip #2. As new customers arrive at the bar, if at all possible, let them know that they will soon be waited on by placing a drink napkin in front of them, followed by communication. This is likely to ensure that they won't give up and leave on a busy night, costing you a sale.

Doing this also increases efficiency. For the single bartender, this serves as a reminder to whom he or she has already spoken to and informed of the wait. For nightclubs with multiple bartenders, it lets all of them know that another bartender has greeted particular guests and that they need not stop and tell the same person the same thing twice.

TIP #4–Customer Satisfaction First: Do not squabble with customers over the little things. You're in business to make people happy. The nightclub isn't a large department store where some people go into to shoplift or try and get over on a company with bad checks or fraudulent merchandise returns. If a customer returns to the bar and tells the bartender that the screwdriver he ordered doesn't taste like a screwdriver to him, make him another drink to his satisfaction for free. The minimal amount of money it actually costs to make another drink is nothing compared to the customer being happy and bringing his business back on another night.

TIP #5–Use Appreciative Words: Telling a customer "thank you" or "please," always strengthens the relationship between the customer and the nightclub. These are small words that most people take for granted but are very powerful in the business world. These words used sincerely, can cause customers to feel that they have received genuine service. Simple, appreciative words result in repeat visits and increased tips for both the wait and bartending staff.

TIP #6–The Right of Way Behind the Bar: Bartenders should develop a system for delivering drinks, especially on busy nights. As far as efficiency is concerned, a bartender that can deal with and pour more drinks at one time, can serve more customers and close more sales.

This trait often comes with experience or is taught. Any bartender in the process of preparing a larger order than any other bartender has the right of way. Meaning he or she should have priority access to all drink inventory and equipment. Other bartenders should yield, and give that bartender clear and unimpeded access from the preparation area directly to the customers or wait station. Doing this will eliminate unnecessary drink spillage and/or glass breakage should two bartenders collide with each other.

TIP #7–Train the Wait Staff: A properly trained wait staff can alleviate many of the burdens placed on the bartenders during a busy night. One of the biggest bartending complaints is brought on from the small orders that the wait staff brings to the bar when it's busy. Instead of a waitress or waiter approaching the bar with one or two orders from one customer, the wait staff should be doing a better job and check with more tables and more customers and build bigger drink orders before they approach the bartenders. This action causes them to be at the bar less, which means that they'll be with the customers more. The bartenders can also spend more time focusing on the customers at the bar.

TIP #8–Stop Problems From Escalating: The bar is a very popular place for people to congregate around and unfortunately sometimes when people are brought together in large crowds, some will sometimes irritate each other. The reasons they do vary, but with human nature and alcohol combined together, you can bet the reasons are usually about nothing at all.

Because the bar is often a center of attention, the bartenders will have contact with many people. The bartenders will often see problems or potential problems occurring between patrons. Talking to guests and being present is often the key to preventing a scene from ever escalating. Bartenders will often hear all sorts of conversations between customers and an alert bartender who hears a disgruntled customer upset with another customer can often intervene with casual conversation and usually take that customer's mind off of the problem. This is also the time to involve security to see to it that nothing further occurs.

Presence can sometimes be just as powerful as conversation. Even though bartenders usually don't double as the security staff, the simple fact that they're there within an earshot of a problem conversation or situation may be enough to quell a bad scene from escalating or from even ever happening at all.

TIP #9–When to Cut Someone Off: This without a doubt is one of the hardest things a bartender has to do. Serving an intoxicated person can have consequences. Not always, but the chances for trouble should out-weigh everything else. It's fair to say that most people who happen to drink too much become "happy drunks," but some become problems or the "mean drunks." The other type of drunk is the "passed-out drunk."

All of these drunks can potentially cause problems nightclubs don't really need. This isn't even to mention the possible civil liabilities someone might hold against you. A common scenario of civil liability a nightclub could face by serving an intoxicated patron too much to drink is if later, after that person left, he or she jumped behind the wheel of a car and started driving. Later, if that patron became involved in an alcohol-related accident and killed someone, there's a strong chance that a nightclub could be named in a lawsuit.

Therefore, bartenders should be alert and aware of the state of the guests they serve. On a busy night where a bartender deals with hundreds of drink orders, monitoring the sobriety levels of guests is impossible to do. Fortunately most overly intoxicated people seem to have the ability to draw attention to themselves and stand out like sore thumbs. These are the customers bartenders should focus on, when determining whether to serve or cut someone off. Good common sense and an awareness of the ramifications intoxicated guests pose will usually be enough to get bartenders through this, which makes the club run smoother and also keeps other guests happier.

The wait and security staff should also keep a constant vigil for over-intoxicated guests. The wait staff, while making their rounds *will* see intoxicated customers. A waitress should keep mental tabs on what and how much the customers she has served, have had to drink. Knowing this, a waitress has the ability to prevent someone from becoming too intoxicated. Security staff members, should easily identify intoxicated customers who draw attention to themselves and deal with them appropriately. For instance, someone sleeping or passed-out at a table, should be asked to leave— passed-out guests paint a bad looking scene.

TIP #10–Keep Track of Money: Often on a busy, crowded night, the problem of keeping track of money denominations arises. A common reason this happens is when the bartenders are dealing with multiple customers at the same time, it is very likely that on occasion that they'll forget who gave them what and how much. Situations such as this will cost you money. Inevitably at some point during a bartender's career, a customer will state that they gave the bartender a ten-dollar bill but didn't receive the correct change. The bartender will swear that the customer only gave him a five-dollar bill, but how can he be sure? To satisfy the customers, in instances such as this, you'll take a loss, if the bartender's instinct was right and pay the customer what he thinks he should have gotten.

To avoid money problems, stress to the bartenders to only handle the money of one customer at a time. Bartenders should pay close attention to the amount of money that customers give them and make an effort to make a mental note of the transaction before they reach the register. You'll find that customers will make the mistakes and confuse themselves about how much money they gave to the bartender. If the bartender only deals with their money and makes a mental note of how much that customer gave them before they ring up the sale, they can confront the customer confidently and set it straight and the club won't have to lose any money.

PROMOTIONS AND SPECIAL EVENTS

KEEP THEM COMING
BACK FOR MORE

In today's highly competitive nightclub market, you must have a plan to win customers over. Convincing customers that a nightclub is the place to be can be accomplished in different ways. Nightclub patrons are a very complex and demanding group of people and usually no one promotional effort or special event standing alone can compete against customers' time and interests over a long period of time. The point is, if customers become bored with a nightclub they will find something else to do somewhere else. So, it's important to constantly provide new, fresh and seemingly exciting events or entertainment to draw customers in, keep them in longer and hopefully convince them come back next time.

You'll find that in order to convince people to enter your nightclub, sometimes they'll need a little coercing through advertising and good promotions. With a little time and an understanding of your club you'll learn how to properly publicize it to the clients it'll be built around. Advertising, promotions and special events all go hand in hand to work together to bring a distinct style and reputation to a club. So, take the operational workings of your nightclub very seriously if you hope to survive in the long run.

Managing any nightclub is a combination of staying on top of *"Your Sales, Giving Patrons Something to do, Promotions and Special Events"* and more. The key to successful management of a nightclub relies on an operator knowing the venue and knowing what's needed to make it work day in and day out. It takes much more than opening up a club and selling drinks to make it all happen smoothly.

The nightclub industry has evolved so much that many aspects of an operation must come together as one to keep customers happy and coming back for more. Managing never stops and the decisions that are made can often determine the fate of a nightclub. Everything from a nightclub's employees to managing special events must be given serious consideration to increase the likelihood of success and maximize overall profits.

> THE NIGHTCLUB INDUSTRY HAS EVOLVED SO MUCH THAT MANY ASPECTS OF AN OPERATION MUST COME TOGETHER AS ONE TO KEEP CUSTOMERS HAPPY AND COMING BACK FOR MORE.

MANAGING DRINK SPECIALS

Drink specials are very important promotional tools. Proper management of specials can influence repeat visits and increase customer traffic. The specials that are promoted can encourage customers to choose one nightclub over another when they decide to go out.

Managing specials is a combination of knowing how to price drinks and still make a profit, knowing what days the specials will work best and knowing when to end the specials and charge regular prices for drinks.

All specials should be designed to draw in customers on any given day of the week. The best specials should be used together with cover charges and special events to get the best results.

Here's a drink special schedule to illustrate the management of specials assuming a nightclub were to open for business 7 days a week:

Monday:
$1.50 Draft Beers
$2.50 Bottled Beers
$2.50 Shots
$2.00 Cocktails
ALL NIGHT LONG

Tuesday:
$1.00 Draft Beers
$1.00 Bottled Beers
$2.50 Cocktails and Shots
ALL NIGHT LONG

Wednesday:
.50 Cents Cocktails
.50 Cents Draft and Bottled Beers
Free Corona All Night Long
$2.50 Shots
UNTIL 10 PM

Thursday:
$2.00 Two For One On All Cocktails And Beers
Except Shots
$2.50 Shots
UNTIL 9 PM

Friday & Saturday:
.75 Cents All Cocktails
UNTIL 11 PM
$1.25 Draft And Bottled Beers
$2.50 Shots
ALL NIGHT LONG

Sunday:
$1.00 All Draft and Bottled Beers
$1.00 All Cocktails
$2.50 Shots
ALL NIGHT LONG

Of course this is just an example, and you'll need to modify this schedule to best suit your nightclub and the expectations of your clientele. Be prepared to be flexible—you may find that you'll need to change or modify your schedule from time to time to get them to work best. The drink schedules of competing nightclubs in the area will also sometimes dictate your schedule to a degree if you want to stay competitive. Some special events that don't occur on a regular basis may also prompt a temporarily change in drink specials to maximize customer traffic and profits.

MANAGING COVER CHARGES

There is a direct correlation between cover charges and drink specials. Your door and alcohol profits often will depend on both working together. Usually, when the drink specials are cheap, charge a little more at the door to get in and a little less when the drink specials aren't so cheap. Some nights, especially slower nights, you probably shouldn't charge any cover charges at all. If you so choose to do so, you *don't ever* have to charge a cover to enter your club. Just realize that if you don't, you'll be missing out on the huge profit potential. Be consistent with the going rates for club entry fees in your area. The worst thing you could do with cover charges is to make the price too high. If the cover charge is too high, it usually won't matter what your drink specials are because many customers won't bother coming in.

A good way to address cover charges is to mix it up a little and make it fun to get in. You don't have to charge everyone all the time. Depending on the venue, most customers will appreciate the recognition they receive by not being charged a cover charge. Let them in for free now and then during special events or circumstances, such as a "skirt night" (women wearing a skirt get in free). Or maybe let your customers in for free for showing off a tatoo anywhere on their bodies.

Here is another sample schedule, but one that covers *door cover charges* to go along with the schedule in *Managing Drink Specials* and *Managing Events,* in the next session:

Monday:
No Cover

Tuesday:
No Cover

Wednesday:
$1.00 Cover Until 10 PM
After 10 PM $3.00 Cover

Thursday:
No Cover Until 10 PM
After 10 PM $3.00 Cover
SKIRT NIGHT: Women Wearing Skirts Get
In Free All Night Long

Friday:
Show Your Tattoo And No Cover All Night Long
No Cover Until 9 PM
After 9 PM $2.00 Cover

Saturday:
No Cover Until 10 PM
After 10 PM $2.00 Cover

Sunday:
$1.00 Cover Starting At 8 PM
No Cover After 11 PM

Notice that on Thursday and Friday nights, customers are allowed to avoid cover charges by showing a tattoo or wearing a skirt. These sorts of door promotions are real winners. Develop special incentives like those that'll be exclusive to the style of your nightclub to set you apart from the competition. Customers may not remember all of the details about a club, but regular customers, in the above schedule, will associate Thursday nights with "Skirt Night" at your club. Little things like that can encourage repeat visits.

MANAGING EVENTS

Events such as bikini contests are used to draw in customers. The number and types of events that you can sponsor are endless. For the most part, all events should be consistent with the style of a nightclub and cater to the personalities of the clientele. An event can be just about anything, from a live band to a competition. You can also designate certain nights of the week such as skirt night, in *Managing Cover Charges* to be an event of a particular evening every week.

Here's one more sample schedule detailing a few common nightclub events. Keep in mind that you'll want to change your events on a regular basis in order to keep the action fresh. Most events, especially contest, work well for a few weeks before a new event is needed.

Monday:
80's Night:
Nothing But The Best 80's Tunes played All Night Long

Tuesday:
Live Band: Darkstones
Show Starts @ 9:30 PM

Pool Tournament: First Prize is $50.00 For The Winner
Tournament Starts @ 6 PM (See Bartender For Details)

Wednesday:
College Night
.50 Cents For All Drinks Except Shots
Coronas Are Free All Night Long

Thursday:
Skirt Night: Women Wearing a Skirt Get In For Free All Night
Karaoke Contest
Contest Starts @ 10 PM
First Place - $100.00

Friday & Saturday:
Free Give-Aways Regularly All Night Long
DJ Eric KeepTheBeat: Alternative/House and Hip-Hop All Night

Sunday:
Swimsuit Competition
1st Place - $150.00
2nd Place - $ 75.00
3rd Place - $ 25.00
Contest Starts @ 8 PM (Contestants Must Arrive And Sign-up Before 7 PM)

You should see how powerful events, drink specials and cover charges are. When you combine the three, you give your nightclub a direction in which to work towards. Customers also know what's going and there are generally no surprises. Just make sure to properly promote and advertise your schedules as a whole.

ADVERTISING, PROMOTIONS AND PR

If you fail to market and advertise the nightclub's special events, you may as well consider them failures because few people will know about them. The importance of marketing and advertising cannot be over stressed enough. A marketing and advertising plan can be implemented in a number of ways, but the key to a successful campaign is innovation and persistence. Marketing and advertising can be a powerful tool that when used wisely can greatly influence overall sales. Advertising a nightclub is a task that should be an ongoing managerial mission that never stops throughout the existence and life of the club.

In order to maximize success, promote what you'll be selling to your intended customers. Even nightclubs need to be able to communicate with its target customers through advertising or some sort of promotional effort to let people know the club exists, what's going on inside and to tell them how they can enjoy themselves if they come. Effective communication with potential and regular customers can determine the fate of any club and can cause repeat visits, increased traffic and more sales. On the other hand, the lack of a solid promotion and advertising plan doesn't do much and a club would have to rely on its target customers to find out about the club on their own. People won't look too hard on their own when it comes to finding out where to go for a night out and the competition will only benefit.

Because of that, you'll have to tell them about your club and then convince them that your nightclub is the place to be. This can be accomplished with a good marketing strategy. All nightclubs, regardless of size, should thoughtfully research a marketing plan and include it into the business plan. Here you should identify some important questions that'll help define what your goals are: *Who are the target customers? What makes your nightclub/events different from your competition? Where will the campaigns occur? When will the campaigns begin? And, how much will be spent on the plan and how much business do you expect to evoke from each campaign?*

Establishing a marketing plan of action will increase the likelihood of success and can set in motion any atmosphere you wish to create. Soon after, you'll begin to build up a steady clientele base that could be loyal for years. You'll constantly receive new clients, who'll come routinely. Other guests will come occasionally and you'll lose some who'll never come back again for whatever reasons. Usually, your guests will progress through all three cycles over a period of months or even years. This turnover is normal, but because of it, you'll need to constantly be thinking and working on the next marketing project to keep the process of turnover flowing to your advantage.

ADVERTISING

Advertising is usually a paid form of communicating to both regular customers and potential customers. The goal for any advertisement should be to interrupt anyone who sees, reads or hears about it. After the ad gets customers' attention, it should tell, enlighten, convince, educate and remind them about the nightclub and the events that may be coming up.

All advertisements should touch on several important areas if they are to be effective. Each advertisement must be able to tell the customer what they need to know in a brief, concise manner that leaves an impression on them. An impression causes an ad to be remembered. People remember both good and bad advertisements alike. For that very reason, any ads you decide to use to influence foot traffic and sales should be carefully thought out.

Use these basic tips when creating ads to sell your business to customers:

❑ **Be Honest:** Honesty goes a long way. If you lie to customers, they may resent it in the future. Dishonesty can also cause you to lose many customers. False or deceptive advertising is also against the law and could set in motion legal problems you don't need. It may be tempting to advertise something a little too good to be true in order to get customers to come. And, if it's not true, they'll only be let down once they get there. Don't do it!

❑ **Keep it Simple:** If you expect customers to remember an ad they saw, read or heard, it had better be simple. Regardless of what means you choose to advertise through, get to the point quickly and deliver the message. For instance, if the concept for an ad were to promote a drink special for a particular night, get the message across swiftly and say so. The remainder of the ad should revolve around the that single message. Doing this will enforce the message and make it easier to remember.

❏ **Choose a Style:** Advertisements represent the business and should reflect the atmosphere the business hopes to project. Give ads a style and stick with that style. Once you have a style don't change it unless you absolutely have to. If you change it too many times, the ads may confuse customers and it may be counterproductive. A style helps readers, viewers or listeners quickly relate to a business. Think about it. If you watch a lot of TV, you actually know what most commercials are all about, what they are selling and who's selling it before they even tell or show you. That's because those companies advertise their products with individual styles. In other words, a style leaves an impression and is easier to remember.

❏ **Ask for their Business:** Don't be afraid to tell people to come and visit your club and to take advantage of whatever you're promoting. After the message is delivered, let people know where you are. Assume that no one knows where your club is, so give them the address and the hours of operation if you need to. Amazingly, just asking customers to come, will cause many to do just that.

❏ **Stay Competitive:** Being on top of a nightclub, knowing the clients and competition is the key to producing competitive advertisements. You'll want ads to be different from that of the competition and stand out. Strive to be unique. Ads that are much different from competitors' ads can cause a substantial increase in customer traffic.

❏ **Back-up Your Ads:** Backing up what you say in ads goes hand in hand with being honest. Your credibility should stand up to your offers. If you advertise that on Monday nights there's no cover charge, it should be so. Also, don't say things like, "we have the coldest beer in town" if you don't, or "our steaks are the cheapest, best-tasting sirloins around." Those are subjective opinions and if too many customers disagree with the analysis it could do more harm than good. Be prepared to deliver whatever you say if you expect customers to believe you during ad campaigns.

❏ **Keep All Ads Professional:** Consider hiring professionals to customize your advertisements to avoid appearing amateurish. Customers will often base their decisions on advertisements and if ads don't look or sound professional, it could have a dramatic impact on their opinions about your nightclub. If you're going to produce ads, take the extra step and spend some money to have it done right, or don't do it all.

There are many channels which you could choose to send messages through to your intended audience of customers. Many channels of advertisements have been around for years. Some, such as word of mouth has probably been in use since the very first business was opened centuries ago. Another channel, the internet, is the newest form of advertising and is becoming an increasingly popular way to get the message out to customers.

Which channels of advertising will work best for you will be unknown until you try them. Advertising can sometimes be unpredictable and can backfire without a solid approach. It's recommended to implement several channels of advertising on an ongoing basis and constantly evaluate each one of them as to their effectiveness. Some may work very well for your nightclub and some may not. The same types of ads, that may not work for you, may for some reason work well for your competition and vice versa. Take full advantage of the channels that do work and exploit them to increase sales.

The follow are the most typical channels of advertising channels that can work well for you— or against you in some cases:

WHICH CHANNELS OF ADVERTISING WILL WORK BEST FOR YOU WILL BE UNKNOWN UNTIL YOU TRY THEM. ADVERTISING CAN SOMETIMES BE UNPREDICTABLE AND CAN BACKFIRE WITHOUT A SOLID APPROACH. IT'S RECOMMENDED TO IMPLEMENT SEVERAL CHANNELS OF ADVERTISING ON AN ONGOING BASIS AND CONSTANTLY EVALUATE EACH ONE OF THEM AS TO THEIR EFFECTIVENESS.

- **Radio:** This is a common and probably the most popular medium in which many nightclubs turn to advertise through. Radio commercials allow any business to reach a large number of potential customers. People mostly listen to the radio while traveling in automobiles or while at work. This means that the average person is exposed to thousands of radio adverts each year and if the radio is used for advertising, make sure that the ads are catchy and can make listeners stop whatever their doing to pay attention.

- **Newspapers:** Newspapers have huge readerships and are very economical to advertise in. Newspapers are very good sources to advertise specials and events in for any particular day of the week. The key to using newspapers is creating eye-catching and interesting ads that get readers' attentions.

- **Television:** Advertising on television is usually more expensive than other forms of marketing but can be an effective means of getting the word out to a much larger audience. If you utilize this media form, make sure that any commercials that you plan to air are done in very good taste and represent your nightclub in an appealing manner.

- **On-Premise Marketing:** This type of advertisement comes in many different forms. From signs, billboards, posters, memorabilia, to name a few. Using advertising inside of a nightclub is very effective and can often cause impulse sales from customers who are exposed to them. Advertise your specials of the night or day to remind customers to take advantage of them or use on-premise advertising to announce events or specials that are to come the following day or week. Clients that enjoy a club will take notice and many will act upon the ads.

- **Word of Mouth:** Word of mouth is perhaps the most powerful type of advertising. This is a direct means of communication. This interaction can take place between customers talking with other customers or a nightclub's employees getting the word out by telling customers relevant information. For example, having the wait staff tell guests what the food specials are, is a form of word of mouth advertising. Utilizing the DJ to announce drink specials, upcoming events or other activities is the same thing. Guests will communicate with other guests inside and outside of a club by either recommending or passing along their disapproval of a club. Past customers can keep opinions for long periods of time and people who have never been to a particular club before will give word of mouth more weight than any other form of mention. So, make sure to do your best and satisfy as many customers as possible each and every night.

- **Phone Books:** Do make sure you have a listing in the phone book. Phone books are huge resources that people use to find other people and businesses. As a business, a nightclub will be listed in the yellow pages under a listing such as "taverns, bars, restaurants or nightclubs." The listing will normally include only the phone number and address of the nightclub. If you really want a club to stand out from the competition, instead of just being listed, place a display ad in the yellow pages about the nightclub. Include anything you want about the club to make sure it gets seen and read. If the nightclub will rely heavily upon daytime food sales, for instance, think about purchasing an *entire page* and displaying a menu. Or tell readers more about the club, events, special nights, etc. and how they will enjoy themselves when they come. Display advertising in the yellow pages is an easy way to get noticed and easy to invoke a positive response from potential clients.

- **Internet Web Site:** Using the internet to advertise nightclubs is a fairly new form of advertising. The benefits of a web presence are unprecedented. More and more people spend a lot of time online and use the internet to stay informed about many current events and other subject matters. Use this trend to your advantage and let people in your area know what's going on inside your club through a web site. Organize a web site to introduce any special events, cover charges, food specials, hours of operation and whatever else your customers may need to know. If you establish a web connection, be sure to have it professionally done to project the right image.

Another issue you'll need to concern yourself with is the *frequency* in which you run or display your advertisements. Develop a working schedule that will maximize the chances of your ads reaching a greater number of people over a period of time. In other words running one display ad in one local newspaper for a week will do little good in the long run. Instead, get creative and do something like running a slightly different ad each week for several months.

Both radio and television advertising *need* to have frequency schedules. Preferably you'll want them to be aired as many times as possible during the hours of the days to reach the prime clientele candidates. If you properly plan your advertising venture, you'll budget a certain amount of money to use during campaigns to stay on track. Make sure enough money is allocated to allow for multiple exposures over a given period of time. Plan ad

> DEVELOP A WORKING SCHEDULE THAT WILL MAXIMIZE THE CHANCES OF YOUR ADS REACHING A GREATER NUMBER OF PEOPLE OVER A PERIOD OF TIME.

frequency that'll be consistent with the cash you've appropriated so that you stay within your plans.

PROMOTIONS AND PR

Promotions are more or less what's happening inside your club at any given point in time. This can be anything from free or no cover charges, a contest, a special night (ladies' night), drink specials (free beer all night) or a live event. Promotions are a very important part of operating a nightclub and first-class management of promotions can determine the success.

Promotional events give clients incentives to come, stay longer and spend more money. Promotional events can also influence clients' decisions as to come back again. The sky is the limit as far as which promotions can be used to make customers happy. This is where your knowledge of your customers, nightclub and your imagination come into play. Strive to be different from your competitors but still use the ideas that work to draw people in and keep them there. Promotions like lunch or drink specials, happy hours and other events still work well and probably will for some time. What you need to do is to variate your promotions to best fit the atmosphere of your nightclub and to your desired clientele.

Stay on top of promotions, properly plan and organize them to get them to work best for every occasion. If something can be done better or not done it all, address it and change it. Don't be afraid to make both minor and major changes in the ways that your promotional events are hosted. If something is working well, that's good news and the only thing you should be thinking is how to make it just a little bit better. If something isn't working or if something is needed to bring it all together, find it, eliminate it or add it. Don't let problems with promotional activities go on for too long. Otherwise, you'll begin to see a decrease in sales, which will force you into a position to start all over again and convince your clients to come back through advertising. If customers aren't happy about the events in your club, it'll be harder to win their devotion a second time.

PR or public relations, is unfortunately a rarity in the nightclub industry. PR is an indirect means in which a business attempts to promote a positive image of itself. A successful PR campaign can shed a nightclub in a prosperous light and increase overall sales. PR includes a wide variety of activities to accomplish the task. If you seek to use PR to your advantage you must first know your community before you even think about implementing any PR activities. Jumping right into it without thoroughly knowing what you're getting into, could backfire and have little results and cost more money than it was worth.

Public relations stem from activities such as sponsoring a local amateur softball team, working with nonprofit businesses to raise money for needy causes or sponsoring/donating money toward local events. Getting involved in public issues or crusades can help to shape public opinions about nightclubs. Be careful if you want to get involved in these sorts of things. The worst thing that can happen is a PR activity having a negative effect. It could cause people to be leery of your intentions. If you plan to get involved in public relations, start small and slowly work your way up to larger activities.

MAKING THE DECISION TO EXPAND

USE SUCCESS TO COMPOUND PROFITS

Deciding to expand any venue is a true indicator of a successful operation. Expansion in some way shape or form will probably be necessary at some point in time for all clubs, regardless of the size of the operation. At the very least, most nightclubs will have to undergo a face lift on occasion to give the venue new life. To stay competitive, renovation and remodeling may be necessary and can make loyal customers feel as if they have walked into an entirely new club. The feelings that a remodeling project can create can often spark unexpected customer traffic and increased profits. Renovation is just that powerful, but before diving into an expansion project, such as remodeling, careful considerations must be given.

Some owners feel content with operating just one venue which they have operated to success. That's fine, but why limit yourself? Start a franchise and sell your ideas to other operators. Or, duplicate your success by building multiple nightclubs, which of course would multiply your profits. Regardless of what you decide to do about expansion, don't take the subject lightly and don't rush into it without properly researching and planning all the moves.

RENOVATION AND REMODELING

Choosing to remodel, renovate or build onto an existing facility is usually the first choice for many operators. Changes such as replacing furniture, re-carpeting, painting or changing themes can have impacts and make a huge difference. Renovation can transform any venue into almost a completely new club.

Renovation can be a very expensive undertaking for operators who plan to completely redo the entire nightclub. But if you compare the costs of building another venue in another location to the costs of renovating and by far renovating is the cheaper of the two.

Before even considering a renovation project, for any nightclub, operators should carefully evaluate the many aspects of the operation already in place. If operations are working well and the only thing holding the club back is the need for more space or the need for a little change to keep customers inspired, then go for it. If the club is lacking or struggling in certain areas, then an operator should concentrate on improving any problems that exist before deciding on costly investments, like construction, replacing furniture or equipment. It makes no sense to expend more money on a club that isn't running efficiently or as planned.

BUILD ANOTHER VENUE

Building a second venue is an exhilarating endeavor and obviously one that deserves some considerable thought and planning before anything is finalized. The key to building another venue is duplication. This means applying the same methods and principles that made the first venue a success.

Only once your venue reaches peak performance and you build a solid, favorable clientele base should you even think about building another venue. As you well know, a lot of planning, thought and implementation must go into the daily operations of any venue. It often takes time to perfect it all to find out what works and what doesn't. Every venue should be operated according to a game plan and should move through several stages of that plan. When the club advances through each phase of the plan and reaches the pinnacle of success and has no where else to go, why not double profits and build another one?

If you decide to open another venue, beware that it isn't as simple as copying what you've already done. Although, as mentioned before, duplication is the key to a successive venue. Each and every nightclub is very different from each other in ways. That means that you cannot just use the same plan for a second venue and expect it to work. A new plan will have to be conceived, which lays out all of the specifics, such as the new location. Location and demographics have a strong influence over nightclubs. If you were to take your successful existing venue, pull it out of the ground somehow and plant it in another location, it would almost be like starting over, because in essence your clientele would change. That means you would need a new plan in order to build another customer base.

Duplication comes into play by using some of the same ideas, concepts and principles that worked in the first venue. It may take awhile to develop a unique style and once you find it, there's nothing wrong with using the same style in a new venue because you know it already works. For instance, you can use the same uniforms, drink/food menus, drink specials, lighting effects, style of music or themes, to name a few, that helped to make the first club successful. These elements all played an important role in giving the first club an identity and distinguishing it from the competition.

The only major drawback to operating multiple venues is learning how to divide your time and run them all. Two separate venues in the same city will probably be a little hectic but it can be done. Once an operator expands to three or more venues, it increasingly becomes difficult to effectively run them. It becomes impossible if the venues are spread out in different cities. The solution to this is to appoint managers, who work underneath and report directly to you.

In a case where a manager will assume the major role of responsibility, establishing a high degree of employee trust is essential. Perhaps the best way to select a manager to lead a new venue is to promote from within. If you are directly involved in the daily operations of the first venue, then it's likely you'll take notice of the work ethics of employees. You'll establish a professional and sometimes even a personal relationship with them. It will be very easy to identify a high level of leadership and integrity qualities within some employees. These are the employees that will make the best candidates to operate a venue on your behalf.

After you've built a second venue, operated it, advanced it through all of the planning phases and doubled your profits, why stop there? You can keep compounding your profits as many times as you want to with multiple venues. Build three, then four and so on. Before you know it, you may own twenty or more venues bringing in multimillion dollar annual profits. The sky is the limit but it can only happen with successful operations time and time again.

START A FRANCHISE

Owning a chain of nightclubs for many operators seems like an impossible dream. It isn't impossible and it doesn't have to be a dream. Franchising may not be for all venues, especially smaller ones, but it is always possible.

For some operators, the idea of running multiple nightclubs in various locations is an unforeseeable goal because of the time demands and management aspects of doing so. The answer for these operators is to give serious consideration to franchising their existing operation. Franchising is a unique opportunity for entrepreneurs. An entrepreneur, the franchisee, purchases the right to open a franchised business from a franchiser. What the franchisee buys, is a tested, proven operation that has a very high likelihood of success. The franchisee gets to set up the same operation as the franchiser, including using the same club name, look, equipment, food/drink menus, operational management techniques and everything else that makes a nightclub different from another.

> OWNING A CHAIN OF NIGHTCLUBS FOR MANY OPERATORS SEEMS LIKE AN IMPOSSIBLE DREAM. IT ISN'T IMPOSSIBLE AND IT DOESN'T HAVE TO BE A DREAM. FRANCHISING MAY NOT BE FOR ALL VENUES, ESPECIALLY SMALLER ONES, BUT IT IS ALWAYS POSSIBLE.

Franchisers also usually offer a complete comprehensive training program to get the new operators and management up to speed with what they need to do to make their club successful. On going training, marketing support, evaluations and the sharing of new products and ideas are also normally offered in a franchise contract during the life of a franchise to assist the operators in continued success.

The franchiser profits from the actual sale of the franchise, which is set and determined by the franchiser. The cost of a franchise usually varies anywhere from $10,000-$175,000. That's just the cost to own the rights to a franchise. Those figures don't include the costs to actually *build* the franchise, equipment costs and other operational expenses. The franchisee is responsible for raising that money. In addition to that, most franchisers also profit by taking a percentage of the franchise's profits every year.

As you can see, a franchiser can find him or herself in an advantageous position. For each franchise that is sold, the franchiser is handsomely rewarded. The owner/operator of the parent franchise, gets a chance to own part of every franchised club that opens up. This is definitely one way to quickly grow and expand a nightclub throughout a region or even the entire country. Operators also are relieved of the burden of having to run multiple venues, because the purchasers of franchises have vested interests in the success of their clubs. Therefore, they will probably work just as hard as you did to make it work.

Franchising any business is a complicated legal commitment. You should consult with a franchise advisor and your attorney for legal assistance. If you should decide that franchising your operation is right for you, you'll need both an advisor and an attorney to assist in research and developing a sound franchise marketing plan. Franchising can be a long and difficult process and the services of professionals who know what they are doing are invaluable.

DON'T FORGET TO RESEARCH AND PLAN
Before any type of expansion is done, it must be properly researched and planned. Regardless of the type of expansion an operator might want to do, it's likely to be expensive. Mere expense alone should be enough to prompt an operator to investigate numerous possibilities

before making any final decisions. It's impossible that everything will always go or happen as planned, which is why businesses are sometimes risky endeavors. But a good approach toward research and planning will make all projects calculated risks, rather than just risks.

Research and planning includes knowing who your market is, choosing the appropriate location for expansion and carefully studying and exploring different ways to achieve a specific goal. There are many nightclub consultants that may be able to assist you in planning an expansion. If you choose to utilize the services of a consultant, make sure you get one that is on your level and has a thorough knowledge of nightclub designs and operations. Employing a consultant may cost some money, but if you're thinking about spending $175,000 for example, on a renovation project, then every penny spent on a good consultant should be considered a wise investment.

Successful nightclubs will also find that the money for projects will come much easier than say, capital for a start-up operation. Clubs that have proven that they can generate profits on a yearly basis, have a much easier time obtaining loans from banks, investors and other financial institutions. Although, the best way to do business is to stay out of debt. Obtaining a loan from a bank means that eventually the loan will have to be paid back with interest. The best way to expand a nightclub is to have expansion worked into a long-term plan. That way, some of the club's profits are put right back into it and an operator can eliminate a bank loan from the equation which in the long run will save more money for the next project.

THE SOUND SYSTEM

SOUND FACTS

Another important feature to any nightclub or bar is the music and lights. No nightclub is complete without music. Some small bars can do very well without any but it's not recommended to go without at least a jukebox. Larger nightclubs, however, will require a superior sound to satisfy customers and cause repeat visits. Building a sound system is an important aspect that requires the right equipment, placement and know-how. The sound and music inside of a nightclub is so important that customers will deem it either good or bad. If it's bad, they may not come back again. If it's good, well, you know what happens.

The role that sound combined with lights and lighting effects, play is a crucial one that cannot be underestimated. Lights and sound together is one of those things people take for granted and don't realize how important they are until they're gone. Together they are tremendous influences which can help give any nightclub a name and a level of respect among clients.

THE SOUND

Sound is a nightclub's heartbeat. Without sound, the club is dead. The importance of a good sound system cannot be emphasized enough. During the research and planning phase of a new venue, you may feel compelled to cut costs here and there by eliminating or reducing funding towards certain facets of the nightclub in order to save some money. Cutting costs is okay if you know where to cut them but, whatever you do, don't even think about skimping on the sound system, especially if you want to operate a respectable nightclub that expects to bring in a decent crowd.

Be prepared to invest a considerable amount of start-up capital towards a quality system. If you don't, the system will be plagued with technical problems, not to mention the noticeable differences between a high quality sound and a poor one. Believe it or not this can actually affect your bottom line because the sound has a lot to do with how customers will perceive a club.

You ask what kind of system should I invest in? This depends on a number of factors. The major factors should be decided on the type of venue you are planning to operate. If you're going to operate a dance club for instance, then you should strive for quality. Build a system that can withstand the needed bass and volume to entertain customers. On the other hand, if you are operating a smaller venue and don't plan to have a DJ or a dance floor, then most likely a good jukebox and a so-so set of speakers will be enough to get by.

A smaller bar can also consider building a smaller, less expensive system of components: Small amps/receivers, CD players, tape players, small speakers and maybe even an equalizer. Smaller bars usually don't need to place an emphasis on sound quality, therefore any combination is probably good enough to do the job. For smaller bars, with a small system, the bartender can also double as the DJ if the equipment is set up behind the bar. The only thing a bartender needs to do is change out the CD's and play the songs.

Regardless of how you plan to build your system read on and familiarize yourself with all of the following basic components.

THE COMPONENTS

At a minimum you'll need speakers, an amplifier, a mixer, and CD players. Then you'll need some top quality wiring and cables to link everything together. Each of these components have their own individual functions but work together to deliver sound. The trick is to have the best components money can buy so that these components don't just deliver sound, but deliver an awesome sound! Remember this, *you'll get what you pay for.*

Because the sound system is such an important element to a nightclub, as well as a significant investment, seriously consider hiring a professional to assist in the setup of the system. Working with a professional can be very beneficial and can help to eliminate a lot of potential problems with the design, selection, build and installation of the sound system. The services of a professional sound person are well worth every penny you spend on him.

SPEAKERS

Seems like a no-brainer. The sound has to come out somewhere right? That's part true. Yes, the sound has to come from somewhere but the quality of the sound has a lot to do with the quality of the speaker. A good speaker system should be better than your amplifier. Meaning, your speakers should be able to handle more watts than your amplifier is able to produce. Speakers should be able to play crisp, clear sound with thunderous bass at very high volumes to even be considered acceptable in most nightclub settings.

> THE TRICK IS TO HAVE THE BEST COMPONENTS MONEY CAN BUY SO THAT THESE COMPONENTS DON'T JUST DELIVER SOUND, BUT DELIVER AN AWESOME SOUND! REMEMBER THIS, YOU'LL GET WHAT YOU PAY FOR.

You'll likely need many speakers placed throughout the nightclub in order to provide an *even* coverage of sound. How many will depend on the design and size of the club. Multiple speakers also add a degree of depth to nightclubs and the phenomenon of surround sound can be created.

There are many different manufacturers of nightclub/commercial quality speakers. Some better than others. Expect to pay anywhere from $600 on up per speaker if you want quality.

CROSSOVERS

A crossover is a component that allocates the right frequencies to the right speakers. A crossover sends high, mid and low frequencies to the amplifiers which then sends the frequencies to the appropriate speakers. The result of this processing is a commercial quality sound that is fit for any nightclub. If you need many speakers, you'll want a crossover to regulate frequencies to get the most from the speakers.

AMPLIFIERS

This is one of the most important components that your DJ will have in his arsenal. It's also one of the most demanding ones too, so it's very important to purchase an amplifier that's of the highest quality that can be afforded. The amplifier will determine how loud the system will be. The loudness of the system is determined by the power rating of the amplifiers.

Although today's amplifiers are very powerful, one probably won't be enough to power a large sound system. Therefore, most likely more than one amp will be needed to get the job done. Typically, most clubs utilize at least two amps. One for the treble and one to power the bass or low frequency woofers. If needed, a system can be powered with more than two amps to boost all of the frequencies further to get even more performance from the speakers.

You also need to prepare and expect an amp, no matter how good it's manufactured, to eventually *burn out*. Burn outs usually happen during the busiest part of the night just when everything is just starting to happen. Burn outs are the result of amplifiers becoming too hot and more or less, a melt down occurs. All nightclubs are subject to amp melt downs, it comes down to a matter of when and how often. With the cheaper, less-capable brands of amplifiers, melt downs will probably occur more frequently and in the long run, cost more money to keep replacing them with other cheap models.

You should now realize the necessity for *back-up amps* in case of a burn out. Chances are, you won't know when a melt down will occur so it's important to have amps standing by, ready to go, to keep the sound system up and running in the event of a small disaster. Otherwise, if a blow out were to occur and there was no back-up amp, the night would pretty much be over because you wouldn't be able to give your customers any music entertainment. A nightclub is worthless to a dance crowd without music.

In case you didn't know, amplifiers are the workhorses of a sound system. Amps provide speakers with power so, invest only in quality brand name amps to add to the system. The standard amplifiers that are durable enough to withstand the rigors of a nightclub's demand range in price from several hundred dollars to several thousands dollars.

MIXERS

Next along the lines of necessities comes the mixer. The mixer is the most commonly used component within any sound system. Mixers allow the DJ to control and adjust the sound and the volume in order to play clean, clear, dynamic music. Mixers can also cross fade channels which let the DJ smoothly transition from one song to another.

All of your components will be routed through the mixer which makes it the centerpiece of the sound system. You'll need a mixer that has enough channels to accommodate at least two CD players and two turntables. So, four channels are the absolute minimum. A mixer with more than four channels is very nice because it lets your system become more versatile by allowing more components, such as a tape player, to be added.

Make sure to get a mixer that can withstand heavy DJ use. As stated before this is the most commonly used piece of equipment and is subject to more wear and tear than any other component simply because the DJ will constantly need to manipulate the controls and buttons on them. Quality is the key to durability.

EQUALIZERS

You'll also want to consider investing in a good equalizer. The sound system can probably get by without one, but it will be very limited. Equalizers are used to fine tune the sound by smoothing and enhancing the frequencies and bass.

The dynamics or the actual sound of music inside of a typical nightclub constantly changes during the course of a daily operation. There are a number of common reasons this happens. One reason is that the sound of your system will vary at different volume settings. It's highly unlikely that during the afternoon, when food sales are at their highest, that you'll be blaring dance music as loud as the system can play it. Rather, it's likely that the music will be at a much lower, casual volume. The differences in volume will probably require a little equalization to maximize the quality of the music at the different volume ranges and frequencies.

Acoustics is another reason you'll want an equalizer. Acoustics play a big part in the overall sound. For instance, you could test and tweak your system to sound perfectly at high volume in an empty room. But, fill the room up with people on a busy night, and it's a certainty that the perfect sound you thought you had, now sounds different or distorted. Sound bounces off of objects, people included, and you need to realize because of that, it is subject to constant change. You or your DJ will need to monitor the sound of the music throughout the course of a working day and be prepared to make minor changes in equalization in order to achieve the music clarity customers expect to hear while they are there.

The trick to working with an equalizer is to establish pre-settings for different types of songs and for the different times of the working day. Once you've figured out the settings don't change them! All nightclubs are laid out differently, so each will require their own individual sound settings to compensate for such things as acoustics and for the type of music that is played. Some music sounds better with more bass and some sounds better with more treble. Once you find those settings, the DJ should just need to adjust them according to presets. If subtle adjustments are needed, the DJ should use the mixer band equalizer and leave the system equalizer alone. If he's messing with the system equalizer, inevitably he'll screw up the settings.

COMPRESSOR/LIMITERS

These components protect the system and the speakers from being blown up. CL's prevent overloads to the speakers and amps which could otherwise permanently damage them. Overloads typically occur when the DJ isn't properly monitoring the system at high volume levels. Heavy base that's too much for a system to handle will result in problems. Systems are too expensive to have some DJ, who claims to know what he's doing, come along and blow up the speakers.

TURNTABLES/CD PLAYERS

Next you'll need to choose a platform in which to actually play music. Turntables and CD players are the two most common platforms used in a nightclub sound system. Most nightclubs use one or the other. Some nightclubs utilize both. Which platform you opt to use is entirely up to you. The DJ may also want to have a say in the matter since he'll be the one working with the equipment.

In the past, turntables and vinyl records dominated the nightclub scene. But, fairly recent technological breakthroughs such as the CD and the CD player, have emerged and easily surpassed cassette tapes and vinyl records as the most economical and ideal media for playing music. In addition to the clear, high quality sound compact discs offer, their small sizes makes them very easy to handle and their designs make selecting the songs you want to hear, just a push of a button away. For these very reasons, CD's have fast become the platform of choice for many club operations.

Although turntables are deemed by many to be an older method of playing music, there is no indication that they are going out of style anytime soon. Many DJs still prefer vinyl records over the compact disc. DJ preferences usually have a lot to do with the style of music that they play. For instance, hardcore dance or rap music DJs usually like to become more interactive and manipulative with the music. Turntables allow that to happen. With CD's that is hard to do. Trying to manipulate a CD while it's playing will probably only result in it skipping which will ruin the whole song.

To stay versatile, you should consider adding both turntables and CD players to the system. By adding both components the DJ is able to do much more than he could with just one or the other. If you hire a competent DJ who knows what he's doing with the system, the club sounds will really come alive.

The only downfall to having both instruments in your system is being able to properly adjust for equalization. Normally what happens is that there is an offset of equalization. CD's have a much higher output than records and if the DJ were to switch inputs from a turntable to a CD player, without compensating for the differences in dynamics between a CD and a record, a sudden increase or *spike* in volume would occur. Spikes could easily ruin your speakers in no time at all and obviously, when and if they occur, are rather annoying and very noticeable to customers.

This problem is easily solved with a knowledgeable DJ who can carefully fine-tune the equalizer to suit both platforms. Take care that the DJ doesn't configure the equalizer to play well for one or the other because if he does, there will be a distinct difference in sound between the two. One platform will sound way better than the other and you don't want that. Since playing a CD produces more output than a record does, it's important to monitor volume levels, to prevent spiking, when switching from a turntable to a CD player. Properly utilizing a compressor/limiter can take part of the burden off of the DJ during a switch and will allow him to turn up the volume at will without worrying about blowing up the system.

> TO STAY VERSATILE, YOU SHOULD CONSIDER ADDING BOTH TURNTABLES AND CD PLAYERS TO THE SYSTEM. BY ADDING BOTH COMPONENTS THE DJ IS ABLE TO DO MUCH MORE THAN HE COULD WITH JUST ONE OR THE OTHER.

MICROPHONES

How else can a DJ directly communicate with the crowd? The mic is an important tool that must not be over looked. A good DJ can speak to the crowd and sometimes get them riled up when needed. The mic also allows the DJ to advertise drink specials and other up-coming events which can boost sales.

There are cordless and wired microphones. Some mics sound better than others and some aren't designed well and can't handle excessive use and eventually fail. It doesn't really matter if you go with a cordless or one with a wire as long as it's a quality, rugged mic that when used, allows the DJ to talk clearly, crisply and without any static or crackling.

CABLES AND WIRING

Lastly, the cables and wiring that link a system together deserves some serious consideration. This is probably the easiest thing to deal with, in order to get the most from a system and to make the club sound better. It's often tempting to go out and buy the cheap stuff to save a few dollars. If you do that, you'll lose out. Connect the sound system's speakers and amps with the thickest, shielded gauge cables you can, preferably 10-gauge.

That'll increase the system's overall volume by doing this and eliminate the common problem of hissing and humming that some systems have. Unshielded wiring picks up RF interference, such as radio signals, electrical noises or even air conditioner units. These annoying RF signals will be amplified right through the system if not protected against them. Proper cabling also reduces wear and tear on amplifiers because they won't have to work as hard and therefore can stay cooler.

You need to also replace the wires and cables that actually come with each of your components. These are the wires that actually connect the components such as the mixer, the equalizer, the turntables, CD players and so on. These cables also pick up RF and will ruin the music just as easily as unshielded speaker and amplifier wiring. Throw them away and purchase some commercial quality wiring.

JUKEBOX

The Jukebox is a common sight in smaller bars. Jukeboxes provide musical entertainment for those who so wish to entertain themselves and everyone else in the bar. The best thing about the jukebox is that the music that it plays can be a wide variety of genres and artists. This gives patrons a choice to listen to what they want to listen to. If you purchase a jukebox, you'll find they are very profitable investments that require little to no maintenance or attention. Occasionally, you may want to add or remove different selections/CDs or even records, but that's about it.

Make sure to also have a decent speaker system hooked up and that the jukebox is properly plugged into the speakers. Speaker placement should be such that the music can be heard throughout the entire bar. The worst thing that can be done is to set up the jukebox with an inadequate speaker system. The music will lose its meaning because of poor quality or the inability of all of your guests to hear it.

CONCENTRATE THE MUSIC TO THE DANCE FLOOR

One of the biggest mistakes made by nightclubs is failing to concentrate the music onto the dance floor. The dance floor should be the loudest area in the club. When people are dancing, bombard them with the music. When they leave the floor, they should be able to relax and have a conversation with others without having to yell. Excessively loud music off the floor is considered annoying and can have a negative effect.

Sometimes, the design and layout of a nightclub is such that the entire club becomes the dance floor and the music is played loudly all throughout the club. These clubs are the exception, because their customers know what they're walking into when they get there.

Controlling where the sound is loudest is a matter of speaker placement and the number of speakers inside a nightclub. For most clubs, speakers should be placed and directed towards the dance floors. Doing that will concentrate the music into one area. If set up properly, the rest of the club will receive ambient sound from the dance floor area. The sound will be more than enough to entertain the guests who are not on the dance floor and still allow them to relax and carry on normal conversations.

SOUND SYSTEM MAINTENANCE

It just makes good old-fashioned common sense that anyone operating a nightclub full of high dollar sound equipment would want to maintain the system to get the most out of it and increase the life span of the components. A well-maintained system could very well last forever. Routine maintenance check-ups should be scheduled and conducted by a professional. This procedure can head off potential problems and even prevent system failures when they will hurt business the most.

SYSTEM CLEANING

Aside from regular maintenance visits from a professional, there are things that both you and your DJ can do on a daily basis to keep the system free from contaminants and working properly. A clean system is a healthier system. Dust particles can quickly undermine any system by getting in through the vents. When dust accumulates, it takes its toll by making it harder for components to cool themselves.

With most components, simply following the manufacturers suggested procedures for dusting will be enough to clean them. In addition you should establish a cleaning regiment and make sure that it's adhered to. The DJ should be responsible for cleaning. And, at the very least, cleaning and dusting should be done at the beginning and end of the DJ's shift.

Dusting can be done in several ways without hurting or compromising the system or any system settings you don't want changed. Compressed air is now the popular choice for dusting. You can get compressed air at just about any electrical, stereo or computer retail store. The great thing about compressed air is its ability to dust through the vents, inside of the components. If compressed air is too expensive for your taste, the old feather duster will work fine to rid components of surface dust before it gets a chance to accumulate inside components.

Aside from dust, there is also the matter of liquid contaminates. This can be a problem when a drunk DJ spills a beer on one of the components. The liquid can quickly make its way inside to the heart of the component and cause an electrical failure, thus rendering it useless. The DJ booth is often a very popular place and many guests may congregate around this area. Forbid them from entering. They may not intend to cause problems but sometimes all it takes is just a drop or two of liquid from their glasses to cause a catastrophe. Also consider establishing an employee policy which restricts the DJ and all other employees from bringing liquids into the booth to prevent this very problem.

VENTILATION
Make sure that all components are properly ventilated and have access to cool air. Sometimes, if the amount of space you have to work with is limited, this is hard to achieve. Stacking components on top of each other can cause excessive heat buildup and prevent cool air from reaching the vents. Over time, poor ventilation could cause them to overheat and probably fail. Ideally, your components should be separated and installed away from other components so that they are allowed to breath a little.

Fans are one way to help components keep cool, especially if you are forced to stack your system. Just make sure your DJ doesn't point the fans at himself because he feels he's too hot.
Even if you think the components are well ventilated, it won't hurt any to have a few fans working on them, keeping them even cooler.

If you place your equipment inside of a stereo cabinet, make sure that the cabinets themselves are also well ventilated and have good air circulation. Even if you separate your components, it's no good if the shelves they're placed on don't have a smooth air flow. The components will just sit on the shelves and bake in their own heat.

THE MUSIC

PLAY THE RIGHT SOUNDS

Choosing the right music for a nightclub doesn't have to be a difficult thing to do. The music selection for the most part should stay consistent with the type of venue you'll be promoting. There are several different music genres. Many nightclubs only play specific genres, such as a Country and Western venue. Other venues, especially dance clubs, sometimes incorporate almost all genres of music and put them into the play list.

Whatever is played is up to you, but to satisfy the clientele, follow the constantly changing music trends. Select music that will have a wider appeal to the majority of the clientele. Also remember that music has the ability to change people's moods and even cause an increase in food and alcohol sales. So, take the music seriously, there's more involved to choosing the right music than just throwing on a record or a CD and expecting everything to go smoothly.

The following are the most common types of music genres. To give you examples, check out the artists and album titles. See if you recognize any of them.

Dance:
Moby/Play
Dido/No Angel
Eiffel 65/Europop

Classic Rock:
Tom Petty & The Heartbreakers/Greatest Hits
Eric Clapton/Unplugged
Aerosmith/Big Ones

Rock:
Pearl Jam/Ten
Alanis Morissette/Jagged Little Pill
Dave Matthews Band/Crash

Alternative:
Red Hot Chili Peppers/Californication
Papa Roach/Infest

Pop:
Madonna/Music
Matchbox Twenty/Yourself Or Someone Like You
Christina Aguilera/Christina Aguilera
Britney Spears/Oops...I Did It Again

Country & Western:
Faith Hill/Breathe
Shania Twain/Come On Over

Hip Hop:
DMX/...And Then There Was X
Lauryn Hill/Miseducation of Lauryn Hill
Sisqo/Unleash The Dragon
Lil' Kim/The Notorious KIM
Eminem/The Marshall Mathers LP

R & B:
Destiny's Child/The Writing's On The Wall
Macy Gray/On How Life Is
Pink/Can't Take Me Home

Of course this is a very small list of songs/artists, but you understand. You may have also noticed that there is a specific genre for dance. That doesn't mean that is the only category that has music worth dancing to. Virtually all categories of music have songs that people love to dance to, so keep that in mind.

THE DJ MUST CONTROL THE TEMPO

Assuming that you'll be operating a nightclub that will bring in a dance crowd, the DJ needs to control the flow of the night with the music. Timing and tempo is everything. Poor management of song selection can ruin the energy and mood on the dance floor and inside the entire club.

The DJ needs to be able to mix up the songs that the target audience wants to hear. The trick is to make the changes in music selections noticeable to customers. If the music all sounds the same, it will eventually become boring to customers and will probably have an opposite effect.

The DJ must keep up the tempo. If he loses the tempo, he loses the audience. The tempo or beat of the music is what keeps people dancing. The DJ must have a feel for the crowd and anticipate what they want and need. The DJ shouldn't be playing for himself, but rather for the target customers. If the excitement levels in the club are high and there's a lot of energy flowing, keep it going with the right upbeat, danceable music selections.

The worst thing a DJ can do is to disrupt the tempo of the club with bad selections when customers aren't ready. This is usually done by dramatically changing the type of music being played. The best example of this would be entertaining very energetic customers, early in the night with popular dance music, and then suddenly breaking the tempo with some slow, golden oldies songs. The slower tempo, in that case would probably only discourage many energetic guests.

Conversely, when the crowd is in the mood for a slower pace, soft songs may be just what they need. Slower tempos are going to happen and there's nothing wrong with them at all as long as it's what customers want. During a slow period, don't start blaring R & B, expecting everyone to immediately respond and hit the dance floor because it won't happen.

All songs have their time and place to be played. Knowing when to play them and when not to, is the key to keeping with the tempo. Let the clientele decide what they want to hear. Keep a careful eye on the crowd, their body languages, moods and attitudes will tell you when it's time to up or lower the tempo a little. With experience this will become second nature.

Timing is just as important as the tempo. A good DJ should be able to recognize, by reading the customers, when it's time to change-up and play something totally different to recapture customers' attentions and keep them entertained. In other words, if the DJ were to play hip-hop music song after song after song, eventually it'll get old to the dance crowd and the dance floor will slowly start to empty. The DJ needs to be able to see this coming several songs ahead of time and switch to something else that's new and exciting. Timing is crucial and will cost you if it's not done correctly.

> ALL SONGS HAVE THEIR TIME AND PLACE TO BE PLAYED. KNOWING WHEN TO PLAY THEM AND WHEN NOT TO, IS THE KEY TO KEEPING WITH THE TEMPO.

MAXIMIZE DRINKS SALES

Usually, a nightclub that can draw in many people will have excellent alcohol sales. Sometimes though, a DJ does such a great job of keeping the action on the dance floor going that the majority of customers are more interested in dancing, and less interested in drinking. This is going to happen sometimes but it doesn't have to cut into drink sales.

When the house is packed and the excitement on the floor is so intense that it begins to affect drink profits, leaving sales only so-so or mediocre, the DJ should shift the action to the bars. This goes hand in hand with proper timing. When the floor is packed and the bars are empty, it might be time for the DJ to change the tempo by playing a song that's out of the ordinary or a song that doesn't have much dance appeal. Customers may look at you funny and wonder what it is you think you're doing but they'll leave the dance floor and the action will slow down a little. This change in tempo will serve as a break. You're almost guaranteed that the bars will become flooded with customers and drink orders.

A break in the action is also a good time to begin promoting drink specials or even to begin a transition towards another event inside a nightclub. The break doesn't have to last a long time either. It may only take the completion of the one song that drove everyone off the floor, before shifting back to the action songs. The break will give customers a chance to congregate around the bars, gather themselves and order some drinks. This will increase mediocre sales and maximize drink profits if done properly several times during the night. Don't overdo it, because customers will begin to hate you for it. The trick is to be clever about it and not too obvious.

Once the break is over, the DJ should slowly transition back to the floor packing songs. If the transition is too fast, and the DJ plays a song that's really popular, then it's possible that the floor will fill back up just as quickly as it emptied out, causing customers to abandon the lines at the bars.

CREATE A PLAY LIST

As stated before the DJ needs to be able to mix it up to keep the action on the floor fun and exciting. This can often be done ahead of time by compiling a list of songs that will be played during the course of a night. This will alleviate the need for the DJ to guess what the next songs should be during the action. The result of creating a play list, is a well calculated, organized lists of different songs that will be played at the right times throughout the evening.

You and your DJ must have a clear understanding of what you want, who the customers are, which songs are currently at the top of the music charts, which songs work best for the particular nightclub, which songs people are more likely to dance to and which aren't. The answers to these issues should define what a club is all about and what kind of music it should play to maximize success.

Taking all of that into consideration, create a play list by arranging music selections into sets of 4-6 songs. Group together the most popular dance songs into several sets. These are the songs that you'll want people to crowd the dance floor to. Then group several sets of average, less-popular songs together. Use these songs to pass time, in between breaks and before the night takes off.

Lastly, create several sets of fun songs. These are the songs that consistently pack the dance floor full of energetic customers. These types of songs for some reason, seem to have a longer life span than other songs and can be played at just about any moment to get people in the mood to dance and what else? Have a little fun! One of the best examples of a fun song would be "YMCA" by the Village People.

Start each night off with a few sets of average songs. Before the night gets going people will need a little time to get wound up so the sets should be just enough to hold customers' attention and keep them wanting a little more. Early in the evening is when the dance crowd should begin to arrive and this is the time to capitalize on drink sales and drink specials. The average set of songs should by no means be second rate songs, but should still be songs in which people can dance to and enjoy. In fact many people will but, it's unlikely that most will take to the dance floor early in the night to these songs.

After giving customers ample time to take advantage of any drink specials and allowing time for the club itself to get as busy and as full as it's probably going to get, kick off the night by playing a set of some current, very popular music. Again, these are the songs that should fill the dance floors every time they're played. You'll also want to turn the volume up. Way up! The songs themselves and the increase in volume will send a fever of enthusiasm through the place as people scramble to hit the dance floor.

After the night is started off, mix it up with different music sets and keep a good tempo going. Play several sets of less popular music in between a set or two of popular, top dance music. During peak times of action, throw in a set of fun songs to really get people excited. Fun songs played just at the right time will boost energy levels and bump up the tempo. After finishing the fun set, transition back to the average set of songs and start the cycle all over again.

This formula works well but make sure that the sets are played in a different order each night otherwise, regular customers will begin to predict what the next song is going to be. That will take a lot of excitement from the dance floor. Lastly, don't forget to control the tempo with timing. If the DJ is doing his job, he'll be watching the crowd and the bar. He should have a feel as to which sets need to be played and when.

INVENTORY CONTROL

There are many services and products available on the market to assist in controlling inventory. Because controlling inventory is such a critical task, failing to accurately track inventory can cause a dysfunctional nightclub.

Staying on top of the inventory situation is a must. Can you imagine what would happen if on the busiest night of the week, a club suddenly ran out of beer? Most likely, a lot of customers would be lost and as they go, so do profits.

MAINTAIN ENOUGH

The basic inventory should consist of a realistic and reasonable stock of alcohol and food products to cover normal sales demands placed on a nightclub. If you'll be opening a nightclub for the very first time, you initially may need to rely on a business plan to estimate a year's sales to calculate the needed inventory.

As a nightclub owner you should always keep your ear firmly planted to the ground and stay up to date with current events. The things that happen in peoples' everyday lives can often stimulate a busy night—Like weddings, concerts, sport events, festivals, holidays, reunions, etc. Try not to let those fluctuations catch you and the staff by surprise. If you know what's going on outside of the nightclub, it's possible to prepare the club and have adequate inventory for any unusual occurrences. Poor inventory control will equate to lost sales when not ready for anything at anytime.

A common problem for new operators when calculating inventory is to neglect *lead time*, which causes inventory levels to fall short. Lead time is the time it takes after you place your order to the time it takes for your order to actually arrive inside your nightclub ready for use.

KEEP TRACK OF INVENTORY

Fortunately, unlike many other businesses, tracking inventory in the nightclub industry can be a lot easier because nightclubs don't carry as many products to sell. A nightclub's typical product or inventory lines usually consist of alcohol and food. That's it. Even though a nightclub doesn't have to deal with numerous product selections like a retail business would, it's still easy for a nightclub operator, who neglects the books, to fall behind and get into trouble because of a lack of inventory attention.

You could choose to track inventory manually or opt to use one of the many inventory tracking systems made specifically for tracking alcohol inventory and distribution. Consult with your accountant in regards to how you will set up an inventory control system. A good system, manual or computerized, should be able to tell a lot about the state of the inventory.

POS or *(Point-of-Sale)* systems allow operators to carefully track inventory and can do a number of different things such as; Keep track of inventory usage, monitor changes in sales, track sales data and also offer the ability to *analyze* sales data.

One of the POS systems greatest attributes is that they allow operators the ability to track sales histories of each individual drink or food item sold by recording each sale as it happens at the cash register. This tells you which drinks are most popular, sell the most and which aren't moving out of the tappers so fast and need a little advertisement.

This is a great piece of information to have handy when it comes time to reorder alcohol inventories from the venders. Based on POS reports that can be generated, an operator can compare the relationship between their physical inventory and all sales that the nightclub has closed with very reliable accuracy.

Other benefits to POS software systems are electronic cash drawers, credit card readers, credit verification equipment and numerous other beneficial accounting features. In all, probably the greatest worth POS software systems offer is that they allow operators to gain control over their entire inventory by allowing them to thoroughly examine and break down the sales performances of each product through detailed POS reports.

VENDERS

Your venders or suppliers are without a doubt, extremely essential to the success of the nightclub. You'll generally need at least two venders. An alcoholic beverage distributor, and if your going to be in the food service industry also, you'll need a food distributor. When seeking venders you'll want to deal only with venders who will be reliable. A good alcohol vender should be

> BASED ON POS REPORTS THAT CAN BE GENERATED, AN OPERATOR CAN COMPARE THE RELATIONSHIP BETWEEN THEIR PHYSICAL INVENTORY AND ALL SALES THAT THE NIGHTCLUB HAS CLOSED WITH VERY RELIABLE ACCURACY.

able to timely respond to the nightclub, possibly several times a week to restock alcohol inventory as needed. You'll need a food vender that can deliver at least once a week. Also, if at all possible, the food vender should be able to deliver all of the food products required to eliminate the necessity for multiple food venders to cover all of your food inventory needs.

Compile a list of possible venders and get quotes, prices, proposals, discounts and terms of delivery. Carefully research each potential vender and ask for references. Don't hesitate to contact the references and speak with past or existing customers to find out how they feel the vender has performed.

After establishing your venders, you'll then need deliveries to begin arriving. Some distributors will extend credit and bill at a later date. This is usually the case with food sales. In most states however, it is illegal to purchase alcohol on a credit basis and therefore every time a nightclub receives a delivery, the inventory will have to be promptly paid for— cash on delivery (C.O.D.). So, be prepared to have plenty of working capital written into the business plan to avoid suffering from shortages during the beginning weeks or months of the nightclub's life.

RECORD KEEPING

For some, this is perhaps the most dreaded of all managerial functions an operator must perform. But, it is vital to the success of any nightclub. A successful operation depends on a record keeping system that carefully tracks all financial aspects of a nightclub. This activity can sometimes be tedious and demanding on your time, by leaving you to tend with paperwork, but it is a very necessary process. Improper management of the books could very well cause serious problems or even cause you to lose money if you let it go too long without accurate conciliation. Bad book management could possibly even lead to going out of business and you really don't what that to happen.

Many of the financial record keeping elements of running a nightclub can be left to a knowledgeable accountant if you would be willing to pay the fees associated with such services. Most accountants can assist with just about any record keeping you want, including handling the payroll and issuing pay checks to employees. Generally speaking though, the more work an accountant does, the more the services will cost.

If you decide to cut down on the cost of accounting services, especially in the beginning of a nightclub's life, be prepared to tackle most of the accounting work on your own. Carefully keep track and document the income in relation to outgoings and other financial obligations. Recording income and expenses is important to accurately figure your taxes to satisfy the IRS and can even help you to look better in the future if and when you need to approach a bank for money to use towards renovations or expansion.

The bottom line is that staying on top of your records will keep you informed with what's happening within your club and eliminates headaches later on. It could be difficult to determine a nightclub's financial situation at any point in time if the books aren't up to date. Failures such as that could lead to catastrophic problems, like not having enough money to pay employees because you thought there was more than enough in the bank account to cover it. So manage the records with great care. You don't have to be especially good with numbers, a calculator will do wonders, but you do have to keep track of all financial matters in a clear and easy to understand format that you can be easily referenced to make important financial decisions on a daily basis.

Here are the basic financial details you'll likely need to keep track of with a record keeping system. Of course, no two nightclubs are the same, so there may be more or less that will need to be dealt with.

Income:
Game Profits.
Alcohol Sales.
Food Sales.
Door Cover Charge Profits.

Inventory/Outgoings:
Alcohol.
Food.
Payroll/Employee Incentives.
Equipment Rental/Payments.
Rent/Mortgage Repayments.
Business Loan Repayments.
CDs/Records.
Special Entertainment Fees (i.e. live bands, featured DJs or other entertainers).
Promotions and Advertising (includes prize monies and prize give aways).
Other Expenses (such as employee training, services and uniforms).

Utility Bills:
Electricity/Gas.
Water.
Garbage Collection Bills.
Cable/Programming Networks.

Other:
Profit and Loss Statements.
Taxes (Employee, federal, state and local).
Employee Schedules.

ADULT CLUBS

ENJOY THE EASY PROFITS OF
AN ADULT ORIENTED VENUE

Call them what you want, strippers, exotic dancers, topless dancers or just dancers—Whatever. The fact is that adult clubs offer a source of entertainment that draw in millions of paying customers each year all throughout the world. Operating an adult club can be a very financially rewarding opportunity that usually carries a lower risk of investment and the chances of an adult venue failing are significantly less than that of a standard nightclub or bar.

This is so because the main product of an adult club really never changes. The product is entertainment in the form of nude dancing. The faces of the dancers may change, but the type of entertainment always remains the same. People, men and women alike, who go to an adult club do so because they expect to be entertained by professional dancers. Not for any other reason. Although, good drinks, drink specials, games (Darts, billiards, video games) and good hospitality still helps to create a positive atmosphere to enhance an adult club's value to its customers.

THE CUSTOMERS

High prices by way of door charges and drinks aren't enough to keep millions of enthusiastic customers away from adult clubs. Adult club customers come in all shapes and sizes from men or women to the young, old, married, single, divorced and on through the blue collar workers to the wealthy.

Adult clubs aren't just limited to male customers either. Though, the vast majority of all adult clubs in existence throughout the world, feature dancers who are women, there are still a few that are designed primarily for female customers and feature male dancers. Even so, an adult club that exclusively hosts nude or topless female dancers will have customers who are both men and women and vice versa. Many customers, men and women alike find that being entertained by a professional dancer to be sexually erotic. Some couples find their way to these venues just for that reason.

Other customers go to get away from reality. How often does one get to see a beautiful woman, in the nude, dancing on a stage? A good dancer is one that is able to capture the attention of the customers and make each customer feel like they are the only one the dancer is dancing for. Some customers can lose themselves during performances as they visualize themselves in an intimate encounter with a dancer. This is the case primarily with male customers.

Yet, other customers enter an adult nightclub just for the enjoyment and sensation of being entertained by good looking and talented dancers. These are the people who go to have fun.

THE DESIGN

As with any venue, marketing and research should be a major concern before the front doors open up for business. A good floor plan for the most part, should be set up like any other nightclub, where comfort and efficiency are the primary concerns. There should be few choke points where traffic can congest. It should be relatively easy to travel to and from points with the use of pathways. The wait and security staff should be able to get anywhere quickly and unimpeded to serve customers and to handle any problems that arise.

The floor should be designed around the stage(s). The stages are where most of the action takes place, so it's important they are visually accessible from all areas inside of the club. As for the design of the stages, there are many ways to build them. How they are built should be determined by the layout of the club to maximize space and be consistent with the atmosphere that the club will project. Probably the most important piece of equipment that a stage should have are stage poles. Many acts or routines that the dancers perform, involve the use of stage poles. Dancers tend to complain or feel uncomfortable performing on a stage without poles so make sure each stage has at least one.

AS WITH ANY OTHER BUSINESS, AN ADULT CLUB WILL NEED TO OBTAIN THE APPROPRIATE BUSINESS LICENSES AND PERMITS TO LEGALLY OPERATE. MOST CITIES HAVE ALREADY ISSUED ALL THE PERMITS AND LICENSES FOR ADULT VENUES WITHIN THEIR CORPORATE LIMITS THEY INTEND TO AND PROBABLY WON'T ISSUE ANYMORE BECAUSE OF ALL OF THE SOCIAL ISSUES SURROUNDING ADULT OPERATIONS.

Lights and special effects should also be used on stage. Proper lighting and effects can make the experience more interesting by enhancing the acts of many dancers, especially the more upbeat and faster routines.

THE PROBLEMS WITH ADULT CLUBS

Fortunately, there really aren't too many problems associated with operating an adult venue. Perhaps the largest obstacle an operator will have is just being able to establish the club itself in a city. Any operator, who has the desire to open up an adult venue, will find that in just about everywhere in the country, he or she may meet some resistance from the city they wish to set up in.

As with any other business, an adult club will need to obtain the appropriate business licenses and permits to legally operate. Most cities have already issued all the permits and licenses for adult venues within their corporate limits they intend to and probably won't issue anymore because of all of the social issues surrounding adult operations. An operator may also find that some cities won't even consider issuing licenses for *any* adult nightclubs period! These cities have no adult clubs anywhere within their limits and don't plan to ever allow any in.

If you're lucky enough to obtain the necessary permits and licenses, you'll still have to contend with city zoning plans. Most cities place adult venues in zones far away from residential areas in an attempt to avoid problems between residents and the adult scene. There are just too many rumors floating around about adult nightclubs, some true, but most not true. Rumors have such an influence on the way that many people perceive them and as far as many citizens are concerned, adult clubs fall into the *NIMBY* category. That's, "Not in my backyard!"

All of this leaves the aspiring operator with two options. The first option is to seek and purchase an existing adult club operation. This is sometimes almost impossible to do at a reasonable price. If the adult club is successful, then chances are, the price tag will be staggering. Why would anyone in their right mind sell a successful adult club for next to nothing? Conversely, if an operator approached an owner and the owner was eager to sell the business for a price that seemed too good to be true. That should leave the potential operator wondering what's wrong with the club? A very careful evaluation should be made in a situation such as this. Why buy a failing business of any sort unless you are absolutely positive that you have what it takes to turn it around and generate some profits?

The second option that many adult operators have turned to is setting up business out in the county, away from city limits and social pressures. In most cases, it will be easier for an operator to obtain a county business license and required permits. Most counties are less populated or unincorporated than cities and so the social woes aren't as influencing.

The only downfall to clubs situated away from cities is that it forces customers to have to drive longer distances to get there. For some this may be a reason not to go, but for others it won't make too much difference at all. Frequenting an adult club is something that many customers specifically plan to do and the drive will just become part of the plan.

The last major problem that adult venues have to deal with is abiding by any and all specific laws placed on them. These laws are often more stringent than the laws any normal nightclub has to abide by. Adult nightclubs are in the business of promoting sexuality. A nude dancer on a stage dancing in a provocative way is doing just that. Because of that, many states have felt the need to get involved and pass laws regarding such activity.

Depending on which state you live in, laws vary and it's important that anyone wanting to get into this business learn the specific laws of his or her state regarding an adult nightclub. Generally speaking, most laws will forbid any sex act to be committed between a dancer and a customer. Sex acts are actions that involve any contact with the genitals and direct contact with the nipples of a female. Sex acts also include intercourse, oral or genital and it doesn't matter whether the act is really sex. Simulating sex counts too. That means that any sexual positions between the dancer and customer are out, even if sex isn't really occurring!

Finally, unless you live in the state of Nevada, sex for money is illegal. This is otherwise known as prostitution. Adult club prostitution isn't something that's going to be visible for all to see. Typically, some sort of private transaction is made between the dancer and the customer and the act is done somewhere else.

SEX ACTS ARE ACTIONS THAT INVOLVE ANY CONTACT WITH THE GENITALS AND DIRECT CONTACT WITH THE NIPPLES OF A FEMALE. SEX ACTS ALSO INCLUDE INTERCOURSE, ORAL OR GENITAL AND IT DOESN'T MATTER WHETHER THE ACT IS REAL OR SIMULATED.

Not all dancers are prostitutes and in fact very few of them are but if an operator was unfortunate enough to have a dancer or two engage in this sort of activity, the club legally could be considered as a *brothel* and it's illegal to operate a brothel. This could cause the operator legal trouble in the form of criminal or civil litigation. A brothel is a place, any place, where a person can go to hire a prostitute.

The point to all of this is to be careful. No one probably opens an adult club with the intention of breaking the law whether they agree with them or not. An operator will need to have a properly trained security staff that is thoroughly knowledgeable about every aspect of the club and a staff that can take proper steps to avoid illegal activity. Often, an overindulged customer will initiate some sort of illegal contact with a dancer and that customer should immediately be dealt with. The most common occurrence will be how the customer touches the dancer and the next are how the dancer touches the customer. The dancers as well as customers, should be warned or disciplined for any inappropriate behavior. Usually all it takes are verbal warnings by making both the dancer and the customers aware of the problems. If that doesn't work, you'll need another approach.

The reality is that all adult nightclubs are different. In the interest of business all of them will do what they have to do in order to become successful. Have you ever been to an adult club, made an observation and noticed that there was a lot of body contact between the dancer and a customer during a performance? Then at a different adult club, make a similar observation, and saw that there was hardly any contact all between the dancers and the customers? In both cases, the dancers are just conforming to the standards of the nightclub that they happen to be working in. This happens because of the different styles of the operators who run the clubs. Pressure from law enforcement or the lack of it also plays a role in what's acceptable in many different adult clubs.

BASICS OF A TYPICAL ADULT CLUB OPERATION
There are generally three different kinds of adult clubs. The first one is the small, run-down club, that seems to attract a questionable clientele and has problems booking or hiring quality entertainment. They are usually forced to accept the bottom of the line dancers. These clubs fall into the "sleazy" category to many people.

The second type is what all adult club operators should strive for. These are the more upscale, somewhat glamorous adult clubs. These clubs usually feature several dancers at anyone time on a daily basis. Usually these clubs can afford to be very selective in the type of entertainers they book and hire and normally there is no shortage of entertainers wanting to work for these clubs. These are the adult clubs that most customers prefer to go into.

The third type of an adult venue is better known as a *"juice bar."* Juice bars have come into their own in recent years. These clubs feature entertainers that perform completely in the nude. Their entire bodies, genitals and all, are exposed for customers to see. Because most states and municipalities have set clearly defined laws regarding nudity, exposed nipples and genitals, they will not issue liquor licenses to juice bars. Therefore, juice bars cannot legally sell alcohol.

Juice bars have gotten around this dilemma by charging higher door cover charges to make up for lost alcohol sales. Most juice bars also allow customers to bring in their own alcoholic beverages. This is completely legal to do.

RULES

The rules inside of an adult club usually slightly vary but for the most part, they're all pretty much the same. The rules apply to the dancer and to the customer. The rules keep the club in compliance with the laws and also serve to protect the dancers. Rules address what the customers and the dancers can do. Rules address how the customer is allowed to touch the dancers and answer such questions regarding whether a customer can place his hands on the dancer's legs, buttocks or breast.

Likewise, rules lay out how the dancer is able to perform for the customers. What kind of allowances are they given? What can they show customers? Pubic hair, nipples or everything? How close are they allowed to get to the customers during a performance? Are they allowed to touch the customers and if so, how? These are all questions that each adult venue must carefully evaluate and address.

WHO GETS PAID AND HOW?

Industry standards vary depending on the locale of the adult club about how dancers are paid. Aside from the tips that dancers receive from customers for their entertainment, many are paid a base salary from the clubs they work in. Some venues are so successful, that the dancers actually have to pay the clubs in order to work there. The fees that the dancers pay are small peanuts in comparison to the huge amounts of money they can make from tips on an average night.

DJs and bartenders normally are also compensated for the work that they do for the dancers. Dancers should appropriately tip DJs and bartenders a percentage of their tips. The tips they receive from dancers of course, should be on top of their hourly wages.

STAGE DANCE

Stage dances give customers the most frequent exposure to the entertainment. On the stage is where the dancers' talents are revealed. Each dancer's individual stage performances can separate them from other dancers. These stage shows often set up lap dances and private dances after they finish their acts. Dancers take the stage for a specified period of time, usually a set of music between 2 and 6 songs. After a dancer finishes a set, a new dancer takes the stage. This cycle will repeat itself until closing time or until the end of a dancer's shift.

> DJs AND BARTENDERS NORMALLY ARE ALSO COMPENSATED FOR THE WORK THAT THEY DO FOR THE DANCERS. DANCERS SHOULD APPROPRIATELY TIP DJs AND BARTENDERS A PERCENTAGE OF THEIR TIPS.

Using a cycle like this will allow the dancers to stage dance more than once in a shift, so long as there aren't too many dancers in the rotation. A general rule of thumb is that the first dancer in the rotation should be the first one out. Therefore, the last dancer in the rotation should be the last one of the shift or night (at closing time).

LAP DANCE

Lap dances are also known as table dances. The dancer performs for the customer while the customer is seated at his or her table. This is an up close and personal encounter that lasts anywhere from a few seconds to several songs. After the dance, the dancer is tipped by the customer. The tip is usually no less than one dollar.

PRIVATE DANCE
Private dances are a one on one dance that are usually a little more intimate and longer than lap dances. Private dances normally last for at least an entire set of songs in a secluded area away from the rest of the customers. These dances are more costly than lap dances and typical prices range anywhere from $10-$50, sometimes even more depending on the quality and success of the club.

THE MUSIC
There are two ways to utilize music in adult venues. The first way is the least preferred way among dancers, which is to have a DJ that plays whatever he wants, when he wants in an effort to control an overall atmosphere. Dancers in general don't like having any control over the songs that they have to dance to. This seems to be one of those things that can cause a lot of stress between the dancers and management.

The other option of course is to allow the dancers to choose their own set of songs. Prior to each dancer's stage performances they should check in with the DJ and arrange with him the set of songs they want to dance to. This method works well and alleviates stress among the dancers, but can cause the music in the club to go all over the place. One dancer might go with a set of R & B, the next with Country & Western and the next might choose Classic Rock.

The variety of music may not go over well with customers as the sounds in the club go from one extreme to another. There's nothing more annoying, for many customers than enjoying a certain type of music for several minutes and then having to listen to a completely different type of music afterwards.

For the very small adult venues that don't have a DJ and don't plan on getting one anytime soon, a decent sound system that allows the dancers access to a tape or a CD player will suffice. The entertainers will need to provide their own songs, but the dancers who work in those smaller clubs usually won't have too many problems with that.

Adult clubs with multiple stages and dancers performing stage sets at the same time may get around the song dilemmas by just letting the DJ take control of the music. All of the dancers will have to dance to whatever the DJ plays. This only makes sense because it's impossible to play several songs in one room at once. The key to making this work is to have a DJ that is playing music which is easy to dance to. Second, the songs themselves should be generally entertaining for the type of customers that frequent the club. This formula will work well in most adult clubs and has a long track record of success.

DOOR FEES AND DRINK PRICES

Because adult clubs often carry a stimulus of being culturally unacceptable or "dirty" places to go to, especially for many Americans, this enhances the marvel of actually going inside one. In the U.S., to promote or see nudity and especially sexuality is taboo. And so, entering an adult club is not even close to being the same as entering any other type of nightclub. People go to nightclubs to socialize with and meet others in relaxed atmospheres. People go to adult clubs to be entertained by the opposite sex! It's not every day, a beautiful, nude woman performs up close and personal for most people. For some customers this is fun, for others it's like a secret seductive world that they can enter. And yet others feel that the experiences of an adult club can enhance their sex lives with their partners.

> PEOPLE GO TO ADULT CLUBS TO BE ENTERTAINED BY THE OPPOSITE SEX! IT'S NOT EVERY DAY, A BEAUTIFUL, NUDE WOMAN PERFORMS UP CLOSE AND PERSONAL FOR MOST PEOPLE.

For all this, the adult club operator needs to be well compensated for providing a place for unique experiences to occur. Typical adult venues charge much higher cover charges and drink prices than other nightclubs. It isn't unreasonable to do this and it won't hurt business at all. Operators of adult clubs find themselves in positions to profit handsomely simply because of the value that the customers themselves place on these venues.

THE DANCERS
Since the dancers take center stage in any adult club, figuratively speaking, it's very important that an adult club's dancers provide fresh and exciting entertainment. An adult club relies solely on the dancers and they'll be judged by what they do, what they don't do, how they look and how they treat customers. The personal appearances of the dancers, plays the largest role in whether or not customers will be satisfied with the entertainment. Let's face it, people go to adult clubs for their own various reasons, but what good is it to go to one if the dancers aren't attractive? Very attractive, busty women or attractive muscular-toned men make the best candidates for dancers most adult club customers (men and women respectively) desire to see.

DANCER MANAGEMENT
The biggest challenge in operating an adult club is that of managing the dancers. An operator has to keep the entertainment fresh, which means that he or she must deal with many different dancers on an ongoing basis. Dancers are in a league of their own and usually are quite different types of people than what most people are used to dealing with. This isn't meant in a bad way, but is meant to prepare prospective operators for reality.

Ideally, all of the dancers in an adult nightclub would be perfect. That is, they would be exceptionally attractive and would have great personalities as well as putting on award-winning stage performances. The sad fact is that this isn't the case. All dancers come with their own individual personalities, talents and some with their own problems. These traits will be either good or bad for business.

Operators should keep a keen eye on what's going on with the dancers. Problem dancers can translate into problems for the club. Any serious problems that cannot be resolved between the operator and the dancer should result in the dancer being let go.

Dancer management also includes keeping the stage full of entertainment from night to night. Today, an adult club needs many different dancers to be successful. An operator cannot get away with only having one or two dancers a night. Customers need a lot of variety. No two dancers are exactly the same and the more variety or diversity an adult club can throw at the customers the better the chance there will be of those customers returning again.

Weed out the dancers that aren't drawing in a crowd. Anyone who has ever gone to an adult club on a regular basis has seen a dancer that cannot keep the attention of customers. This usually happens because the dancer isn't physically attractive and the customers become disinterested by the presence of the dancer.

Some dancers try to dance as many years as they possibly can because the money is usually too good to just walk away from. Their primes come and go and inevitably, they are perceived as too old or unattractive. This isn't fair but it's the hard truth for many entertainers.

An operator has to be prepared to replace those dancers that are bad for business. This isn't sometimes the easiest thing to do but this is what business is all about. It's hard to tell an entertainer that they're not working out because of their age, looks, personality or the lack of talented performances. Adult nightclubs are businesses of entertaining by promoting sexuality and beauty in a relaxed social atmosphere. If that isn't happening because of a particular dancer, an operator should be honest and tell the dancer straight out what the problem is and let the dancer go. *Most* dancers will appreciate honesty and any constructive criticism that can be given.

Keep an open mind. All dancers are different and all have their own individual capabilities. It's quite possible that an older experienced entertainer can still draw in a crowd and make profits for the nightclub verses the older dancers' counterpart, the younger, less experienced dancer. The bottom line is that customers go to see a good show and to be entertained. As long as that happens, ages and physical appearances should take a back seat.

WHERE DO THE DANCERS COME FROM?

Although there are a few clubs that cater to female customers and feature nude male dancers, most adult clubs around the world are oriented toward the male clientele and predominantly feature female dancers. This is so because there is a larger market for men wanting to be entertained by female dancers than women wanting to be entertained by male dancers. These dancers can and often do come from all walks of life. Thousands are lured into the business by the idea of being able to make huge sums of money. Yet others enjoy the thrill of power and being watched on stage.

Luckily, there aren't too many times when an adult club operator is faced with a shortage of willing entertainers. For the successful adult nightclubs, it isn't uncommon that the entertainment finds them. Many successful adult clubs have so many eager candidates seeking employment that they have a waiting list and can afford to be very selective in deciding which dancers stay and which one go.

The adult market has become so huge that many dancers have agents. Those dancers actually pay an agent to ensure that they have venues to work in. The agent's job is to book their clients into adult clubs and make sure they have work every week. This often means that agented entertainers do a lot of traveling from venue to venue. Usually dancers that are booked by agents only work inside a club for a very short period of time before moving onto the next scene. Normally, they'll work anywhere from just one night to one week.

In some cases, an adult operator may seek out and become a client of a talent agency. These operators contract with an agent and the agent places entertainment inside the venues according to the operator's preferences. Talent agencies are the preferred choice for many owners because they usually only need to deal with their agents to keep the entertainment fresh. Owners pay these agents a fee and enter into a contract with them but, the terms are usually easier to deal with than them having to go out and hire the entertainment on their own.

Some adult entertainers have become so successful and in demand that adult clubs profit immensely when they are booked to work. These entertainers are well-known and so popular that they sometimes even travel with a small entourage of body guards and followers. When an adult club is able to book such an entertainer, the operator needs to take advantage of the promotions and properly advertise the event.

Customers do respond to adult club advertising and will likely line up to get in just for the chance to see and get next to a popular or well-known entertainer. For the operator, this is the time to reap all of the benefits of the adult market and increase the door entry fees. Higher door cover charges won't turn too many away and the house is likely be packed.

If at all possible, in the interest of quality control, an operator should audition all dancers who express a desire to work inside the club, especially dancers who are inexperienced and new to the business. Auditions give an operator the opportunity to see first-hand how a dancer performs. This is the time to identify which dancers fit into the scheme of the club and which ones don't.

All auditions should be followed up with personal interviews. The process of an interview allows an operator to learn more about a dancer's personality and experience. The results of both the auditions and the interviews should be used together to make hiring decisions.

As with any nightclub operation, one of the many keys to success is innovation. Innovation allows an operator to keep the atmosphere fresh and entertaining. An astute adult venue operator takes full advantage of every situation and is able to turn it into entertainment for the customer, thus increasing customer traffic and gross profits.

To illustrate effective innovation, hundreds of adult venues throughout the U.S. now take advantage of the many inexperienced dancers wanting to get into business by offering them the opportunity to participate in special nights called something like an *"Amateur Night."* These amateur nights are highly promoted and usually draw in healthy crowds of customers who want to see dancers who have never danced before. The amateur dancers get a chance to put on a show and entertain for the first time. The customers get to witness the dancers' debuts. The club itself gets easy publicity, more customers, more profits and more repeat visits. Amateur night is just one example of how an innovative operation used such an event to a club's advantage. Now this event has become so popular that it is done all over the country.

APPENDIX A

"The Equipment"

Obtaining the necessary equipment and inventory to properly run a nightclub will require the help from other companies to deliver an assortment of products and services. During start-up, hundreds of important decisions must be made regarding the look and style of the club and everything else that will occur on an operational basis. Choosing the right equipment and inventory is a substantial part of the decision making process.

Everything from employee uniforms to promotional products, eventually must be decided upon. Once the decisions have been made, you'll have to turn to other businesses to obtain the necessary equipment. Nightclubs rely heavily upon other businesses to fulfill inventory orders and render services. In most cases, you'll need to establish accounts with other businesses, such as distributors or wholesalers, to begin a working relationship with them.

There are hundreds of companies and other businesses that specialize in selling to or servicing nightclubs and nightclub/restaurant operations. Because there are so many and because they are usually localized, meaning they are specific only to a given area or region of operation, it's impossible to list all of them within the confines of this book. You'll have to do some homework to find the companies in your area that will best suit your needs. Once you start looking you'll see they aren't too hard to find. The trick is to find the ones that'll be reliable and will serve you well.

The internet, the phone book yellow pages, trade publications and business reference guides are excellent places to start looking. Word of mouth is also a useful source for information. Don't be shy, ask other nightclubs and restaurants in your area which businesses do what for them. Chances are they'll tell you and any leads they provide are worth following up on.

Contact as many like companies as you can to keep your options open. Request as much information about them and their products or services that they can provide you with. Study everything, compare offers and make educated decisions. Wise decisions can keep a business healthy and save money.

The remainder of this appendix, outlines some basic equipment, inventory and services you may require and each includes a checklist to assist you in determining what you need or should consider adding to a nightclub. Figuring out what will be needed to make an operation work is also important when creating the business plan. Researching and adding the costs of services and each piece of equipment that'll be required can help accurately determine exactly how much money is needed during start-up.

BEERS, WINES, SPIRITS AND OTHER BEVERAGES

With the exception of teen clubs, nightclubs cannot survive without alcoholic beverages, which means you'll need lots of drinks to satisfy customers. If you plan to be successful you'll have to serve large volumes of beverages on a weekly basis. The services of alcoholic beverage distributors, venders or wholesalers are going to be necessary to replenish the inventory and prevent the club from having a shortage.

Set up an account with at least one stable distributor, vender or wholesaler who can deliver the much needed beverage products to the nightclub on a regular basis. How often you'll require deliveries will depend largely on how busy you'll be or how many drinks you'll serve in a given time period. A typical delivery schedule could vary as much as twice a week to once a month depending on the club and the strength of its business.

It takes a combination of alcoholic beverages to accomplish the task of delivering a quality venue to guests. Regardless of the size of the operation, you'll need *at least* four *different* brands of beer to keep customers happy. When it comes to beer, variety matters—Not all guests enjoy the same beer. Most successful clubs sell anywhere from ten or more brands of beer and some host more than one hundred different beers. Brewpub operations should especially focus on beer variety because beer diversities are strong selling points for these clubs.

You'll also need to be adequately supplied with wines and spirits. Wine is a great beverage for special occasions and good to have on the menu to compliment good food for the customers who enjoy drinking it. Spirits are necessities to create the endless numbers of cocktail recipes or to serve straight as shot drinks.

With each type of spirit, there are numerous brands that fall into its category. For instance, whiskey is a type of spirit in a class of its own, but there are dozens of different manufacturers and variants/brands that are all slightly different from each other, but are all still whiskeys. Those variations are usually noticeable in the taste and smell of the different spirit brands which means a cocktail could taste somewhat different depending on which brand was used as an ingredient.

Which spirits taste better than others are subjective opinions so, you'll have to determine which types and brands of the different spirits you'll serve and use in cocktails based on your own preferences. Nevertheless, you'll need to be supplied with the spirits of your choice by a distributor or wholesaler.

It may be necessary to have multiple distributors or wholesalers to deliver all of the needed alcoholic beverages, because some may not carry everything needed on their product lists. This is especially the case when it comes to adding dozens of different beers, wines or spirits to the drink menu. One distributor may not carry all the beverages you want so it may take more than one to get everything you'll serve.

Distributors should be able to deliver the following beverage products in any brands, labels and styles you need:

❑   Beers/Lagers (Draft and Bottled)
❑   Spirits
❑   Wines
❑   Champagne
❑   Liqueurs
❑   Pre-Mixed Drinks (i.e. Wine Coolers)

NON ALCOHOLIC BEVERAGES/COCKTAIL INGREDIENTS
Not all drinks served in a nightclub are alcoholic. Not everyone that frequents a nightclub drinks alcohol and because of that, you need to be able to serve them too. Non alcoholic drinks are important for a dinner crowd and early in the morning prior to closing time. Many non alcoholic drinks are also used to mix cocktails or to add flavoring, such as the case with a "Jack and Coke."

Most distributors and wholesalers do deliver non alcoholic products for order as well as alcoholic beverages. Typical non alcoholic beverages include:

❑ Coffee
❑ Cappuccino
❑ Soft Drinks
❑ Fruit Juices
❑ Tea
❑ Mixes/Flavoring

BAR EQUIPMENT
Setting up the bar requires some unique facilities to make the process of bartending a system. Bartenders will need several items in order to make their jobs more productive and serve drinks with efficiency. On top of serving drinks, the bartending station should be responsible for cleaning dirty glasses and keeping the bar itself clean and presentable to clients.

The bar obviously, is where a great deal of sales will be made and it will need to be constructed almost as its own business inside of a business. Bartenders will need easy access to sinks, reach in refrigeration and freezer systems to keep drink mixes and fruits cool, cocktail utensils in order to make certain drinks, ice cube machines, ice storage bins, CO_2 systems, tappers, cleaning and disinfectant agents, a good beverage dispensing system and more to effectively do the jobs.

Locate several companies that manufacturer or wholesale bar equipment and request a catalog of their products. They'll be more than happy to work with you. Carefully, examine their products, compare prices and look for at least the following suggestions—You're bound to find a lot more than what's listed below and that's good. You'll probably come across products that your specific operation will need that others may not:

- ❑ Bar Sinks
- ❑ Refrigeration Systems
- ❑ Cocktail Accessories
- ❑ Cocktail Shakers
- ❑ Cocktail Strainers
- ❑ Bottle Spigots (For spill-proof pouring)
- ❑ Blenders
- ❑ Coffee/Tea Brewers
- ❑ Espresso/Cappuccino Machines
- ❑ Ice Machines
- ❑ Ice Buckets
- ❑ Ice Crushers
- ❑ Glass Cleaners/Scrubbers/Sanitation Agents
- ❑ Hand Towels
- ❑ Beverage Service and Dispensing Systems

BEVERAGE SERVICE AND DISPENSING SYSTEMS
You are going to need some way to deliver beer from the keg to the beer mug. You'll want the beer to be cold and fresh. Right? There are many systems on the market that can help to accomplish just that. Most of these systems are user-friendly and utilize few working parts such as the liquor gun, which can dispense dozens of different beverages, alcoholic and non alcoholic alike, with the touch of a button and all from one station.

There are draft beer meters that aid in monitoring usage and determining inventory. There are sophisticated systems that portion drinks and some that have foam controls. Most of these systems can also be set to keep and maintain beer at specific temperatures that are set. Some can even track the brands of beer which generate the greatest profits. System controls come in many different forms including computerized, mechanical or manual.

Decide which type of system will best meet your needs. This decision should be based in part on what you can afford. Try to find a system that has multi-beverage capabilities from as few stations as possible. These types of systems may cost more money but will be easier to maintain and a decent system will work more efficiently. If you find a quality system to do the job, you'll get your money's worth in the long run.

KITCHEN EQUIPMENT AND INVENTORY
The ability to serve food is going to require some very specific equipment. How much equipment and which types should be determined on how much emphasis you plan to put on serving food. For example, if your operation will only serve pizza, then it's likely all you would need is a pizza oven. But, if you plan to host an extensive food menu, more equipment will be necessary.

Some knowledge of cooking and dish preparation is required before you begin purchasing kitchen equipment. Kitchen equipment is expensive and so you need to acquire what you can afford and need to do the job. Call upon the expertise of an experienced cook or restaurant consultant to learn as much as you can about kitchen and cooking components before buying anything. The basic restaurant/cooking appliances are:

❏ Convection Ovens
❏ Conveyer Ovens
❏ Freezers
❏ Dishwashers
❏ Fryers
❏ Griddles and Grills
❏ Microwave Ovens
❏ Pasta Cookers
❏ Pizza Ovens
❏ Gas or Electric Ranges
❏ Refrigerators

- ❏ Steamers
- ❏ Pot Washers
- ❏ Rotisseries

UTENSILS AND FOOD PREPARATION EQUIPMENT

On top of major appliances, smaller appliances such as toasters, blenders and prep equipment/areas such as prep tables, provide the means in which to properly prepare and cook a variety of dishes.

- ❏ Blenders/Liquidizers
- ❏ Cutting Utensils/Knives
- ❏ Pots and Pans
- ❏ Prep Tables
- ❏ Sinks
- ❏ Food Mixers
- ❏ Slicers
- ❏ Toasters
- ❏ Can Openers
- ❏ Bottle Openers
- ❏ Meat Cutting Machines
- ❏ Corkscrews

FOOD PRODUCTS

Which foods are selected for distribution is dependent on the food menu. Therefore, knowledge of the menu must be a consideration beforehand. A food distributor should be able to deliver a wide variety of food products, including meats, fruits, vegetables, diary products and so forth. Plan on ordering enough food inventory to suffice for one working week. Close to the end of the week, careful inventory should be taken of the remaining food products and the following week's food should then be ordered as needed and delivered.

- ❏ Meat Products
- ❏ Pasta

❑ Pizza Bases
❑ Poultry
❑ Sea Foods
❑ Cheese
❑ Eggs
❑ Diary
❑ Potato Products
❑ Desserts/Cakes
❑ Fruits and Vegetables
❑ Frozen/Fresh Foods
❑ Flour/Mixes/Sauces/Dressings/etc.

SAFETY AND SANITATION EQUIPMENT

Safety and sanitation are a major concern. Regardless of the type of operation you decide to run, these are issues that must be addressed on a daily basis. Not only do you not want employees or guests to get hurt, from slips, falls or any other injurious episodes, you don't want them to get sick either from unsanitary conditions. To address these problems you're going to need some simple, yet effective equipment such as, trash cans and disinfectants to handle it.

Cleaning regiments help to keep a nightclub presentable to customers and keep it in good shape for a much longer period of time. Look over the safety and sanitation checklists and be sure to acquire like equipment before you even consider opening the front doors for business:

❑ Waste Disposal Equipment
❑ First aid/Medical Supplies
❑ Dishwashing Detergent
❑ Anti Slip Floor Mats
❑ Trash Receptacles
❑ Hand Soaps
❑ Hand Towels
❑ Safety Signs ("Caution wet floor")
❑ Vacuum Cleaners

- ❏ Brooms
- ❏ Mops
- ❏ Mop Buckets
- ❏ Dusters
- ❏ Dust Pans
- ❏ Disinfectant Agents

RESTROOM EQUIPMENT

Restroom equipment is equally important as everything else. Restrooms allow customers to relieve themselves and practice good hygiene. The state of the restrooms says a lot about a nightclub and customers expect to use clean restrooms with adequate hygiene supplies. The following checklist is probably common sense to most, but none-the-less, make sure that at least these items are in the restrooms:

- ❏ Sinks
- ❏ Toilets
- ❏ Liquid Soap Dispensers
- ❏ Hand Towels
- ❏ Hand Dryers
- ❏ Mirrors

DESIGN, DECORATIONS AND FURNITURE

The designs, as well as decorations and furnishings, are crucial expressions of the atmosphere a nightclub hopes to create. There are countless ways in which an operator can lay out a nightclub and however it ends up, is entirely up to you. The end product is what customers see, sit on, smell, touch, how the place makes them feel and other comfort creating features. Therefore, consideration should be given to various decorative equipment, furniture and other details such as, temperature appliances and air quality.

- ❏ Air Purification Systems
- ❏ Air Conditioning
- ❏ Humidity Controllers

- ❏ Heating
- ❏ Ventilation
- ❏ Bar Stools
- ❏ Bar Rails
- ❏ Railings
- ❏ Chairs/Couches
- ❏ Tables
- ❏ Paintings/Pictures
- ❏ Mirrors
- ❏ Memorabilia
- ❏ Aquariums
- ❏ Carpet/Flooring
- ❏ Wall covering/Finishes
- ❏ Dance Floors
- ❏ Doormats
- ❏ Rugs
- ❏ Ash Stands
- ❏ Coat Rooms
- ❏ Coat Hangers

SERVICES

Because design and layout is such an important element, you may elect to involve the services of a professional. This option will be contingent on several factors such as the state of the building you buy or rent to operate a nightclub in. You don't necessarily need to hire any services but the pay off can be significant if you do. If you do choose to employ professional services, get many estimates and proposals before you make any final decisions and figure the costs into the business plan.

- ❏ Design and Bar Planning
- ❏ Architects
- ❏ Interior Designers
- ❏ Landscaping
- ❏ Signage
- ❏ Bar Design (The bar itself)

GLASS AND TABLEWARE

The drinkware at the minimum, should consist of beer mugs, glasses and shot glasses. If you really want to show some style have plenty of wine glasses on hand too. Just as important as the beverages are the drinkware that they'll be served in. What good is a shot of liquor without a glass to pour it in?

Stock up and make sure to have plenty of glasses of all types to contend with heavy customer traffic. The absolute worst thing that can happen is to run out of glasses during the peek of business. Customers won't wait on you too long and will probably take their business elsewhere. Consider having additional supplies of glasses on hand stored away in a back room ready to be used upon demand. Also figure on losing a few glasses here and there to accidental breakage and theft. Some customers will steal glasses and keep them as souvenirs.

Try and be consistent with the types of glasses you have. For instance, all of the beer mugs should look exactly alike and all shot glasses should look exactly alike. Your consistency should and will add professionalism to the nightclub.

Tableware includes the details surrounding food service and the items that sit on top of the tables. This covers just about everything from silverware, place mats to ashtrays. Much like glassware, all tableware should be consistent and of the same styles.

❏ Glassware (Mugs, glasses, shot glasses, shooters, martini glasses, coffee cups, etc.)
❏ Plates/Hot Plates/China/Pewterware/Serving Dishes
❏ Silverware/Cutlery
❏ Table Mats
❏ Table Skirts/Table Cloths
❏ Baskets
❏ Ashtrays
❏ Condiment Trays
❏ Napkins
❏ Coasters
❏ Menu Holders

COIN OPERATED EQUIPMENT

Using Coin-fed machines to your advantage can make thousands of dollars in supplemental profits with little to no extra work and without having to hire more employees. Coin-fed machines do all the work for you and even advertise themselves. All you need to do is figure out where to put them to maximize their selling potentials.

VENDING EQUIPMENT

There are several types of vending machines that all have the ability to make easy money from customers' pocket change. While putting together a nightclub, whatever you do, don't forget these simple additions:

- ❑ Condom Dispensers
- ❑ Candy Machines
- ❑ Medicines (Aspirin, Tylenol, Ibuprofen)
- ❑ Cigarette Machines

GAMES

Games are almost prefect money makers because they have the ability to captivate and hold the attention of customers for long periods of time. The longer customers stay, the more they eat, drink and tip. And, the longer a game can hold their attention, the more change customers pump into them as they relax, socialize and compete. This is a win/win situation for both the customers and the nightclub.

You'll be better off purchasing games like dart boards and pool tables because they'll always make huge sums of money. You'll do best to contact a game vender for video games and sports simulators. Large video games are expensive to buy and eventually people will stop playing the same old games as the years pass. When that happens, you'd be stuck with it if you owned it. Therefore, consider splitting the profits with a vender.

Venders can place key money making games and rotate out the ones that are no longer making profits. Take some time and look into the possibilities of money making games such as the following—Don't worry too much about costs because games will quickly and easily pay for themselves:

❑ Darts
❑ Pool Tables
❑ Foosball
❑ Air Hockey
❑ Sports Simulators (i.e., virtual golf)
❑ Video/Computerized Games

PAY PHONES

Pay phones offer customers a way to reach others who aren't there. The best place to place a pay phone is near the front entrance. In addition to allowing the luxury of phoning others, they allow patrons to call for rides or taxi cabs freeing you to attend to the other duties within the nightclub. If you won't have a problem making calls for patrons, or letting them use your phone lines, then don't worry about getting any pay phones.

CIGAR AND TOBACCO PRODUCTS

Many customers will feel the need to enjoy a cigarette or cigar and you need to be prepared. Make sure you have an adequate number of ashtrays or they will without a doubt use the floors, the tables, the chairs, the bar itself and anything else they can find as an ashtray to dispose of ashes and put out their cigarettes or cigars. Cigarette holes and burns in your carpet are unpleasant sights.

Another not so bad idea is to have match books and have those match books imprinted with your nightclub name/logo on them. Imprinted match books also double as promotional products.

Cigar and Martini bars obviously need to be prepared for smokers. They need to have a wide variety of cigars for customers to choose from. Have cigar selections laid out in a menu, complete with a description of each cigar and the prices, that can be passed out to customers upon demand.

Cigars and cigarettes can be obtained directly from wholesalers and manufacturers. Mail is the typical method that tobacco products are delivered so find a company that has a wide selection in which to choose from and establish an account.

❑ Cigars/Cigarettes
❑ Matches/Lighters
❑ Vending Machines
❑ Cigar Cases
❑ Cutters
❑ Cigar Holders
❑ Humidors
❑ Ashtrays

MUSIC AND VIDEO

Quality should be first and foremost when it comes to music and video equipment. The sound system plays an integral part in serving customers. A good sounding system is imperative. Customers can easily tell the difference between a good one and a bad one and they are known to judge a nightclub on that standard of alone.

Video, though not as crucial as the sound system, is more of a bonus for clients. Video includes television and programming that allow guests to watch live TV, recorded events and special adaptations, like live action on the dance floor inside of the nightclub. Sound, Video and DJ equipment can be found through a variety of manufacturers and wholesale companies. Look for brand names such as JVC, Carver, Gemini, Numark, JBL, Denon, Yamaha, Vestix, QSC, Technics or Pioneer to name a few.

SOUND AND VIDEO SYSTEMS

This checklist contains some basic equipment needed to fill a nightclub with quality and entertaining sound and video:

❑ Amplifiers
❑ Speakers
❑ Equalizers

❏ Crossover
❏ Mixers
❏ Compressor/Limiters
❏ Microphones/PA System
❏ CD Players/Turntables/Tape Players
❏ Jukebox
❏ Karaoke Equipment
❏ Sound Accessories (Cables)
❏ Televisions
❏ DVD Players
❏ VCRs
❏ Cameras
❏ Cable/Satellite Programming/Networks

SERVICES
An electronic specialist might be needed to properly install and hook up the sound and video systems to make sure it's done right. Hiring a professional can eliminate future problems with connections, acoustics and general problems with the system. Professional services may cost some money but not using them could end up costing even more money in the future. So, unless you know what you're doing when it comes to sound and video equipment, get a pro on the team. Typical sound services are:

❏ Music Programming
❏ Sound System Professionals (Installation and Servicing)
❏ Video Programming

LIGHTING AND SPECIAL EFFECTS EQUIPMENT
Much like the sound system, lights are just as important if not more, and play a role of their own. Lights are needed to create environments and manipulate moods. Take your time with light selections and approach lighting schemes with great care to ensure they work together as needed to project the proper image. Light effects come in a variety of shapes and sizes and all of them can do different things. Many of today's light

effects are programmable and can perform to preset routines or synchronized to play to the beat and sound of the music. Good light effects can definitely make the dance experience memorable for guests. Other special effects, such as fog, are excellent nightclub paraphernalia that can greatly enhance lighting effects to push the envelope even further.

Because there are so many variations in lights, light effects and special effects, you should thoroughly study and view demos, of any devices your thinking of adding to the nightclub to be sure their performances and features will be what you need. By doing this, you can eliminate surprises when the equipment is installed. Also, because there are so many different products in this area, there are many different companies that manufacture or sell them. Many of these companies all sell similar, but different, equipment and it will be prudent to contact several companies and request information regarding their products. In a lot of cases, just when you think you've found the perfect light equipment from one company, something even better for your club might lay in the hands of another company.

Here's the checklist for the lights and special effects you'll want to look into:

- ❏ Light Fixtures
- ❏ Light Dimmers
- ❏ UV Lights
- ❏ Effect Lighting
- ❏ Smoke Machines
- ❏ Hazers
- ❏ Foggers
- ❏ Lasers
- ❏ Mirror Balls
- ❏ Gobos
- ❏ Pin Spots/Helicopters
- ❏ Scanners
- ❏ Beacons
- ❏ Projectors
- ❏ Strobe Lights

ELECTRONIC TECHNOLOGY

Many of today's business are equipped with all kinds of technical electronic equipment which are capable of performing numerous tasks and can simplify operations. Technology such as computers and the internet have made it easier and faster to handle daily book work, communicate with people, broaden the scope of advertising by reaching a greater number of people and even increase sales. Other technologies like ATM machines and the ability to accept credit cards have helped to push sales even further.

Why should the nightclub industry be any different? Modern nightclubs should also ride the technology wave and take full advantage of all the benefits. System such as POS (Point of Sale), have made it much easier to accurately track sales and inventory. ATM machines and credit cards have their obvious advantage by allowing guests easy access to their bank accounts or charging their bills to a credit card. Those transactions, spell more sales and more profits for the industry. Computers, with all their sophistication, have made it easy to run a business with just a few programs. Everything from payroll to futuristic projections can be saved, edited, tracked, calculated, stored, retrieved, printed and more with ease.

The downfalls to these kinds of technologies is that they can become pricey. But, if you think in terms that you have to spend a little to make a little, you'll find that technology will be worth every penny you invest in it. Electronic technology equipment is easy to find but just be sure to keep everything in perspective, so don't go overboard and purchase things you don't really need.

Essential equipment you should consider making permanent additions to your nightclub are:

- ❑ Pos Equipment
- ❑ Cash Registers
- ❑ Computers
- ❑ (Software) Microsoft Office, Quicken, etc.
- ❑ Internet Services
- ❑ Age and Id Verification

❑   ATM Machines
❑   Credit Card Acceptance and Processing Equipment

ATM MACHINES AND CREDIT CARD PROCESSING
ATM machines and the ability to accept credit cards, will greatly increase the profit margin. Putting an ATM machine in the bar allows customers to replenish the cash in their wallets or purses. Generally when people run out of money, they leave. With an ATM machine inside the nightclub people have instant access to their bank accounts and more money to spend on drinks, food, games and whatever else you have to offer.

Place ATM machines in highly visible locations so that your customers can easily find them. Sometimes, the mere sight of an ATM machine can cause customers to take out additional cash. ATM machines will surprisingly increase business because many customers who don't have cash on them before they leave their houses, will know that if they go to your nightclub they'll be able to quickly obtain money.

If you opt for an ATM/debit machine, see to it that they are stocked with small denomination bills such as $5 dollar bills. It's much easier for customers to spend $5 than it is for them to spend a $10 or $20 dollar bill at once. Even if they spend four $5 dollar bills, they've obviously spent $20 dollars but may not even realize it.

Credit cards will also boost your sales off the charts. Some customers may not carry much cash on them and will prefer to deal and make their transactions by credit cards or checks. Accepting credit cards allows you to secure their business. You'll need credit card processing equipment to verify all transactions. There are several different ways to obtain an ATM machine or get the equipment needed to process credit cards. You can start with your local bank. Most banks will be more than happy to set up a merchant account with your nightclub so that you can accept credit cards. The fees for this service can vary from several hundred dollars to several thousand dollars.

ATM machines typically can either be bought outright or rented. When dealing with companies that sell or rent this equipment make sure that you calculate several aspects of any possible deals before making final decisions.

- **Make sure you fully understand everything:** You're understanding of any deals you enter into with companies can save you a headache later on. Compare cost and add up fees to see where you'll stand.

- **Measure cost effectiveness:** Compare whether leasing or buying equipment will be cost-effective. Leasing agreements can range anywhere from $100-$250 a month. It could cost upwards of $3000 to buy a machine outright.

- **Find a company that will effectively maintain the machines:** ATM machines aren't perfect by any means and will eventually break down and have problems. The company that you choose should be able to quickly respond and fix any problems that arise with the machine.

- **Look out for bad deals:** Don't give your trust to just any company. There are some bad companies out there looking to take advantage of the misinformed. Find a reputable and stable company in which to do business with. You'll be less likely to end up with a shoddy deal.

PROMOTIONAL PRODUCTS

Promotional products can pay off big. Sometimes the little things keep people coming back again and again. Most of the promotional products you'll initially need shouldn't be very expensive. But, if you want, you can go all out and open with a big bang and spend a lot of money buying promotional products. Promotional products are anything that draws attention to a nightclub which ultimately draws customers in and encourages repeat visits.

Promotional signs placed in the front windows lets people know a lot about what's going on inside. You can advertise drink specials there or a special event that's coming soon. Signs can be made up anyway you want and you can create them yourself, have employees create them or hire an advertising agency to do it for you. Don't just limit signs to the front windows. Place them inside, in several different areas to keep your patrons informed.

Other promotional products can include such items as key chains, posters, matchbooks, free beer mugs, T-shirts, decorative glassware, banners, floor graphics, coasters and any other promotional products that customers will view, read or take with them when they leave. Keep promotional products in mind when your thumbing through product catalogs looking for general nightclub equipment and items.

- ❑ Logos
- ❑ T-shirts
- ❑ Banners
- ❑ Posters
- ❑ Matchbooks
- ❑ Drink Coasters
- ❑ Signs

SECURITY

The Security that is provided inside a nightclub is both beneficial to customers and to the nightclub itself. There are many security products on the market that can help keep order inside. How much security you want to establish is up to you.

Security equipment can vary from sophisticated camera and monitoring equipment to just employing a bouncer or two to keep an eye on everything. You'll have to tailor any security issues you may have to the specific problems within the nightclub. It's highly suggested that if you are opening up a larger nightclub to have cameras stationed and fixed in the busiest areas. The busiest areas are those most likely to have problems among guests. It's a good idea to place the monitoring equipment in locations where your security employees, better known as bouncers, can watch the action away from the crowd. The front door area is also a good location for monitors to be placed since the front door area is a common place that bouncers protect. Behind the bars, in a back room or even inside an office are also excellent places to have monitors positioned.

Beyond that, decisions will have to be made regarding personal defensive weapons for the security staff. This is a big decision because the use of such weapons could place more liability on the nightclub. For most nightclubs, security weapons probably won't be a necessity but for others, especially the ones set in rough areas where problems and the threat of violence are part of daily life, might give weapons some serious consideration to protect bouncers and innocent customers. If you are considering whether or not to buy such equipment, consult with an attorney to find out which applicable laws apply in your area.

SECURITY EQUIPMENT
Security equipment can usually be found with major companies that specialize in security or police gear. Bouncers should be properly training in the uses of all equipment that they are given, including surveillance, prior to them using the equipment in a normal capacity. Getting the equipment is not enough. Be sure that any gear you buy comes with easy to understand instructions and then hold training classes with security employees, which they must pass before they can use the equipment. The services of a professional or police officer to teach the sessions would be a good idea.

These are some common pieces of equipment that security teams have in their arsenals:

❏   Cameras/Surveillance Equipment
❏   Mace/Pepper Spray
❏   Handcuffs
❏   Stunguns

AGE IDENTIFICATION
Trying to avoid serving minors alcoholic beverages should be a concern for every nightclub. This problem becomes exceptionally difficult for nightclubs that allow underaged patrons inside(18 or 19 and up bars) because once they're inside, there is a good chance they may deceitfully obtain alcohol behind the nightclub's back. The preferred way to address this problem is to try and identify those who are or are not old enough to drink, by branding them with hand stamps or wristbands.

If a nightclub will allow people under age 21 inside, look into obtaining the following ways to identify customers:

❑ Hand Stamps
❑ Wristbands

UNIFORMS

Although selecting appropriate uniforms may not be the easiest of tasks, selecting a uniform vender or retailer is not so hard to do. Most venders are very eager to work with you and can give you many ideas to chew on. Uniforms can range from just T-shirts to entire outfits. With outfits, they can help out with styles, embroidering, logos and fabric selection— Good designers are familiar with the occupational requirements of uniforms and will suggest a durable uniform.

Designing custom outfits should be a capability for any venders you consider hiring. Most of them won't have any problems with custom designs and do excellent work.

Uniforms are big decisions and if you want your employees to stand out from the guests, you'll have to dress them up. The following employees will need consideration for uniforms:

❑ Wait Staff (Male and Female Uniforms)
❑ Bartenders/Bar Hops
❑ Security Team
❑ Cooks/Kitchen Staff
❑ Hosts/Hostesses

APPENDIX B

"Mixing The Drinks"

No modern day nightclub can survive without alcoholic beverages. And sorry, but just serving beer on the menu isn't going to suffice if the nightclub hopes to be successful. Nightclub customers are a demanding group of people with varying taste and preferences for alcoholic drinks so you had better be prepared to deliver.

Thousands of different types of alcoholic drinks exist— all with their own names and unique characteristics. Nearly all of them are born as a result of experimentation. There are so many drink recipes that it is impossible to even attempt to name them all. Some creations find fame only within the local clientele of a nightclub that spawned it as a house specialty that can't be bought anywhere else. Other invented drinks enjoy success and notoriety on a nationwide, and sometimes even a worldwide level after quickly gaining popularity with nightclub customers.

Who knows maybe your bartending staff will invent a fresh, new exciting drink that will soon be in demand. If it does, add it to the drink menu. Maybe it'll become so popular that your competition will beg you for the recipe.

This appendix, assumes that you are an aspiring operator looking to break into the industry and have little or no practical experience in bartending or with preparing various cocktails. This segment is also meant for the seasoned operator looking to enhance his or her drink selection menu by giving it a new start or just to add a few more selections to the list. Therefore, this chapter is dedicated to giving you and your bartending staff a solid beginning and some fresh ideas to assist in creating a drink menu with a wide variety of popular selections.

BEERS

As stated before, a nightclub cannot depend on beer alone to support alcohol sales if it expects to be successful in today's competitive nightclub industry. But, ironically, nightclubs cannot thrive without beer sales either because beer is the most common and popular of all drinks. The majority of alcohol sales will most likely be that of beer sales. Beer comes in many brands, shapes, sizes and even tastes. From light beer to dark beer, imported, domestic or micro brewed. They all have their own separate personalities, characteristics and properties. These traits include the different bodies, textures, tastes, sweetness or bitterness of beers.

Because of the different characteristics of each beer, customers will have beers they like and beers they don't like. Therefore, it's important that you at least provide several brands of beer for sale to offer customers a variety to choose from. Some nightclubs feature hundreds of brands while others only offer a few. The number and types of beer brands you sell should be conditional on the style of your operation.

If an operation is that of a Brewpub, then one should focus and promote a wide selection of *many* different types of beers in addition to the club's own micro brewed house signature beers. Most customers frequent Brewpub to experience such diversity in beers.

The following is a list of some of the more popular beers of which to choose from. Depending on the combination that you choose for your nightclub, you may need more than one distributor because it is unlikely that one distributor will carry all of these beers on their products list.

HAND-CRAFTED MICRO BEERS:
Pete's Wicked Ale
Pete's Wicked Honey Wheat
Pete's Wicked Strawberry Blonde
Gordon Biersch Marzen
Gordon Biersch Blonde Bock
Pyramid Apricot Ale
Pyramid Hefe-weizen Draft
Sierra Nevada Pale Ale
Samuel Adams Boston Lager
Anchor Steam Red Hook EBB
Red Hook Hefeweizen
Samuel Adams Cherry Wheat

Samuel Adams Summer Brew
Samuel Adams Pale Ale
J.W. Dundee's Honey Brown Lager
Grant's Perfect Porter
MacTarnahan's Amber Ale
Genny Cream Ale
Hooper's Hooch Orange Brew

AUSTRALIAN BEERS:
Foster's Lager Old
Australian Stout

CANADIAN BEERS:
Labatt's Blue
Wyder's Peach Cider
Molson Ice Molson Golden
Moosehead

AMERICAN BEERS:
Budweiser
Bud Light
Bud Ice
Busch
Busch Light
Miller
Miller Light
Miller High Life
Lowenbrau
Lowenbrau Dark
Michelob
Michelob Light
Icehouse
Coors
Coors Light
Rolling Rock

George Killians Irish Red
Mickey's Malt (Big Mouth)
Henry Weinhard's Private Reserve
Henry Weinhard's Private Reserve Dark
Henry Weinhard's Private Reserve Amber
Lone Star
O'douls (Non-Alcoholic)
O'douls Amber (Non-Alcoholic)
Sharps (Non-Alcoholic)

MEXICAN BEERS:
Bohemia
Carta Blanca
Tecate
Dos Equis Amber Lager
Dos Equis Special Lager
Modelo Especial
Negra Modelo
Sol
Corona
Corona Light
Pacifico

HOLLAND BEERS:
Heineken
Heineken Special Dark
Amstel Light
Grolsch (Swingtop)
Oranjeboom

GERMAN BEERS:
Beck's
Beck's Dark
Warsteiner
Paulaner Hefeweizen

St. Pauli Girl
St. Pauli Girl Dark
St. Pauli Girl (Non-Alcoholic)
Ayinger Brau-Weisse
Ayinger Ur-Weisse
Ayinger Alt Dunkel
Celebrator Dopplebock

ENGLISH BEERS:
Bass Ale
John Courage Amber Ale
Theakston's Old Peculiar Ale
Samuel Smith's India Pale Ale
Samuel's Smith Lager
Samuel Smith's Imperial Stout
Samuel Smith's Pale Ale
Samuel Smith's Nutbrown Ale
Samuel Smith's Taddy Porter
Samuel Smith's Oatmeal Stout
Watney's Red Barrel
Watney's Cream Stout
Newcastle Brown Ale
Caffrey's

IRISH BEERS:
Guiness Stout Draught
Harp Lager

JAMAICAN BEERS:
Red Stripe

CHINESE BEERS:
Tsing Tao

SCOTTISH BEERS:
McEwan's Export Ale
McEwan's Scotch Ale
MacAndrew's Stock Ale
Traquair House Ale
Belhaven Scottish Ale

This short list of beers should be more than enough to get you started. Another method to go about your beer selection process is to let your clientele to tell you what they want. This can be done a couple of different ways. Without a doubt some beers will sell better than others. Some will not sell at all. When you see such trends, maybe you should consider dropping the beers that aren't so popular from the menu. Customers will often tell you what they want so listen to them. Many requests for certain beers should prompt you to add those beers to your drink menu to satisfy your clientele.

Finally, the last question about beer that must be addressed is how you plan to serve your beers. This decision will say a lot about a club. Will you serve your premium beers by the bottle, can or both? Also, decide how you will serve your draft beers—In a glass or in a beer mug? And which sizes and styles?

BEER DRINKS

Beer drinks have been around for a long time and have been very successful in Europe and Australia. Beer drinks have only been in the United States for a few years but have taken off in popularity. If you want to add some innovation and creativity to your drink menu, consider including beer drinks to give customers some delicious alternatives to just drinking the standard beers.

Beer drink recipes involve the mixing of beer with beer and often with other forms of alcoholic or non-alcoholic ingredients. Some consider it an art that involves carefully selecting beers according to their opposing properties (taste, sweetness, bitterness, body and texture). Consider experimenting with your own beers to produce your own beer drinks or choose from the following proven and popular beer drink recipes to incorporate into your operation:

Beer Buster
Requires a chilled beer mug
Pour in 1 oz. of Vodka, 2 or 3 dashes of Tabasco sauce and fill the rest of the mug with draft beer.

Bumble Bee
Requires a chilled beer glass
Fill the glass half full of Guinness Stout and half full of Hefeweizen or honey lager.

Dr. Pepper
Requires a chilled beer mug and a shot glass
Fill mug with about 7-8 oz. of any draft beer. Pour 1 oz. of Amaretto in a shot glass and drop the shot into the beer.

Black and Tan
Requires chilled beer mug of glass
Fill glass half full of Bass Pale Ale. Fill the other half with Guinness Stout by pouring in the stout slowly, over a spoon. Allow to settle and layer before serving.

Half and Half
Requires a chilled beer glass
Fill beer glass with ½ of bitter ale and ½ with Pilsener.

Black Velvet
Requires a chilled beer glass
Fill glass half full of Guinness Stout and the other half with hard apple cider.

Black Velveteen
Requires a chilled beer glass
Fill glass ½ full of Guinness Stout and ½ full of Champagne.

Koala Beer
Requires a chilled beer glass
Fill glass ½ full of Foster's Lager and ½ full of Guinness Stout.

Gold and Lager
Requires a chilled beer glass
Fill glass with 1 1/4 oz. Goldschlager and top off with draft beer.

Bloody Bastard
Requires ice, a bucket or a specialty glass
Add 2 oz. of Bass Ale, then fill with Bloody Mary Mix and add ½ tablespoon of horseradish. Serve with peeled shrimp and garnish with a lime wedge.

Lunch Box
Requires a chilled beer glass
Combine 1 oz. of Amaretto, 1 oz. Orange Juice and 3 or 4 oz. of draft beer.

Purple Death
Requires a chilled beer glass
Fill glass 3/4 full with Bass Ale, 1 oz. of Chambord and top off with hard apple cider.

Lockhart Zoo
Requires ice and a house specialty glass
Combine 3/4 oz. of Tequila, 3/4 oz. of Vodka, 3/4 oz. of Gin, 3 oz. Cranberry Juice in a shaker. Shake well and strain into a glass and then fill with draft beer.

Shandy Gaff
Requires a chilled beer glass
Fill half of the glass with draft beer and the other half with Ginger Ale.

Rock 'n' Bock
Requires a chilled beer glass or mug
Combine equal parts of Shiner Double Bock and Rolling Rock.

SPIRITS
Many people confuse all alcoholic drinks— beer, wine and spirits to all be liquor. However, this is incorrect. Beer and wine are produced by a method called fermentation. Spirits on the other hand are produced by distillation. Liquor is defined as alcohol made by distillation rather than fermentation. So from now on when you refer to liquor, you are actually referring to spirits.

There are several different categories of spirits which make up the hundreds of different types of liquor products. The most common categories that you'll be dealing with are Liqueurs, Gin, Rum, Brandy, Whiskey, Vodka and Mezcal (Tequila).

The best thing about liquor is its versatility. Most liquor can be served straight as a shot, used in combination with other alcoholic beverages or other additives to create cocktails or mixed drinks. To see how this works, read the next section *Cocktails/Mixed Drinks (page 286)*.

Below, each liquor category is broken down, described and includes some of the more popular drinks that are consumed by nightclub customers as straight shot drinks or used as ingredients to create great tasting cocktails.

LIQUEURS
Liqueurs offer a wide range of variety. They can flavor a base spirit to make a cocktail or can be drank as is. Some spirits such as Rum, Whiskey or Brandy also fall into the liqueur category because they too can be used to give flavor to other spirits.

Liqueurs are either flavored artificially or by fruits, nuts, herbs, flowers, roots or barks. The types of liqueurs that you'll most likely be dealing with most often, to prepare certain cocktails, are Cream Liqueurs, Creme Liqueurs and Triple Sec. Cream Liqueurs are a thick and creamy liquor. Creme Liqueurs are not creamy but will become thick because of their sugar content. Triple Sec is a sweet orange liqueur. The most popular brand of Triple Sec is Cointreau. Other popular liqueurs are:

Cointreau
40% alcohol. Regarded as the best Triple Sec. As an orange liqueur it's usually used as an ingredient but is also drank straight.

Bols Triple Sec Curacao
39% alcohol. A little bitter but sweet. Not as good as Cointreau.

Galliano Liquore
35% alcohol. Yellow in color, has a very strong anise and vanilla flavor.

Galliano Amaretto
28% alcohol. Has a very strong almond flavor. A commonly used liqueur to flavor mixed drinks.

Jagermeister
A popular liqueur that has a very unique taste. A great bar drink that is typically drank straight.

Galliano Sambuca
38% alcohol. Sweet. Has a strong anise flavor.

Jacquin's Apricot Flavored Brandy
Fruity tasting and has a strong apricot smell.

Amalfi Lemon Liqueur
Very strong tasting. Just like its name implies, it has a lemon base, and it tastes like strong lemonade.

Bols Coconut Creole Liqueur
24% alcohol. Very strong coconut taste, smell and flavor.

Bols Apricot Liqueur
24% alcohol. Another popular additive which gives certain drinks the right touch. Tastes and smells strongly of apples.

Chambord
17% alcohol. Very strong sweet and fruity taste. Made from black raspberries and other herbs and fruits.

Drambuie
Very popular Scotch liqueur that has a herby taste but isn't too sweet.

Kahlua
A nice flavored versatile coffee liqueur. Another nightclub favorite.

Malibu
24% alcohol. Coconut and White Rum liqueur. Releases a strong coconut smell but easy to drink.

Bols Misty Peach Liqueur
24% alcohol. A peachy tasting and smelling liqueur.

Midori
21% alcohol. Very sweet tasting. A green melon liqueur which makes it a fruity tasting drink.

Baileys Original Irish Cream
17% alcohol. One of the best cream Liqueurs on the market. Smooth and creamy with a mild chocolate taste.

Bols Creme de Cacao
Sweet chocolate taste. Easy to drink but more often used to flavor a base spirit.

GIN
Unlike liqueurs, Gin is flavored by a method of redistilling the flavors with more Gin. With liqueurs, after distillation, flavor is added. Juniper berries are used to flavor all types of Gin. Gin is not considered a liqueur but still can be used to create a mixed drink such as a Gin and Tonic. Gin is a white spirit.

Tanqueray
Perhaps the easiest drinking Gin on the market.

Seagram's London Dry Gin
Good, cheap Gin to consider stocking behind the bar. This is a basic Gin that works well for mixing Gin cocktails.

Beefeater London Distilled Dry Gin
Very popular Gin throughout the world which makes for a good Gin to drink straight and to use in many cocktails.

RUM
Produced either as a White Rum, Dark Rum or Golden Rum.

Bacardi
A world famous White Rum. Can be drank straight and makes for an excellent drink mixer.

Bacardi Gold
Very different from Barcardi (White Rum) because this one is a *Dark Rum*. It has a smooth taste and is light gold in color.

Captain Morgan Dark Rum
40% alcohol. A Canadian Rum with a thick molasses flavor. A little harder to drink straight but is a good liqueur.

Captain Morgan Gold Rum

40% alcohol. Very similar in nature to Captain Morgan Dark Rum. Has a very mild molasses flavor and smell. Much easier to drink straight and still makes a good liqueur.

Captain Morgan White Rum

40% alcohol. Very mild smelling and flavoring. Not as popular as other Captain Morgan spirits.

Malibu

24% alcohol. A coconut flavored White Rum liqueur. Malibu is a hard tasting spirit that has a strong coconut smell and taste, which makes it a little harder to drink straight but excellent for mixed drinks requiring a coconut liqueur— like the Pina Coloda.

Stubbs

An Australian White Rum. Very flavorful, smooth and tasty.

Coruba

Dark, sweet Jamaican Rum.

BRANDY

A brandy is made from distilled wine and wine is made from the fermentation of grapes. Before you continue you need to know that there are many variations of and specific terms for brandy. These are as follows:

- Applejack = Apple Brandy.
- Pisco = Brandy from South America.
- Cognac = Brandy from a western France region.
- Armagnac = Brandy from South West France.
- Calvados = Apple Brandy hailing from Normandy.
- Metaxa = Greek Brandy
- X.O. = Indicates that the Brandy is more than six years old.
- V.S.O.P. = Indicates that the Brandy is five years old.

• V.S. = Indicates that the minimum age of the Brandy is three years old.

Examples of Brandies are:

Godet Fine Champagne Cognac X.O.
40% alcohol. Light and has a good smelling aroma. Very easy to drink.

Massanez Calvados Vieux
An apple Brandy. Has a strong smell of cider. Very easy to drink straight and is a good candidate as a liqueur for mixed drinks requiring an apple base.

Janneau Grand Armagnac V.S.O.P.
Another easy to drink, smooth tasting Brandy that adds a little class to any nightclub.

This is a very small and incomplete list of Brandies. A better way to determine which Brandies you'll have behind your bar is to establish your drink menu (cocktails) and stock Brandy as it is needed to make those drinks requiring a Brandy liqueur. Also choosing and having a house brand or two will satisfy most of your straight Brandy drinking customers.

All Brandy tastes and smells different from each another. Very flavory Brandy is often used to give food extra flavoring during cooking, in addition to being drank straight or mixed into cocktails.

WHISKEY
Bourbon, Scotch Whiskey, Irish Whiskey, Rye, Canadian Whiskey, Corn Whiskey, Single Malt Whiskey and Tennessee Whiskey are all different kinds of whiskies. Whiskey is often drank straight in the form of a shot drink and is commonly used as a base liqueur in cocktails. Here are some of the brands:

Black Jack Kentucky Straight Bourbon Whiskey

37% alcohol. A harsher tasting whiskey that makes it hard to drink. Hardcore whiskey enthusiast/customers may like this one.

Canadian Club

Very flavorful Canadian whiskey that is very easy to drink straight.

Chivas Regal Blended Scotch

Premium Scotch whiskey.

Crown Royal

40% alcohol. A Seagram's whiskey.

Glayva

35% alcohol. Scotch whiskey liqueur. Much like Drambuie but not as flavorful.

Drambuie

Drambuie is a very popular Scotch Liqueur with colorful flavoring that is consumed straight as often as it is used as an ingredient in cocktails.

Jim Beam Rye

Very good and very popular. Jim Beam is a common base liqueur for mixed drinks.

Jim Beam Kentucky Straight Bourbon Whiskey

Another popular Jim Beam product. This is a cheap Bourbon Whiskey that makes a good liquor to have behind the bar.

Southern Comfort

There are several versions of this famous liquor. Southern Comfort is a smooth drinking and flavorful spirit and makes for a good liqueur in cocktails.

Wild Turkey 101 Proof Straight Rye Whiskey
Among the most famous whiskies in the world. Extremely flavorful and intense.

Jack Daniel's Old No. 7 Tennessee Whiskey
Another famous whiskey that is smooth tasting and an excellent mixer.

VODKA
Vodka is perhaps the most well-known spirit of all. It's a very versatile spirit which often is consumed straight as a shot drink, but usually serves as a base spirit and is responsible for the existence of hundreds of different cocktails.

Consider having the following brands of Vodka behind the bar at all times:

Smirnoff
A cheaper liquor that makes a good house Vodka.

Stolichnaya
One of the more popular Vodkas that is exported from Russia. Has a very smooth consistency that makes it good for both drinking straight and using to mix cocktails. Great for making Black Russians.

Absolut
Another Popular Vodka. This one hails from Sweden and is very good for mixing cocktails.

Iceberg
A mildly flavored Canadian Vodka.

Glacier
Cheaper Vodka made in France. Harder to drink straight because of its taste.

Wolfe's Aromatic Schnapps

A good smelling and flavored Dutch Schnapps. Good for drinking straight.

MEZCAL

Mezcal and Tequila are Mexican Spirits. Mezcal is produced from a process of mashing, fermenting and double distilling a plant called an Agave.

All Tequila is Mezcal. The name, "Tequila" is simply a town where some Mezcal is actually produced and that's why most brands are called Tequila.

Tequila has grown to be very important to the nightclub industry, not only for the notorious Tequila shots, that require most drinkers to suck on a lemon immediately after drinking, but many cocktails would not be so, without this potent and well-known spirit.

Cuervo Especial Tequila

A Jose Cuervo product. A good quality Mezcal that makes a good mixer for cocktail drinks and can be drank straight.

Sauza Tequila Blanco

A smooth, consistent silver Tequila. Perhaps easier than most Tequilas to drink straight.

Del Maguey Minero

A deep, tasty and flavored Mezcal that boast a sweet and fruity characteristic.

Monte Alban Mezcal con Gusano

Comes with the well-known worm in the bottom of the bottle. The taste of this Mezcal is argumentative.

Mi Amigo

A silver Tequila. Very easy and especially tolerable to drink, Has a milder flavor that may not work best for mixing cocktails though.

COCKTAILS/MIXED DRINKS

All alcoholic beverages that aren't spirit drinks, wines, beers or beer drinks probably fall into this category. Cocktails or mixed drinks are the creations of adding two or more ingredients or beverages together into a glass to make one drink.

Browse the recipes and make a list of the cocktails that you think will work best in your particular nightclub on the menu. Also remember that just because a drink isn't on your menu doesn't mean that some customers won't ask for it. In the best interest of customer service, you'll need to be ready and should be able to prepare almost any drink order that you get. The only way to do that is to be knowledgeable about a great number of popular drinks. This can only be done by having a competent bartending staff that is eager to learn about and prepare various cocktail drinks.

Many drinks have been intentionally omitted from this book because of their sexually explicit or profane names or connotations. However, a few made it that do contain mild graphic language. Don't get offended— remember these drinks are served in bars!

Lemon Drop

One shot of Vodka or Absolute Citron. Serve with a slice of lemon and one teaspoon of sugar poured into a shot glass.

Special Drinking instructions: Put the sugar on the lemon and then put the lemon into your mouth. Drink the shot and suck on the lemon.

Fireball

Mix 1 oz. of cinnamon Schnapps with a dash of Tabasco sauce.

Harvey WallBanger

Fill a Collins Glass with ice, 1oz. of Vodka and 4 oz. of Orange Juice.

Traditional Martini

Combine 1 ½ oz. Gin and 3/4 oz. Dry Vermouth. Stir the combination, strain into a Martini glass and add an olive.

Sweet Martini

Stir 1 oz. Gin and 1 oz. Sweet Vermouth and ice. Strain into a cocktail glass and garnish with an olive.

Apple Pie Martini

Shake with ice - 3 oz. Stolichnaya Vanilla Vodka, ½ oz. Calvados and ½ oz. of Dry Vermouth. Strain into a cocktail glass (chilled). Garnish with an apple.

Long Island Iced Tea

Use a pint glass and fill it with ice, 1 part of Tequila, 1 part of Vodka, 1 part of Rum, 1 part of Gin, 1 part of Triple Sec, 1 ½ parts of Sour Mix, and just a little splash of coke to give it some color. Then pour it all in a shaker, shake it just once and then pour it back into the pint glass and garnish with a slice of lemon.

Screw Driver

Stir 1 ½ oz. of Vodka and 5 oz. of Orange Juice together in a Highball glass.

Lube Job

In a shooter or double shot glass fill half of it with Irish Cream first and then the other half with Vodka.

Kamakazie

Fill a mixer with ice, 1/3 of a shot of Triple Sec, 1/3 shot of Lime Juice and 1/3 shot of Vodka. Mix and shake the contents then strain into a shotglass.

Italian Screw

Fill a Highball Glass with ice and add 1 ½ shots of Vodka, 1 oz. of Galliano and top off with orange juice.

Generation X

Use a hurricane glass and add one oz. each of Tequila, Jim Beam, Triple Sec, Blue Curacao and Melon Liquor. Add ice and pour in a bottle of Zima.

Candy Apple

Take one glass of apple cider and add just a dash of butterscotch schnapps.

Amaretto Jack

Add one oz. each of Amaretto and Jack Daniel's into a Highball glass. Then add in equal parts of pineapple and orange juice and splash it with cherry syrup to give it some color.

Amaretto Mist

Pour in 1 ½ oz. of Amaretto into a glass filled with crushed ice. Garnish with a slice of lemon.

Amaretto Rose

Pour 1 ½ oz. of Amaretto and ½ oz. of Lime Juice into a glass filled with ice and then add Club Soda.

Amaretto Sour

Shake 1 ½ oz. Amaretto, 3/4 oz. of Lemon Juice and ice. Then strain into a glass garnished with an orange slice. **Or,** take 1 ½ oz. Amaretto and 3 oz. of sour mix, shake and then strain into a glass and garnish with an orange slice and a cherry.

Blow Job

Needed is 2/3 oz. of Kahlua and 1/6 oz. of Vodka. Slowly pour the Kahlua into a shotglass followed by the Vodka. Cover the top of the drink with whipped cream.

Special Drinking instructions: Drink with no hands. Lean over drink, put your mouth over the shotglass, then lean back and swallow it.

Strawberry Daiquiri

½ oz. Strawberry Liqueur, 1 oz. of White Rum, ½ Lemon Juice, 1 teaspoon of Powdered Sugar and 1 oz. of Strawberries. Shake together with ice and strain into a cocktail glass. **Or,** use 1 1/4 oz. Spiced Rum, 1 3/4 oz. Sweet and Sour Mix and 3 oz. of frozen Strawberries. Add a scoop of ice and blend it all together and serve in a cocktail glass.

Margarita

Take a cocktail glass and wet the rim of the glass with Lemon Juice and then dip the rim in salt. The salt should now line the rim. Mix 1 ½ oz. Tequila, ½ oz. Triple Sec and 1 oz. Lemon Juice and shake it all together with ice. Then strain into the salt-rimmed glass.

Sex on The Beach

Mix and shake together ½ oz. Peach Schnapps, ½ oz. Apple Schnapps, ½ oz. Cranberry Juice, ½ oz. Pineapple Juice and ice. After shaking strain into a Highball glass.

Snake Bite

Pour 2 oz. of Yukon Jack with ice into a glass and add just a dash of Lime Juice.

Snake Bite

This is a variation which combines 1 ½ oz. of Jack Daniel's Whiskey, 1 ½ oz. of Tequila and 1 ½ oz. Southern Comfort. Use a Lowball glass. Shake the above with ice and strain into the glass.

Something Different

You'll need 1 oz. of Peach Schnapps, 1 oz. of Amaretto, 2 oz. of Cranberry Juice and 2 oz. of Pineapple Juice. Shake them together with ice and serve in a Highball glass.

Fuzzy Navel

Stir 3 oz. of Peach Schnapps and 3 oz. of Orange Juice into a Highball glass. Garnish it with both an Orange slice and a cherry.

Orgasm

Combine ½ oz. Triple Sec, ½ oz. Vodka, ½ oz. Amaretto and ½ oz. White Creme de Cacao into a shaker. Shake with ice and then strain into a chilled cocktail glass.

Orange Margarita

Blend together 1 ½ oz. of Tequila with ½ oz. Orange Liqueur, a dash of lime, ½ cup of ice and 1 scoop of Orange Sherbert (a frozen ice cream like mixture). After the blended mixture is smooth, serve and garnish with an orange and a lime.

Cactus Bite

2 oz. of Lemon Juice and 2 oz. of Tequila combined with 2 teaspoons of Triple Sec, 2 teaspoons of Drambuie, ½ teaspoon of superfine sugar and just a dash of bitters (bitter tasting spirits made up of barks and roots) are needed to make this drink. Shake it all in a shaker, then strain into a cocktail glass.

Cappuccino Cocktail

Requires 3/4 oz. Coffee Brandy, 3/4 oz. Light Cream and 3/4 oz. of Vodka. Shake them together with ice then strain into cocktail glass.

Vodka Sour

Add 2 oz. of Vodka, a ½ teaspoon of powdered sugar and squeeze in the juice from half of a lemon. Shake all of this with ice and then strain it into a sour glass garnished with lemon and a cherry.

Vodka and Apple Juice

Mix Apple Juice with 2 oz. of Vodka into a Highball glass filled with whole ice cubes. Stir and then serve.

Gin and Tonic

Using a Highball glass nearly filled to the top with ice cubes, add 2 oz. of Gin and 5 oz. of Tonic Water. Stir and garnish with a lime slice.

Gin Sour

2 oz. of Gin combined with 1 oz. of Lemon Juice and a half teaspoon of Superfine Sugar make up this drink. Shake well in a shaker filled with ice then strain into a sour glass. Garnish with an orange slice and a cherry.

Whiskey Sour

In a shaker, add 2 oz. of Blended Scotch Whiskey, ½ teaspoon of Powdered sugar and then squeeze the juice from half of a lemon into the mix. Shake together and then strain it into a sour glass. Garnish with a cherry and a lemon slice.

Irish Whiskey

Add 2 oz. of Irish Whiskey, ½ teaspoon of Triple Sec, ½ teaspoon of Anisette, 1/4 teaspoon of Maraschino Liquor and just a sprinkle of bitters. Stir together and strain into a cocktail glass. Add an olive as a garnishment.

Rum and Coke

Pour 1 1/4 oz. of Rum into a Highball glass filled with ice and then add 6 oz. of Coca Cola. Garnish with Lime.

Tequila Sunrise

Build this drink in a Highball glass with ice. Add 2 oz. of Tequila and 4 oz. of Orange Juice and then slowly add 3/4 oz. of Grenadine. Allow the Grenadine to settle before serving.

White Russian

Use a cocktail glass and pour in 2 oz. of Vodka and 1 oz. of Coffee Liqueur. Fill the rest of the glass with Light Cream, stir and serve. You can also substitute the Light Cream with milk or half and half.

Black Russian

Combine 1 ½ oz. of Vodka and 3/4 oz. Coffee Liqueur in a glass and serve.

Cosmopolitan

Using a shaker, mix 2 oz. of Vodka, 1 oz. Triple Sec, 1 oz. Cranberry Juice and squeeze in the juice from a whole Lime. Shake and strain into a cocktail glass with ice.

Southern Comfort Cocktail

Shake 1 3/4 oz. Southern Comfort, 3/4 oz. Orange Liqueur and the juice of ½ of a Lime together with ice, then strain into a cocktail glass.

Eye Opener

Fill a shaker half way with ice cubes, then add 1 ½ oz. of White Rum, ½ oz. Triple Sec, 1 teaspoon of White Creme de Cacao, 1 Egg Yolk, 2 teaspoons of Pernod and a teaspoon of Superfine Sugar. Shake well and then strain into a sour glass.

Jack and Coke

Build into a highball glass with ice and add 2 oz. of Jack Daniel's Whiskey and 10 oz. of Coca Cola. Stir and serve.

Jolly Rancher

Shake and strain ½ oz. of Blueberry Schnapps and 1 ½ oz. of Melon Liqueur over ice into a cocktail glass. Fill glass with Sweet and Sour Mix and add ½ oz. of Grenadine for color. Stir and serve with a cherry garnishment.

Ultimate Mudslide

Blend 2.0 oz. Kahlua Coffee Liqueur, 2 oz. of Baily Irish Cream, 1 cup of milk and 3 cups of Vanilla Ice Cream together. Blend these ingredients for one minute and serve.

Tom Collins

Combine 2 oz. of Gin, 1 oz. Lemon Juice and 1 teaspoon Superfine Sugar into a shaker half filled with ice. Shake and strain into a Collins glass with ice cubes inside. Top of the glass with 3 oz. of Club Soda, stir and serve with a slice of orange and a cherry.

Manhattan

Strain and stir 2 oz. Rye Whiskey, 3/4 oz. Sweet Vermouth and a few dashes Angostura Bitters into a cocktail glass garnished with a cherry. Or, stir 2/3 oz. Rye Whiskey and 1/3 oz. of Italian Vermouth into a collins glass garnished with a cherry.

Pina Colada

Blend (electric) 3 tablespoons of Coconut Milk, 3 oz. of White Rum, 3 tablespoons of crushed pineapple and 2 cups of crushed ice. After blending pour into a collins glass and serve. Serve it with a straw.

Go Girl

Mix 1 oz. Chambord Raspberry Liqueur with 1 oz. of Vodka, 1 tablespoon of Sour Mix and Club Soda into a cocktail glass over ice.

Barcardi Cocktail

Shake 1 ½ oz. Barcardi White Rum, 1 oz. Lime Juice and a teaspoon of Grenadine. After shaking, strain into a cocktail glass and serve.

Rummy Sour

Blend 1 1/4 oz. Spiced Rum, 1 3/4 oz. Lemon Lime Mix and a scoop of crushed ice. After blending, serve in a cocktail glass.

Slow Comfortable Screw

Pour 1 oz. of Sloe Gin and ½ oz. of Southern Comfort into a collins glass with ice. Top off glass with Orange Juice, stir and serve.

Alabama Slammer

Fill a highball glass with ice and add 1 oz. of Southern Comfort, 1 oz. of Amaretto, ½ of Sloe Gin. Top the highball with Orange Juice, stir and garnish with a cherry.

Seven and Seven

Mix and stir 1 oz. of Seagram's 7 Crown with 6 oz. of 7-up. Serve with ice in any glass.

Sex Up Against the Wall

Shake and strain ice with 1 oz. of Vodka, 1 oz. of Pineapple Juice, 1 oz. Cranberry and 1 oz. Sour Mix. Pour into a highball glass and serve.

Bay Breeze

Build in a highball glass and add 1 ½ oz. of Vodka. Fill with Pineapple Juice and add just a splash of Cranberry Juice.

Gin Aloha

Shake 1 ½ oz. of Gin, 1 ½ oz. Triple Sec, ice, 1 tablespoon of unsweetened Pineapple Juice and add just a dash of Orange Bitters. Strain into a cocktail glass and serve.

Tequila Manhattan

Shake together 2 oz. of Tequila, 1 oz. of Sweet Vermouth and a dash of Lime Juice. Strain the combination into a cocktail glass filled with ice cubes, garnish with an orange slice and a cherry and serve.

Dirty Martini

Mix 2 ½ oz. Vodka with 1 oz. of olive juice. Stir and serve in a cocktail glass.

Rolls-Royce

Shake and mix 1 ½ oz. of Gin, ½ oz. Sweet Vermouth, ½ oz. Dry Vermouth and a teaspoon of Benedictine. Shake the combination with ice, strain into a cocktail glass and serve.

Bourbon Cooler

Build in a highball glass and fill it almost full of ice. Add 2 oz. of Bourbon and 4 oz. of Lemon Lime Soda. Stir and garnish with a slice of lemon.

Bourbon Sloe

Shake and mix 2 oz. of Bourbon and 1oz. of Sloe Gin with the shaker filled halfway with ice. Strain into a cocktail glass and serve.

Bourbon Sour

Pour 2 oz. of Bourbon, 1 oz. of Lemon Juice and 1 teaspoon of sugar into a shaker half filled with ice cubes. Shake well and strain into a sour glass. Garnish with a slice of orange and a cherry.

Apple Pie

Pour 1 oz. White Rum, ½ oz. of Sweet Vermouth, 1 teaspoon of Lemon Juice, 1 teaspoon Applejack and a half teaspoon of Grenadine into a shaker half filled with ice. Shake well, then strain and serve into a cocktail glass.

Tequila Sour

In a shaker add 2 oz. of Tequila, 1 teaspoon of Powdered Sugar and squeezed juice from ½ of a lemon. Shake the ingredients with ice, strain into a cocktail glass and serve with a lemon and cherry garnishments.

Pink Lady

Combine 1 ½ oz. of Gin, 1 oz. of Light Cream, 3 oz. of Sour Mix and a splash of Grenadine into a shaker with ice. Shake well and strain into a highball glass.

Brandy Sour

Fill a shaker with ice, 2 oz. of Brandy, 1 oz. of Lemon Juice and a teaspoon of sugar. Shake well. Serve in a sour glass garnished with an orange slice and a cherry.

Flamingo Cocktail

Fill a shaker with ice, ½ oz. of Apricot Brandy, 1 ½ oz. Gin, 1 teaspoon of Grenadine and the squeezed juice from half of a lemon. Shake the ingredients, strain into a cocktail glass and serve.

Chocolate Rum

In a mixing glass filled with ice, add 2 teaspoons of heavy cream, 2 teaspoons of White Creme de Cacao, 2 teaspoons of White Creme de Menthe and 1 oz. of Rum. Shake then strain the contents into an ice filled glass. Top off the glass with 151 Proof Rum and serve.

Fuzzy Screw

Build directly in a highball glass and add 3/4 oz. Vodka, 3/4 oz. Peach Schnapps and top off glass with orange juice.

Doorknob

Fill a shaker half full of ice and pour in ½ oz. of Amaretto, 1 ½oz. of Light Rum, 1 teaspoon each of Lemon and Lime Juice and 1 teaspoon of sugar. Shake well, strain into a cocktail glass and strain.

Hopefully this list of famous cocktails and recipes will be enough to get you started and thinking about which drinks your club will feature to compliment your operation.

It's also a good idea that you and the bartending staff have access to some sort of data base that stores various cocktail recipes. If your nightclub will utilize personal computers or POS systems, these can be excellent places to store recipe information that is easily accessible to bartenders. If they get an order that they're not quite sure of how to make, PC's allow them to quickly refer to the data based information and get the recipe.

If you don't have PC's yet, settle for typed recipes or cue cards that are kept behind the bar. These can be just as good. You'll need to laminate any printed recipe literature because if you don't, it won't take long for them to become illegible or fall apart because they will inevitably become soaked from water, drinks and whatever else is wet behind the bar.

Often, even if you have your recipes stored in a computer of written down on cue cards, a customer will request a drink that isn't on either reference and the staff won't know how to make either. So what do you do? The answer is easy. Chances are if you asked the customer how to make it, the customer will know and be able to tell you what goes in it. As long as you have the right ingredients, it shouldn't be a problem and you'll be able to satisfy the customer.

WINES

Wine is an optional bar staple that offers even more variety and versatility to a nightclub. Wine probably won't be a huge part of the alcohol sales for most venues, but wine comes in very handy during special events. An example of this is to serve free wine to celebrate New Year's Eve. What a classy touch. Other examples include offering some complimentary drinks of wine during birthdays or wedding parties.

There are many different varieties, styles and brands of wine to choose from, each with their own qualities, prices and varying degrees of popularity. Some are suited for the discriminating wine connoisseurs and others will satisfy the casual wine drinkers. If you're considering adding a wine list to the drink menu, carefully choose wines that will best represent the club. Very expensive wines may be a waste of time and money because the average nightclub client isn't going to pay a lot of money for a glass of wine. Therefore, most venues will need to seek out quality, yet inexpensive wines if they hope to establish a wine menu. Some wines such as *Vermouth* may be necessary anyway as mixes for some cocktail drinks. Some wines that just may fall into the category of quality and inexpensive are:

BLUSH WINE:
Weinstock White Zinfandel
Manischewitz Cream Berry
Manischewitz Cream Blush
Rashi Light Pink Concord
Baron Herzog Zinfandel
Baron Herzog Muscat Blush
Kedem Cream Rose
RED WINE:
Baron Herzog Red Zinfandel
Baron Herzog Red Gamay
Kedem 144 Rouge
Kedem Burgundy Royal
Kedem Concord Grape
Kedem Cream Pink
WHITE WINE:
Baron Herzog Chardonnay
Hagafen White Zinfandel
Kedem Classic White
Kedem Dry Vermouth
Kedem Sweet Vermouth
Weinstock Chardonnay

Index